UNLOCKING YOUR INNER COURAGE

Five Winning Strategies to Achieve
the Life You Want and the World We Need

MELVYN L. FEIN

PB Prometheus Books

59 John Glenn Drive
Amherst, New York 14228

Published 2016 by Prometheus Books

Cover design by Liz Scinta
Cover image © Arthimedes/Shutterstock

Inquiries should be addressed to
Prometheus Books
59 John Glenn Drive
Amherst, New York 14228
VOICE: 716–691–0133
FAX: 716–691–0137
WWW.PROMETHEUSBOOKS.COM

20 19 18 17 16   5 4 3 2 1

Library of Congress Cataloging-in-Publication Data

Names: Fein, Melvyn L., author.
Title: Unlocking your inner courage : five winning strategies to achieve the life you want
    and the world we need / Melvyn L. Fein.
Description: Amherst, New York : Prometheus Books, 2016. | Includes index.
Identifiers: LCCN 2016007384 (print) | LCCN 2016014104 (ebook) |
    ISBN 9781633881693 (paperback) | ISBN 9781633881709 (eBook)
Subjects: LCSH: Courage—Social aspects. | Self-reliance. | Conduct of life. | BISAC:
    SELF-HELP / Personal Growth / Success. | SOCIAL SCIENCE / Sociology /
    General.
Classification: LCC BJ1533.C8 F45 2016 (print) | LCC BJ1533.C8 (ebook) |
    DDC 179/.6—dc23
LC record available at http://lccn.loc.gov/2016007384

Printed in the United States of America

UNLOCKING YOUR INNER COURAGE

CONTENTS

Chapter 1

LAND OF THE FREE, HOME OF THE BRAVE

A SEMI-REFORMED COWARD

I have always thought of myself as a coward. No matter how often people commended me on my bravery, I was excruciatingly aware of my many deep-seated fears. Although my bold exterior sometimes fooled outsiders, I knew the truth. That frightened little boy, the one who sat in the corner of the bedroom on East Eighth Street too scared to go outside, was still there. That lack of courage he now tried to conceal was part of who he was—and would never go away.

Hadn't my younger sister learned to swim before I did? Hadn't she also ridden a bicycle first? I was simply too afraid of drowning or skinning a knee to take a chance. Wasn't I also scared of walking down to the end of the block because there was a bully there who might jump out to attack me? Even though he had polio and limped around on a heavy metal brace, I dreaded his assaults. It didn't matter that I could run faster. What if he caught me unawares?

I was even afraid at school. Despite getting good grades and routine praise, there was always the possibility of not knowing the answer to a question. The mere thought of standing up in class and fumbling for a response was mortifying. Then, as I grew older and my peers began dating, I worried about rejection. Because I was small, what girl would find me attractive? I was not an athlete nor especially handsome, so perhaps girls would laugh behind my back.

Then too there was the question of becoming an adult. What skills did I possess that could be turned to earning a living? Yes, I got good grades, but who would hire me merely because I got A's in history? Anything I knew was totally impractical. I could not fix a car; I didn't even know how to drive one. If the plumbing broke in my apartment, I would be at a loss over what to do. Nor could I wield a hammer and saw as well as my father and grandfather could. They were men who knew how to be men, whereas I was destined to be an eternal child. Condemned to an inferiority that I could not escape, the best I might eventually manage was a pale imitation of manhood.

Nor would this change. I was not physically strong. I lacked gravitas. And worst of all, I did not understand how the world worked. Why others behaved as they did remained an exasperating mystery. Just figuring out how sex worked left me red-faced and dumbstruck among friends who got the joke. How then could I function as the businessman that my father wanted me to be? No one, certainly no self-respecting adult man, would take orders from me. No executive would ever be foolish enough to place me in a responsible position. I clearly did not have the right stuff. Something was missing. Something others had in abundance, which I lacked. While I was not sure what this was, I was convinced that I was biologically incapable of acquiring it.

In short, I was a congenital coward. I was afraid of a world that others met head-on. Instead of taking risks, I sought ways to avoid them. Although I could pretend that I was adequate by keeping my mouth shut, if anyone peered into my soul they would find a Nervous Nellie. While I did not literally tremble as noticeably as Don Knotts, inside I experienced something similar. Nor would my trepidation go away. It was deeply entrenched in who I was and hence there was nothing I could do about it.

In fact, experiences that might have convinced another person he had at least a modicum of courage made no impression on me.

For example, while in college, I hitchhiked alone around Europe for an entire summer. I did this, however, because the friend who was to accompany me had backed out at the last minute. Then, once on the road, upon reaching a strange town, I did not know where to go. Most of the time I stumbled around until I found a youth hostel or visitors' bureau. Only a single time, in Denmark, did I find myself stranded in the middle of farm country and forced to sleep in a field. I survived, but palpably with less aplomb than more intrepid souls. Sadly, each and every time I encountered the unexpected, my heart leaped to my mouth.

Not even my military experience changed my mind. During the heart of the Vietnam War, I was forced to drop out of a graduate program in philosophy and join the National Guard. Though I was mortified by discovering that I detested a subject I thought I would love, I was even more mortified by the prospect of becoming a soldier. My father always warned me that the army would tear me down. Instead of making a man of me, I would be revealed as the child I was. It was therefore with extreme anxiety that I took the PT tests one was required to pass during Basic Training. A failure would mean being recycled and subjected to rigorous punishments. This, I was certain, would be my lot.

When the fateful day came, despite my apprehension, I tried my best. Although I was sure I would fail, the results turned out better than I expected. Out of the fifty men in my squad, virtually every one of which was bigger than me, I came out third best. You could have knocked me over with a feather. How could a weakling like me have done so well? I knew that almost every one of my colleagues was stronger, so what made the difference? It turned out that I was fast and flexible and therefore could speed through exercises like squat thrusts. Nevertheless I was unimpressed. Although I passed, this no longer seemed a significant accomplishment. While I might be quick, quickness was not as important as strength.

Nor did going through the confidence course modify my self-image. This torment was supposed to prepare recruits for the rigors of combat. It entailed crawling under barbed wire in the dark as live ammunition was fired overhead. Many of these rounds were tracers so that it was possible to see them flying by. At first, my squad lined up alongside the course, awaiting nightfall. From here we could see the berm where the bullets landed. The upshot was that many of my peers began to wet their trousers in anticipation of what was to come. I did not. Then, while edging my way under the wire, an explosion went off no more than a foot from me. Suddenly my arm was wet. Was this blood? I could not tell because it was too dark. What then should I do? There was, in fact, no choice. With no one able to come to the rescue, I simply had to keep moving forward. Afterward, I discovered that the field was studded with pots rigged to simulate battlefield explosions. I had been doused because it had rained the previous night and the pots were still filled with water. In any event, I was struck by my fear. Although I got through in one piece, my underlying terrors had once more risen to the surface.

After I left active service, I got a job as a counselor with the New York City Methadone Maintenance Program. Unable to discover any other job for which I was qualified, I was (in my mind) at least morally superior to the addicts with whom I would deal. Many of them, of course, had long criminal records. In fact, a large number carried knives and guns, and/or secreted razor blades in their shoes. I, for the most part, did not want to know. My goal was to stay as far away from the violence as I could. Then one day I was asked to accompany our clients on an outing. They were to play a softball game against another clinic.

All went well for the first few innings, but then a fight broke out between one of our regulars and one of theirs. The two men squared off, brandishing knives pointed directly toward each other. Now the question was, what was I supposed to do? There was no other counselor from my side around; hence it was up to me. I therefore approached the combatants. I did this by coming up from the side and slightly behind. Next, from several feet away, I asked our client, "What are you doing? Surely you do not want to hurt or be hurt." At this, he turned marginally in my direction. Meanwhile, a counselor for the other clinic followed the same procedure with his client. The more I talked, the more my guy turned toward me, while the other guy turned toward his counselor. Soon their knives were pointed not at each other but at us intermediaries. Eventually the combatants were standing with their backs to each other. It was as if my colleague and I were bullfighters who had distracted the fighters from their initial target. Now, no longer face-to-face, they did not have to prove their manhood by engaging in combat. At this point, it was possible to talk them into giving up their weapons.

No one was injured in this encounter. Not one of our clients; not one of us counselors. Meanwhile, I had been in the middle of a knife fight and did not run away. Didn't this imply that I wasn't an unmitigated coward? Well, not from my perspective. After all, what else was I supposed to do? Running away would have been more frightening. It would have exposed my pusillanimity to a playing field full of observers. Had I backed down, I would never again have been able to show my face at work. And so I stayed and did my duty despite my inadequacies.

Many times, in many different settings, I exposed myself to danger. As a caseworker for the New York City Department of Welfare, I walked alone into Harlem tenements armed only with a notebook. As a counselor in a group home for emotionally disturbed boys, I wrestled adolescents to the ground in order to keep the peace. As a counselor in a psychiatric facility, I worked alone in closed rooms with clients who had been convicted of murder. None of this caused me to take flight. But neither did these instances convince me of my courage. So far as I was concerned, I was merely able to put up a good front.

Yet there was this other facet of my character. Over the years, whether at school or at public events, I often stood up to defend unpopular opinions. At such moments I questioned authority figures aloud and articulately championed alternative positions. Whether I was advocating a bureaucratic or political policy, I usually did so with dignity and persuasiveness. Moreover, after these encounters it was not uncommon for my peers to clap me on the back and commend my courage. In saying things they wanted to express, but did not have the stones to dare, I had demonstrated unusual audacity. Still, while I took their words in stride, I continued to believe them misguided. I had merely done what I could not help doing. To have remained silent would have confirmed my spinelessness, ergo I had no choice but to speak up. Besides, this was far less frightening than when, as a child, I had defied my father. Those I now questioned were not going to beat me; thus it took no special talent to assert my views.

I must nonetheless admit that the more often this sort of incident occurred, the more I wondered whether I was quite as gutless as I imagined. What finally got me to suspect that I might be wrong about this lack of bravery was my experience in counseling clients and students. The changeover was gradual. Years earlier, I had spent six years as a client in psychotherapy. This was done in defiance of my father's wishes because I had reached a painful impasse. Totally confused about where I was headed, I consulted my college mentor about the best way to proceed. He advised me that when he had been younger, entering therapy had helped him. And so I took a chance. As a result, I got to delve into my past and explore the sources of my fears. These were many and stemmed from what I would later realize was physical and emotional abuse. Previous to this, I knew that I had experienced a stressful childhood, but I had attributed it to my shortcomings rather than to the way I was raised. It took time for me to realize that many of the punishments I endured had more to do with my parent's limitations than with my own.

In any event, after I started working as a clinician, it became clear that many of my clients were afraid to investigate their histories. They often balked at the possibility of making painful discoveries. This did not surprise me. While in therapy, I was asked to picture myself standing up to my father's blows, and I recoiled at the prospect. He was so much bigger, stronger, and aggressive that, had I rebelled, I would have invited a severe thrashing. As a consequence, I pulled back and did not allow myself to entertain visions of insubordination. Now I realized that my clients were enduring fears not unlike my own. It became obvious that I was not the only person who doubted his courage. I also began to realize that people who were not in therapy had analogous apprehensions. They might more effectively disguise these than I had, but they were there. As a semi-recovered coward, I could see through their defenses. Plainly, they too believed that they did not have the ability to deal with their fears. They too distrusted their courage.

I had another realization as well. It did not matter how often fearful people were assured that they had courage. Like me, they discounted such testimonials. These were regarded as well-meaning but mistaken. Cowards generally assume that they are cowardly to the bone. Consequently, they will not change their minds in response to mere words. They do not trust these; nor do they trust themselves. However much they may hope to face down their fears, they imagine that when the time comes, they will find ways to hide. Only instances of genuine courage might make a difference. Yet these are few and far between. What is more, putative cowards are convinced these incidents are flukes. So entrenched are their anxieties that they resist logic and counterevidence. They defiantly resist assurances that manifestly underestimate the tenacity of fears they know only too well.

The truth is that virtually all of us have fears. Anxieties are part of the human condition. Some people, it is true, are more fearful than others. Likewise some are more risk averse. Nonetheless, most of us are capable to being braver than we realize. We may never fully overcome our uncertainties; nonetheless we can be bold enough to deal with life's challenges. We can even handle our childhood fears if we so choose. As long as we learn how to protect ourselves from our terrors, we can develop the appropriate emotional resilience. Happily, almost all of us, despite our doubts, are stronger than we imagine. Almost none of us are prey to the congenital weaknesses that we dread.

But why should anyone as fearful as I was believe this? Why should they take the word of someone who has not undergone comparable insecurities? This is a good question—one for which I do not have a perfect answer. While I have emerged from the depths of my cowardice, I have come to realize that fear is an unavoidable emotion. Life is dangerous and thus if we do not possess internal signals to warn of potential threats, we will succumb to them. Nevertheless, even people who are not temperamentally brave can learn to cope with these fears. There are methods that may enable them to manage their uncertainties. People do not have to jump on hand grenades in order to prove they are not cowards. All that is necessary is to muddle through during their everyday affairs. This too can be a form of heroism.

In the chapters that follow, I will explain how this can be achieved. I will use my own experience and those of my clients to illuminate the path. This book will therefore be very personal. My goal is to provide persuasive evidence that courage is possible. Why? One reason is to reassure myself. Another is that we, as a nation, have reached a critical juncture. Despite the unprecedented success of the American experiment, too many of us seek comfort rather than confront difficult challenges. We prefer to benefit from the accomplishments of our ancestors instead of risking successes of our own. This is sad and unnecessary. We too are capable of great deeds if we will grasp our capabilities. They are there, but they need to be tapped.

In the rest of this chapter I hope to remind my reader proud heritage that we Americans share. We often forget the daring that it took to carve a modern nation out of the wilderness. We like- wise overlook the valor displayed in our becoming the most powerful nation on earth. This legacy should not be squandered. Isaac Newton wrote that if he had accomplished more than others it was because he stood on the shoulders of giants. We too stand on the shoulders of giants. Thus we ought to endeavor to be worthy of them. Surely the children of giants should be capable of momentous feats.

PIONEERS AND PATRIOTS

The American national anthem tells us that our land is the home of the brave. It also assures us that this courage enables us to safeguard our freedom. Clearly, we have stood up to tyranny in the past.[1] The question is, do we have what it takes to do so in the future? Not every American is certain. Nevertheless, it is evident that our ances- tors did. The proof is all around us. From ocean to ocean, and from the mountains to the prairies, the legacy of countless pioneers and patriots is on display. It is visible in our physical accomplishments, but also in our democracy and personal attitudes. Americans have become a proud people, in large part because we have reason to be proud.

Consider the way the nation began. The colonists at Jamestown were a mixed lot of aristocrats and laborers.[2] Many were not inspi- rational. They had come to make money, even though they were not sure of how. Nor were they considerate of the rights of the natives. Nonetheless, they were a tenacious group. Despite many deaths from starvation and warfare, they persisted. For every settler who perished, more arrived seasick and bedraggled. Eventually they dis- covered that tobacco made a superb cash crop. The demand for this intoxicant far exceeded initial expectations. From this happenstance, a tidewater aristocracy soon arose to dominate Virginia.

In retrospect, we often look upon these doings with embarrassment. The slaughter of the natives, the vanity of the upper classes, the arrival of slavery, and the addictive qualities of tobacco give us pause. And yet, how can we discount the courage of those pioneers? Many of them may not have been nice people according to contemporary standards, but they faced uncertainties far more perilous than we do. Life was hard several hundred years ago. Back then, exposing oneself to death was not unusual. Even so, had these forerunners been paralyzed by their fears, they could not have held on.

Over a decade later, and several hundred miles to the north, the Pilgrims confronted similar hardships. As every schoolchild learns, they came not for wealth but for religious freedom. Back home in Britain, Charles I was making life difficult for dissenters.[3] People were literally put to death for not complying with the dictates of the Church of England. Despite this, the Puritans would not submit. A stiff-necked group, they insisted on a rigid religious discipline that today seems harsh. Accordingly, only by putting thousands of miles between themselves and the authorities could they follow their consciences.

But what did they find in the New World? It was cold, it was desolate, and it did not have the provisions to keep them alive.[4] And so like their contemporaries in Jamestown, they died in large numbers. Still, their co-religionists continued to come by ship until their plantation was secure. At the outset, the settlers had the assistance of the local Native Americans. With time and arrogance, however, they alienated these people. This made families living on the frontier vulnerable. At any moment, they might be slain by their former allies. As for non-Puritans, their presence was not tolerated. These folks were either killed or driven from their colony. The Pilgrims were thus no nicer than their southern compatriots. They were far more principled in their religious zealotry; nonetheless, they were not a touchy-feely bunch.

Yet they were brave. When they perished, they perished with dignity. Of course, like all humans they wept over their deceased. In spite of this, their faith provided the certainty to persevere. Think about it. They were alone. An unfriendly government was too far away to protect them—even had it wanted to. The natives were so different from themselves that they were not a source of security. Meanwhile the land was terribly rocky and the temperatures so bitter that agriculture was unreliable. They could have easily allowed their fears to get the best of them. They could have turned tail and sailed home, there to pledge allegiance to a hated monarch. Yet they didn't! Quite the contrary, they sucked up their courage and continued.

The need for courage was not over. The American frontier did not close until two centuries later. For all that time, an audacious few continued to trickle westward.[5] Nowadays we are likely to regard these folks as heartless aggressors. In setting up homesteads in lands belonging to the natives, they are alleged to have exhibited an unbecoming rapacity. Ours, however, is the censure of hindsight. We are aware of the damages that were inflicted on the aboriginal people. Indeed, in our imagination we have converted the Native Americans into noble savages who were ground under the heel of coldhearted conquerors. In retrospect, they are perceived as peaceful and loving souls. That they too indulged in unprovoked savagery is lost in our rush to be compassionate.[6]

The pioneers enjoyed no such perspective. They moved west, not because they looked forward to butchering the natives. Rather, they were seeking to improve their economic circumstances. With hungry mouths to feed and good jobs hard to come by, they sought opportunities that they understood were fraught with danger. The horrors of what the Comanches[7] did in West Texas and the Sioux[8] did on the northern plains were fresh on their minds. Indeed, the Native Americans slaughtered one another as well, not just the hated settlers. To take up farming under these conditions was terrifying. Survival was not assured, yet the risks were undertaken. Can this be regarded as anything less than courageous? No doubt injustices were perpetrated. They were perpetrated on both sides. This, however, does not detract from tenacity needed to endure unremitting adversity.

Nor should we overlook the patriots who made this westward march possible.[9] To deride them as avaricious brutes does not do them the honor they deserve. The United States is far from perfect, nonetheless the democratic institutions it established have been a beacon for the rest of the world. Here too we are liable to misread the past. Having lived all of our lives with the ability to speak our minds and to enter occupations of our choosing, we assume that this is the way things have always been. Few Americans have any sense of what it was like to live under the authority of a European monarch. Merely to have questioned a king's competence in the privacy of one's own home could have occasioned a gruesome death.[10] To be a so-called traitor could mean a swift hanging, followed by being drawn and quartered. Those Americans who helped create and defend an enlightened alternative ought to be recognized for their valor. Their legacy was not preordained, nor was it achieved without bloodshed.

Neither has our nation been without heroes. Not only pioneer champions but also political ones brought forth a nation conceived in liberty and dedicated to the proposition that all men are created equal. The American founders were a uniquely courageous company. Benjamin Franklin[11] warned them upon signing the Declaration of Independence that they had best hang together or they would surely hang separately. This was not an idle caution. Nowadays many look back upon the Revolution as if it were a high-school pageant. They consider it as an excuse to dress in period costumes and sing patriotic songs. For those who experienced it firsthand, it was a blood-soaked tragedy. Many thousands died from wounds, disease, and exposure.

The war that began in 1775[12] and did not officially end until 1883 was never a sure thing. Numerous losses and privations punctuated an effort that could have failed had not the protagonists stayed the course. George Washington[13] epitomized this tenacity. One of the colonies' richest planters, he had more to lose than most. Nonetheless he volunteered to lead a ragtag army against the then superpower of Great Britain. More dicey still was that Washington was not a particularly competent general. During the conflict, he lost more than his share of battles. Still he did not give up nor surrender to despair. Always on the lookout for opportunities to best his foe, he found one at Yorktown. Even so, he would not have recognized this chance had he not kept his head. Had his fears gotten the better of him, his mind would probably have been too muddled to organize the victory.

Washington's courage did not end there. George III, not exactly the general's biggest fan, opined that if his enemy declined to accept a kingship, this would make him the greatest man in the world. Yet Washington did decline it. Despite the blandishments of his admirers and a military willing to put him in office, he refused to violate his convictions. Having enlisted to overthrow tyranny, he would not impose one of his own. Nor would he allow his officers to march on congress to work their will. It took guts to stand down his supporters—and even more guts to later go home and resume farming.

We ought not trivialize Washington's accomplishments as our first president. Many of this contemporaries feared that he might use his office to impose a military dictatorship. He did not. Others assumed that he would use his position to aggrandize himself. He did not. Almost no one believed he would spurn the third term he was sure to win. He did. Because Washington is no longer with us, he has become a cardboard cutout. Nonetheless, he was a human being who had his doubts and trepidations. Be that as it may, he kept his emotional turmoil under tight wraps. Determined to do what was right, he did not give in to his qualms, nor fold his tent when attacked by rivals. This is virtually the definition of courage.

Happily for the nation, Washington was not an isolated figure. Men such as John Adams, Thomas Jefferson, Alexander Hamilton, and James Madison risked their lives and honor for the sake of a noble cause. Adams[14] did not fight in the war, but he crossed the ocean several times on diplomatic missions; this when such journeys were perilous. Then, notwithstanding his undiplomatic temperament, he fought ridicule and failure to obtain international assistance. Meanwhile Jefferson[15] was the primary author of a document that tempted fate by insulting a powerful nation. Also, as governor, ambassador, secretary of state, and president, he ultimately authorized the Louisiana Purchase in the face of questions about its legality. As for Hamilton,[16] although he was Washington's principal advisor, he left the safety of a desk job to lead an assault on a redoubt at Yorktown. Then as our first secretary of the treasury he invented the department that he supervised and used it to secure the country's credit. Hated for taking on debts that could have been repudiated, he stood firm. Last, Madison[17] was the primary architect of the Constitution, the Speaker of the House of Representatives who oversaw its initial organization, and a president who braved a second war with England. Had he not, along with Alexander Hamilton and John Jay, also fought for the ratification of the Constitution,[18] it is unlikely that the United States would have remained united.

The above inventory is only of men, which might make it seem that only they are capable of courage. This is far from the truth. Women were long denied the opportunity to serve in government and on the battlefield, but this did not preclude impressive contributions. Abigail Adams[19] stands out as an exemplar of what many women accomplished. Left behind by her husband as he traveled on national business, she took over running their farm. Also forced to raise her children during a smallpox epidemic, she never flagged in caring for others. In addition, she collected supplies for the war effort and provided invaluable counsel to her husband. Although women have usually been denied the high profile of public authority, in private they have been no less dauntless. The men in their lives could never have achieved what they did had such women not mastered their fears and provided a stable social infrastructure.

During its inception, the United States could have been undermined by a host of dangers—both internal and external. Those at its helm made many mistakes and yet defied death and humiliation to establish what would become the world's longest lasting republican democracy. Nevertheless, their work might have gone for naught had not another remarkably courageous president taken the rudder. He is, of course, Abraham Lincoln.[20] Perhaps our most revered chief executive, every schoolchild learns of his humble origins. Born in a log cabin and largely self-taught, he became an erudite and successful lawyer. Not quite as successful as a politician, he often failed to win the offices to which he aspired. Even so, he did not give up. His pursuit and capture of the Republican nomination for president was a masterpiece of political maneuvering. Had he not been cool under fire, it is doubtful victory could have been realized.

Furthermore, having already sustained many tragedies in his personal life, Lincoln was well equipped to meet the challenges of a nation rent apart. Surrounded by cabinet members who believed him to be an oaf, and pilloried in the press as not up to the job, he carried on. While his predecessor, James Buchanan, had been paralyzed in the face of Southern opposition, Lincoln acted decisively and intelligently. Although his generals frequently disappointed him,[21] he never lost his nerve. Beset by deaths at home and on the battlefield, he often sank into a deep depression that he never allowed to deter him from doing his duty. He understood the terrible carnage that his directives ensured; yet he kept his eye on the larger issues—most notably maintaining the Union.

With respect to slavery, Lincoln is nowadays faulted for considering blacks inferior to whites. This has been assailed as evidence of his underlying bigotry. In fact, Lincoln was a man of his time, albeit a much better man than most. Whatever his thoughts about the alleged biological deficits of people of color, he did not let this prevent him from protecting their rights. Whatever their abilities, Lincoln insisted that they were human and therefore deserving of the dignity that is every human's birthright. His colleagues may have disagreed, but he was unwavering in his dedication to moral principles. Despite opposition, he issued the Emancipation Proclamation. Also despite desperate resistance, he shepherded the Fourteenth Amendment through Congress to ensure that those who had been liberated would not be re-enslaved. We may take this accomplishment for granted; yet the courage to achieve it was well beyond the norm.

Lincoln stands out as a paragon of valor, but his courage would have been in vain had it not been supplemented by that of hundreds of thousands of soldiers. Over six hundred thousand perished during the Civil War.[22] Although this was by far the bloodiest conflagration per capita in our nation's history, the troops fought with remarkable bravery. Many had doubts about the worthiness of ending slavery; still they put their lives on the line. The novel *The Red Badge of Courage*[23] revealed the fears and misgivings of those who served on the front line. But serve they did. Moreover, this was particularly gory conflict. Thus the Minie balls tore into their flesh, ripped out their innards, and severed their limbs. Nonetheless, the rebels during Pickett's charge at Gettysburg and the Yankees engaged in the frontal assault at Cold Harbor kept coming. They lifted their battle flags off the ground, only to be felled by the thousands. As soldiers, they knew this might happen, and, as men, they did not want to die; yet they did their duty.

Americans have long done their duty.[24] They did it during the Revolution, the War of 1812, the Mexican War, the Spanish-American War, the First and Second World Wars, Korea, Vietnam, and also in the Gulf, Iraq, and Afghanistan hostilities. While I did not fight in Vietnam, I trained alongside men who did. I knew—I could see it in their eyes and hear it in the crackle of their voices—that they did not want to perish. Yet they went and many did die. Moreover, few fell to the ground weeping in terror or calling out for their mothers. They instead pulled themselves together and discovered that they had a courage they did not know they possessed. This mettle, I am sure, is present in more people than realize it. Civilians too, if they set their minds to it, can control their fears. The ability is in our genes—even if we consider ourselves cowards.

THE WRETCHED REFUSE

Like many Americans, my ancestors did not reside in this country during the Revolution. As a result, they did not get to contribute to its inception with their blood or treasure. They were later immigrants.[25] While growing up, I suspected that such persons were inferior. After all, if they could not make it in their homelands, this was probably because they lacked the right stuff. Emma Lazarus's poem at the base of Statue of Liberty seemed to summarize the situation. "Give me," she wrote, ". . . the wretched refuse of your teeming shore." My grandparents were evidently wretched refuse. Not personally daring enough to compete with other Europeans, they were the leftover trash no one wanted.

America has for centuries been a receptacle for castoffs. First came the Puritans, Quakers, and convicts, who did not fit in at home. Then came the indentured servants unable to make a living in England and therefore willing to sell themselves as quasi-slaves. After this followed the Germans who were religious refugees. Next to arrive were the Scotch-Irish.[26] They were an unruly mob who had abandoned their hardscrabble lives in Scotland in search of better land in Ireland, but were then ejected by the native peoples. The American frontier was about the only place left for them. It was likewise a refuge for the Catholic Irish after they were decimated by the potato famine.[27] Mixed in among them were expatriates fleeing the failed revolutions of central Europe. The losers in uprisings intended to introduce socialism, they too now sought safety. Later came the Jews[28] escaping from the pogroms of Eastern Europe, the Poles evading subjugation under the Russians, and the southern Italians[29] taking flight from starvation and oppression. Each nationality found its way across the Atlantic. More recently, Hispanics, Asians, and Africans also arrived in hopes of improving their status. Almost none of them were well educated, wealthy, or sophisticated. All once seemed to me, and many others, to be at the bottom of a not-very-worthy barrel.

But were these folks courageous? Were they cowardly losers or latter-day pioneers? To begin with, their trip across the ocean was often harrowing. During the sailing era, many thousands perished at sea. After the advent of the steamship, their survival was more certain, whereas their comfort in steerage left much to be desired. Once they landed, their adversities did not end. For many, the language barrier was potent. They did not fit in because they could not understand nor be understood by their neighbors. Especially if their culture was different, they were not made welcome. The Irish, for instance, were regarded as lower than dogs. Often forced to reside in squalid inner cities, they had to carve out a niche merely to survive. None of this was easy. Who then would tackle such obstacles? Probably not cowards.

As for blacks, they constituted a separate category[30] in that they were almost entirely involuntary immigrants. The slavery into which they were thrust was far more discouraging than anything encountered by Europeans. Unremitting labor, savage punishments, and chronic humiliation were their daily fare. It might be assumed that courage had nothing to do with surviving this ordeal, but that would be wrong. To not give up under these circumstances demanded the utmost fortitude. To hold back when treated with utter contempt required strong internal controls. These abilities too were bequeathed to succeeding generations. The children and grandchildren of slaves also required courage to withstand the perils of prejudice and discrimination.[31]

I am now going to spend some time discussing the histories of my grandparents, not because their challenges are more significant than others, but because I know them best. Actually, I know comparatively little about my father's family. As a small child, I was too young to ask his father about his parents' past. What I know is this: The Fein family lived in Bialystok, Poland, then a part of the Russian empire. My paternal grandfather, Joseph, was a scribe working for a local aristocratic family; hence he must have been fairly well educated. By 1898, he was married and the father of two young daughters. At this point, the town was ravaged by a nasty pogrom. With his Polish neighbors attacking and murdering Jews, he and his wife, Flora, barricaded themselves in their apartment. Shortly afterward, they decided that prudence decreed they migrate to the United States.

Once the little family arrived, the question was how to survive. Unschooled in English, Joseph clearly could not continue to work as a scribe. Eventually he became a proprietor of a candy store. This required him to work from dawn to dusk, especially as his family grew to include eight children. Ultimately, by buying stores, building up their trade, selling them for a profit, and then moving on to the next store, he earned enough to purchase a house. His clan did not live in great comfort, but nearly all of his grandchildren grew up to be college graduates, that is, doctors, lawyers, and college professors.

That's about all I know. Meanwhile, I learned much more about my mother's side of the family, the Tarriffs, because I was able to query my grandfather Simon about his roots. His parents lived in the Ukraine on the Dnieper River. There his father, a fierce-looking man with a scruffy beard, worked as a riverboat captain. Simon himself started a wagon-painting business as a young man. This provided him with the resources to become a gallant dandy. In his eyes, Ekaterinislav was the Paris of Russia. It main tree-lined boulevard surely rivaled the Champs-Élysées. In time, he even began courting a French maid.

When, however, his lady friend was accused of stealing from her employers, the police called him in for a grilling. Alarmed, Simon's father decreed that it was time to marry. A match was quickly arranged with the sister of the next-door neighbor. Not long afterward, Simon began to fear that he was about to be drafted into the czar's army. The winds of war were blowing in Europe, and being conscripted imposed twenty years of precarious service. The alternative was migrating to America. But first it was necessary to get out of Russia. Three times, Simon attempted to sneak over the border. The first two times, he was caught and sent back home from jail to jail. The third time, he made it out and sailed off to New York and thence to meet relatives in Boston.

Back home in Russia, his new wife, Lizzie, stayed with his parents. The plan was for him to earn enough to send for her. But then the Great War intervened. Simon, still in Boston, obtained employment by working as a wagon painter. Uncomfortable being regarded as a Greenhorn, he struggled to fit in. Nonetheless, he managed to enjoy himself by living what he later described as "the life of a bachelor." When finally the war ended, Simon sent for Lizzie. Unfortunately, Europe was so war-ravaged that she had to make the trip by way of the Trans-Siberia Railway. When she arrived in Japan, however, she came down with typhoid fever. This required months of hospitalization in Yokohama. During this period, all of her hair fell out and later grew back snow white.

It was under these conditions that Simon and Lizzie were reunited. Soon, very soon, Lizzie became pregnant with their first child, my mother, Florence. Now a stay-at-home mom living among strangers whose language she never fully learned, her emphasis was on being a homemaker. She cooked and cleaned and took care of the kinder. Then, when times were tough, her family came first. Accordingly, at dinnertime she made sure that her husband and three children were fed first. Claiming that she had eaten already, she frequently went hungry. This was not discovered until she was later hospitalized for malnutrition.

As for Simon, he always worked. But he was ambitious. His entrepreneurial spirit bridled at having to work for others. And so he started his own painting business, which, despite its many ups and downs, he eventually transformed into a contracting business. At one point, this required a move to New York City. There he began another new chapter of his life, eventually also earning enough to buy a house. In fact, my parents met because they lived next door to each other.

When, late in life, Simon decided to move to Miami, he found it necessary to nurse Lizzie, who had by then developed Alzheimer's. After her death, he survived several years on his own until he developed colon cancer. It was at this time that I asked him to look back upon his life. He did so cheerfully, often chuckling about the adventures he had navigated. His, he explained, had been a good life. There were no regrets—simply pride at having created a family that was doing well.

Were Joseph or Simon, or for that matter Lizzie and Flora, cowards—much less wretched refuse? I, no longer an inexperienced child, do not think so. They piloted a course of challenges in excess of any that I have confronted. Coming to a new land, without much assistance, took enormous courage. They headed into a far greater unknown than I did when traveling alone around Europe. Despite this, they built businesses and families, irrespective of the adversity and discrimination they encountered. In the end, they lived through the Great Depression and endured two world wars, all the while maintaining their dignity. Unlike the parents and siblings they were forced to leave behind, there to be slaughtered by the Nazis, they were able to found new lineages. Was this something to be ashamed of? I don't think so.

Courage consists of much more than storming machine-gun nests. It entails far more than being willing to sacrifice one's life for the sake of others. Normal bravery, the sort that enables us to support ourselves and our families, while at the same time adhering to moral standards, requires that we face life's challenges with relative equanimity. We may be afraid, but if we refuse to run away, that is, if we take on our assigned tasks diligently and intelligently, then we too are brave. We do not have to win; we do not even have for endure with complete grace. But we must persist, despite our fears. That is what counts.

My grandparents did! Yours probably did as well. Clearly, many generations of Americans have dealt valiantly with a variety of frontiers. And they prevailed. They beat back a myriad of dangers and left us with a better world. So what about us? It is now our turn. Do we have the backbone that they demonstrated? Many of us obviously do. The United States remains an economic and military powerhouse. Yet many, too many, of us have decided to run for cover. Swathed in riches, we look for the easy way out, rather than test our mettle. This is a shame because it deprives us of the victories that our ancestors achieved. Nor is this due to a genetic deficiency. Almost all of us can do more and be more, if we choose. The question is, will we? Instead of hoping to be saved from dangers that we do not understand, will we suck up our fears and move forward? Will we prove to ourselves that we are the worthy successors of our intrepid ancestors?

We will not lack challenges to test our courage. Our ancestors faced unprecedented difficulties. They encountered physical and emotional obstacles that might have brought them down. But so do we. They were pioneers in a variety of ways. Whether in fleeing Europe for religious liberty, establishing an enduring democratic republic, or emigrating to a strange land for safety's sake, they encountered formidable problems. So will we. We are teetering at the brink of a middle-class revolution.[32] No previous society has ever been as thoroughly middle-class. We are therefore in the process of discovering how to cope with this novel development. Will we be able to deal with the demands of professionalized employment? Can we become the self-motivated experts needed to sustain a diverse techno-commercial society? How are we to manage the freedom to marry or not? Can we master the strains of this voluntary intimacy or will they tear our families apart? Is our democracy apt to perish on the shoals of apathy? Or will we take responsibility for our destinies? It is too soon to tell. What is clear is that we will need the courage to create previously undreamt-of solutions.

Ours has become a nation of unparalleled wealth and freedom. We thus possess opportunities to fulfill our aspirations in ways that no preceding generation ever could. Yet we might nonetheless fumble these advantages. In our desire never to be bruised, we could decide to hold back from taking any risks? We might therefore demand protections that eliminate every danger. This would be tragic. It would deprive us of the pleasures of conquering a new frontier. It would likewise prevent us from actualizing our potential or providing a solid foundation for our children and grandchildren. This is not necessary. We can do as well as we decide to do. We too can be courageous, every bit as heroic as our ancestors.

Chapter 2

FROM SAFETY NET TO FEATHER BED

THE PERILS OF SUCCESS

Courage has gone out of fashion. Where once it was praised to the skies, today it is an embarrassment. Among the ancient Greeks, heroes were considered demigods. Their valor in battle was retold in stirring song and myth. Alexander the Great[1] was great not merely because of his conquests but because he fought bravely. Among the Romans, Julius Caesar[2] was admired for his military triumphs but also because in the midst of the melee he wore a red cloak that dared his enemies to cut him down. Our own George Washington[3] was first in war, first in peace, and first in the hearts of his countrymen because they recognized his valor. This was a man who had horses shot from under him but never fled the field in despair.

Where are today's heroes? SEAL Team Six?[4] Maybe. But we hide them in the shadows. Their deeds are celebrated, yet for the most part they remain anonymous. After World War II, millions of soldiers and sailors came home to flag-waving parades, whereas Vietnam and Iraq veterans had to plead for recognition. Although we continue to applaud athletic success, in what other endeavors do we admire bravery? Nowadays we often glorify people merely for being famous. Intrepid souls, such as the Kardashians, who are able to get their faces in the media, not necessarily for doing anything noteworthy, are regarded as superhuman. Asked whom they most admire, many Americans respond by citing these pseudoluminaries.

In fact, we are apt to make excuses for people who have done nothing to merit acclaim. We are told that everyone deserves *unconditional positive regard.*[5] Just for being human, whatever their failures or malfeasances, we are to treat all and sundry as if they had earned our esteem. Consider what this implies. The meanest beggar and the most valiant astronaut are to be regarded as brothers in gallantry. The beggar may not have accomplished much, but if we understood the stresses he has endured, we would realize that he too is worthy of our admiration. Mere survival is thus viewed as evidence of courage. One does not have to have stood up to the "slings and arrows of outrageous fortune" to warrant acclaim. Those who have run away are also to receive tribute.

Courage, of course, has not disappeared. The Navy SEALs are not alone. Every day, brave men and women enter military service and put their lives on the line. They do this voluntarily. Many do it for love of country. Or think about the hundreds of firefighters and police officers who rushed into the Twin Towers on 9/11. They understood that this might be a suicide mission, but they undertook it anyway. Their spirit is daily matched by first responders who enter burning buildings or face down armed criminals. Or what about the doctors and nurses who minister to Ebola patients? They are obviously aware of colleagues who succumbed to the disease. Deep inside they must be frightened, yet they continue to serve.

These are unquestionably examples of courage. Many more are less visible. What about the student who is unsure of her math abilities but studies so hard that she passes the test? What of the parent who works two jobs in order to support her children? What too of the entrepreneur who risks his savings on an idea others dismiss as foolish? Every day, ordinary men and women conquer their uncertainties to accomplish difficult tasks. They may not advertise it. They may not even realize that they have done something praiseworthy. But they—not everyone—exhibit the tenacity to cope with formidable difficulties.

Life *is* hard. Personal relationships *are* demanding. Even living up to our own personal expectations can be problematic. Life is easy only for people who construct an impenetrable cocoon of apathy around themselves. Yet even these folks have their moments of doubt. If people are to be winners, if they are to fulfill their potential, they must possess courage. If they do not, if they make excuses and avoid the possibility of failure, they are sure to fail—no matter how strenuously they proclaim their inherent worth.

Americans are in a unique situation. We are heir to opportunities that few others have enjoyed, but we have also inherited an affluence that can sap us of our energies. The Roman Empire[6] surrendered to decadence. After the republic had grown to unprecedented size and wealth, its citizens were no longer prepared to defend their patrimony. Rome did not fall to the barbarians. It fell to its people's unwillingness to resist the barbarians. Under the Republic, ordinary Romans were prepared to take up arms against the Gauls, the Etruscans, and the Carthaginians. When attacked, they fought back. When threatened, they went on the offensive. Their successes bred further successes as they went on to integrate one tribe after another into their domain. Along with this came the grain of Egypt, the tin of Britain, and slaves from just about everywhere.

So prosperous did Rome become that it could not only build monumental structures, such as roads, aqueducts, and amphitheaters; it could subsidize the idleness of its citizens. Diverted by free bread and brutal circuses, these slackers allowed others to do the heavy lifting. This applied at home, where slaves ran their households, and abroad, where barbarians filled the ranks of their armies. Why should they, the most powerful people in the world, engage in manual labor? Wasn't it easier to force others to do the nasty work? Romans, in their superiority, were clearly better fitted for lounging on couches, sipping wine, and reading poetry.

Until, that is, the barbarians got it into their heads that if they were fighting for the Romans, they could just as well fight against them. Why take orders from lazy aristocrats when they could wrest their treasures from them? And so they did. People who are besotted by luxury abstain from the discomfort of fighting, even on their own behalf. Accustomed to being pampered, they fritter away their moral fiber.

Is this what is happening to the United States? Has the nation become so habituated to power and extravagance that its people will not deign to do what is necessary to sustain these? Winning takes courage, yet courage is difficult to acquire and dangerous to act upon. Better then to wallow in the artificial courage of computer games or the vicarious courage of the stadium. These feel good, without the wear and tear, or the jeopardy, of the real thing. Better still to bask in the phony adulation of reflected fame. Why not pretend that you are every bit as valiant as the athletes and movie stars with whom you identify? This is heroism without heroics; it is love without the potential for rejection.

The problem is that the phony is phony. It cannot provide the satisfaction of actual accomplishments. People who pretend to be brave may jump up and down on the couch when they score points in a digital war, but they know this isn't reality. However much they may brag about their victories, they have not actually survived being shot at. Nor is a government entitlement the same as an economic achievement. The money may be the same, but that which is earned is far more valuable. Resources acquired with little effort and praise obtained without exertion are empty. They do not provide lasting satisfactions because they are not secured through personal merit.

Courage—the real thing—does not come automatically. It is valuable precisely because it is not universal. While virtually everyone possesses the capacity to be brave, not all of us are. Courage is attained; it is not granted. No one is born with it. Although we arrive in this world with its possibility, it is up to us to realize it. Cowardice is also possible. We can allow our fears to paralyze us. Yet which of these we choose is up to us.

Nowadays the blandishments of cowardice are everywhere. We are told that we do not have to compete for success. We are assured that we are all winners no matter what we do—or refrain from doing. Nor is anyone supposed to be so unkind as to point out our shortcomings. In a nation as wealthy as the United States, everyone is entitled to respect; no one is to be made uncomfortable. This is our birthright. Those who question our credentials are therefore behaving badly. They are discriminatory; which is self-evidently deplorable.

Nowadays, decent people are not supposed to offend others. Whatever their inadequacies, these weaknesses are expected to be passed over in silence. This especially includes cowardice. No one must be overtly accused of timidity. To do so would be an insult; an abrogation of good taste. We may be aware of another's faintheartedness, but we must keep this knowledge to ourselves. In fact, it would be better if we convinced ourselves that this fragility did not exist. Otherwise the victims might return the favor and expose our own frailties.

Currently no one is permitted to experience pain. With food plentiful, nobody should be allowed to starve. With ample housing available, no one should go without a comfortable abode. Likewise, with medicine capable of miraculous cures, none should suffer unattended sickness. Whatever a person's status or attainments, he or she deserves to share in the pleasures of our affluence.[7] As a result, no one needs to take definitive actions to ensure personal comfort. Bravery is thus no longer a prerequisite for escaping anguish. To the contrary, a cozy well-being has theoretically become our natural condition.

Last, today no one should ever experience failure. A nation with abundant riches and power ought to share these equitably. Whenever anyone is in jeopardy, the community must come to his or her rescue. It cannot put up hurdles that require courage to master. This would be unfair. It might demonstrate that not everyone is equal. Merely because a person has not elected to compete for success does not justify penury or disapproval. An honorable society, a just society, must offer a safety net that protects everyone from misfortune. In short, no one deserves to lose. Nor can personal valor be the criterion for winning.

Americans are a compassionate people.[8] If we have the wherewithal to protect others from their mistakes, we assume that we must try. No one's feelings should be hurt, for any reason, that is, if we possess the means of preventing this. The problem is that we do not always have the means. Life is not only hard; it is unfair. Not everyone wins—certainly not to the same degree. Happiness is assured to none of us. In fact, its possession is correlated with courage. People who are brave enough to stand up to life's hardships have a better chance of surmounting them. They are thus more likely to acquire satisfying jobs and loving relationships. They are also apt to be more highly esteemed. Although this is unfair, it is fundamental to the human condition. Protesting against this is in vain. Consequently, those who desire happiness must also pursue courage.

Most Americans agree that we should provide a safety net for unfortunates. These folks should not be allowed to fall into utter degradation, assuming we can prevent it. Nonetheless, this fail-safe objective has been converted into a feather bed. Not survival, but everlasting comfort is deemed essential. This attitude, unfortunately, is self-defeating. Promising people success without exertion is an invitation to sloth and pusillanimity. It underwrites personal weakness and therefore unhappiness. People who abstain from becoming winners can only be provided with make-believe victories. Sadly, that which is not real is without substance. It is a chimera that offers false hope.

NOTHING OFFENSIVE

Rich people do not want to be offended. They do not want others to say things that might make them feel uncomfortable. What is the point of being rich if the riffraff cannot be kept from the door? Sequestered estates and legions of servants are expected to create impregnable barriers that only light and beauty can penetrate. Why then can't a rich nation banish odious experiences in general? Why should any of its inhabitants be subjected to experiences that upset their equilibrium? Surely everyone deserves what amounts to a moral wall that excludes all distasteful encounters.

The Redskins kerfuffle is instructive.[9] For decades the Washington franchise of the National Football Association has been known as the "Redskins." For most of this period, the name was considered innocuous. If anything, it was regarded as a tribute to the fighting spirit of Native Americans. Much as the Cleveland baseball team was called the Indians; or the Atlanta team, the Braves, the goal was to identify with a winning people. The home team was, after all, expected to win and the name cheered it on to victory.

The same strategy applied to the New York Yankees, the Dallas Cowboys, the Kansas City Chiefs, the Minnesota Vikings, and Notre Dame's Fighting Irish. No insult was intended, nor for the most part taken. But then political correctness entered the scene and suddenly people were offended. How could Native Americans be so casually demeaned? Wasn't it outrageous that the skin color of a much-maligned people should be used to hold them up to ridicule?

Although national surveys showed that most Indians were not affronted by the name, a vocal band of activists was. They would not tolerate so grievous a slur. And so they lobbied to get the name changed. All across the country, schools with Native American–associated appellations hurried to alter them. Ours was a nation that respected all of its inhabitants and hence would not tolerate rudeness. Disrespect hurt. It was immoral. Except that the owner of the Redskins would not cave. He considered the name traditional and therefore worthy of a defense.

And a defense was needed because the PC crowd was out for blood.[10] They turned to the government to withdraw the team's copyright and/or to force a ban on the name's appearance on television. Whatever pain the term caused, they were determined to repay this in kind. The activists assumed that the cowardice of the franchise owner would eventually result in his capitulation. Given that Native Americans did not possess the personal fortitude to endure these unintended insults, their protectors would, in essence, exploit his timidity in order to obtain justice. Indeed, courage was assumed to be in such short supply that mere threats would be enough to achieve the owner's surrender.

How did this happen? How did America become a place where the language police could so easily enforce a bland uniformity?[11] Free speech was once regarded as the most precious gem in the diadem of American liberty. How did it lose its luster? The answer arose from a commitment to extreme egalitarianism. A hyper-tolerance[12] industry surfaced on the assumption that discrimination consisted of more than denying social pariahs jobs or votes. It also entailed making them feel uneasy. To use language that emphasized their inferiority was thus a subtle form of bigotry. Furthermore, in turning their vulnerability against them, it was worse than its narrow-minded forerunners. Because it was difficult to detect, it was harder to fight. More elusive than outright slanders, it was thus tricky to identify.

Embedded in this strategy was the belief that the target community was too weak to protect itself. A lifetime of mistreatment had deprived its members of the resolution to fight back. Society as a whole therefore had to rise up in their defense. Whether the victims were minorities, women, or "different" in some way, the nation required an ethos of universal toleration. Everyone deserved

respect. No one had the right to judge others.[13] Nor was anyone entitled to make others feel bad about themselves. Precisely because
people were weak, nothing should be said that might exacerbate
their distress.

One of the first evidences of this new paradigm was the N-word.[14]
"Nigger" is a corruption of "negro," which in turn means "black."
Nevertheless it has become so vile a pejorative that its mere appearance is taken as evidence of bigotry. Although African Americans
routinely use the word among themselves, in the mouth of a white
person it is perceived as a grave insult—which it often is. Hence
during the O. J. Simpson trial,[15] when Mark Fuhrman, a prosecution
witness, was revealed to have used it in the past, this was compared
with the Holocaust. Its utterance was worse than the blood-spattered
murder of two innocents. Likewise, when Paula Deen, a food guru,
was discovered to have used the term decades earlier, her empire
began to crumble.[16] Nothing she could say, no matter how abject her
apology, could remove the stain.

Of more import was the reception accorded Daniel Patrick
Moynihan's[17] study of the black family. He discovered that by the
1960s, almost one-quarter of all African American children were
born out of wedlock. Accordingly, he sounded the alarm. At this rate,
the black family was becoming an endangered institution. If nothing
were done, this would deprive millions of children of the emotional support they deserved. Yet nothing was done. Why? Because
black leaders objected to an allegation that presumably subjected
their community to disrespect. They insisted that the black family
was strong. It always had been and always would remain a treasured social bulwark. Regrettably, half a century later, nearly three-
quarters of black children are born to single-parent households.[18]
Largely raised by single mothers, they are denied the benefit of a
male parent. With this has come the loss of the personal discipline
that might facilitate economic success.

But blacks weren't the only offended constituency. Feminists decided women had been so brutalized that verbal suggestions indicating that they might be different than men must be forbidden.[19] Difference was equated with inferiority, and inferiority was equated with women-bashing. Such an implication was thus tantamount to physical abuse. In part because women had less upper-body strength, the community had long ago prohibited rape and wife-beating. Comparable protections were clearly needed for verbal slurs. Assumed, albeit rigorously denied, was the belief that women did not have the courage to stand up to insults. As a result, terms such as *waitress* or *stewardess* had to be modified. They were to be transformed into gender-neutral *servers* and *flight attendants*.

But wait. Weren't women every bit as competent as men? Weren't we told that women could do any job men could? No matter. Women were now imbued with the right to decide when they had been offended. The alleged victims are to be judge, jury, and executioner. The fact that a woman felt affronted proved that she had been. Her sensitivity was thus the gauge of whether she was being subjected to a hostile work environment.[20] Accordingly, the most sensitive women were allowed to set the standard. Apparently, the less able they were to cope with their distress the more their injuries mattered. Lauded for their strength, they were nonetheless to be wrapped in cotton batting.

In addition to blacks and women, homosexuals were also eligible for similar treatment. They might be different, but no longer could they be disparaged for their differences. Like women, after being scarred by years of adversity, they were not only encouraged to come out of the closet, they could now punish anyone who objected to their lifestyle. Opposition to gay marriage was expressly despised. It was conclusive proof of homophobia and thus a reason to dismiss people from their jobs.[21] Homosexuals were also evidently too delicate to withstand disagreement. Not even religious convictions could to be marshaled against them. These had to be neutralized despite the offence this gave to the faithful. The irony of this was lost on the prosecutors.

Our schools and universities have become the epicenter of this political correctness.[22] Although once regarded as neutral territory where diverse opinions could be shared and evaluated, a progressive uniformity now reigns. Censorship is thus employed to infuse the young with the correct thinking. In this way, what some call humanism is promoted and negative judgments spurned. Niceness is thereby to become the norm. But, of course, if students are not nice enough to agree with their teachers, these pedagogues must still be nice to them. Tolerance is to become the rule, except that intolerance will not be tolerated.

Let us pause for a moment to examine what it means to be nonjudgmental. To evaluate, and perhaps reject, people is nowadays shunned as discriminatory. No right-thinking person is ever to condemn others. In fact, as noted above, every human being is considered worthy of unconditional positive regard. No matter who they are, or what they have done, they are to receive complete acceptance. They need to be cherished, even if their behavior is considered deplorable. The essence of this attitude is: "I will love you no matter what. You are not your actions and therefore you deserve appreciation whatever your transgressions. You, as a human being, are a tender flower deserving of delicate cultivation. Because you might be damaged by negative evaluations, these must never be voiced. You need to be allowed to grow into adulthood undisturbed by opinions that might cause distress."

This attitude obviously regards humans as lacking the power to withstand adversity. Courage is not to be cultivated, but rather to be made unnecessary. Mere words, whether accurate or not, are to be eschewed if they possess negative connotations. The reason? These appraisals could apparently so warp a child's self-image as to destroy his or her future.[23] The notion that children can master their fears, or correct iniquitous behavior, is thus dismissed out of hand. The young (or for that matter the old) are deemed too delicate to grow stronger. Once criticized, they can never recover; they can never fix what is broken or gain in stature. In other words, their innate cowardice cannot be overcome.

This nonjudgmental viewpoint has an even greater drawback. Taken literally, it rejects all social standards. There is to be no good or bad. There are to be no honorable, as opposed to dishonorable people. The differences between the courageous and cowardly are therefore of no account. They are irrelevant to one's moral worth. According to this thesis, we are all human and consequently moral equals. Yet if this were true, we would live in an amoral world. We would, in effect, be entitled to do whatever we desired. A world without moral distinctions is a world without discipline. When people are not held responsible for their actions, there are no boundaries. All is fair in love, war—or anything else. Nevertheless human behavior does not float in midair. It is attached to particular humans who decide whether to engage in particular deeds. To absolve them of all responsibility is thus to approve of every action, including every transgression.

The contradiction here should be obvious. To protect people by forbidding negative judgments also requires that the condemnation of intolerance be prohibited. Genuinely unconditional positive regard would exclude the disapproval of *all* adverse opinions. Ironically, the current appeals for universal tolerance are prejudicial. They are not really universal. While they endorse some negative appraisals, the PC police disallow those of their adversaries. In other words, what offends a select body of censors is not to be questioned, whereas what they find offensive in others can be suppressed. Given this "heads I win, tails you lose" strategy, the PC constabulary does not need the courage to stand up to its detractors. It is only these others who are forced into silence.

This is no way to survive within a complicated world. It is not a recipe for expanding our knowledge or for resolving our differences. If only one side gets to take the floor, there can be no compromises; no learning from others. To the contrary, this strategy exalts a craven hypocrisy. While it pretends to be the courageous defender of sacred rights, it is a timorous bowdlerizer. Although its advocates denounce intimidation, they employ pressure to suppress unwelcome opposition. Not courageous dialogue, but a spineless duplicity is supposed to become the rule.

The results of this approach have come to pervade grades K–12.[24] Both textbooks and classroom lessons have been expurgated to protect the conventional wisdom. Not a marketplace of ideas, but a one-size-fits-all conformity is enforced. Niceness, as defined by one side of the political spectrum, dominates. The historian of education Diane Ravitch has documented this to a fare-thee-well. Women, for instance, can no longer be shown cooking dinner. This is interpreted as a noxious stereotype. Books must instead present women as engineers and astronauts. Females essentially have to be depicted as active and assertive. Now it is the men who are sent to the kitchen. They are also supposed to be portrayed as caring for their children. The idea is to demonstrate that males too are capable of sensitive nurturing. Images that go counter to the feminist philosophy are, however, banned.[25]

The same applies to other supposedly downtrodden groups. The elderly, for instance, must also be seen as active and assertive. To suggest that the infirmities of age might slow them down is regarded as negative propaganda. Likewise, blacks are to be depicted as executives, Native Americans as engineers, Hispanics as astronauts, gay couples as happy parents, and Muslims as patriotic citizens. These images are to serve as role models for what their authors hope will become the reality. They must in no way indicate that those represented are outside the mainstream. This would be injurious.

Greg Lukianoff, president of the Foundation for Individual Rights in Education (FIRE), has documented how this mentality also infects higher education.[26] Rather than serve as incubators of ideas, contemporary colleges and universities serve as platforms for disseminating politically correct messages. Conservative ideas have largely been banished on the grounds that they promote bigotry. This is especially so in the humanities and social sciences. To suggest, for instance, that affirmative action does not help its intended beneficiaries is rejected as stalking horse for racism. Even to present evidence that unprepared students fail out of school in disproportionate numbers is regarded as insulting.[27] The problem cannot be raised, lest some minority students conclude that they do not have the potential for academic success.[28]

Nor can conservative students voice these opinions openly. Their professors and fellow students might take offence. Feminists cry foul when told that men and women differ. They call this a microaggression and equate it with a full-scale frontal assault.[29] Gays similarly bridle when it is argued that marriage must be between a man and a woman. They insist on being provided with trigger warnings so that they can retreat to a safe room where they will not have to cover their ears.[30] Radicals are likewise affronted by strident defenses of capitalism. All of these potential victims must therefore be protected from exposure to sentiments that disturb their personal tranquility. As a result, the offenders are shunted to remote corners of the campus. Tiny, out-of-the-way, free speech zones are intended to prevent their perspectives from perturbing others.[31] They must certainly not be allowed to distribute provocative materials—such as copies of the US Constitution. These might unsettle students who find them unpalatable.

Nor must "offensive" speakers be invited to campus.[32] Here too conservatives are on notice that their opinions are unwelcome. Graduation ceremonies, for example, almost never feature prominent conservatives. Rutgers University students literally agitated to disinvite Condoleezza Rice from their commencement because of her political stances.[33] Although she was a former secretary of state, her positions about matters such as the Iraq War were deemed too controversial to be tolerated. Only peace activists were wanted. Likewise, anything that might demean Muslims is regarded as off-limits. Thus an uproar arose when author Ayaan Hirsi Ali was asked to speak at Brandeis University's commencement.[34] How could someone critical of Islamic attitudes toward women be provided a college platform? Both faculty and students objected. They did not want to hear viewpoints that contradicted their own. Nothing deemed offensive could be allowed to intrude upon the sensibilities of people who seemingly did not possess the grit to deal with dissent.

NOTHING PAINFUL

Nor do people who are living in a luxurious cocoon wish to experience pain. Pain is for the poor and downtrodden, not the rich and powerful. China's first emperor used his resources to search for the secret of eternal life.[35] Why shouldn't a person of his eminence live forever? Although his quest came to naught, others have also sought escape (e.g., the search for the Holy Grail). Americans are not exempt from this desire. If anything, our wealth has permitted us wider latitude. Many of us do not want our happiness to be troubled by unpleasant events. Neither do we wish to summon the courage to confront such difficulties.

Witness the epidemic of recreational drug use.[36] All sorts of chemical substances are introduced into our systems to anesthetize our pain. And why not? Many people have difficult childhoods. They never live up to their youthful ambitions because they were once subjected to inexcusable abuse. Millions must similarly cope with the deprivations of poverty. Additional millions are brought low by chronic disease. In few of these cases is the attendant pain welcome. Throughout most of history, little could be done to alleviate these sources of distress. Peasants went hungry; women died in childbirth; plagues ravaged entire continents. A resigned fatalism was therefore pervasive. Nowadays, however, a cornucopia of painkillers is at our disposal. What is more, given the money and the time to indulge, large numbers of Americas see no reason why they should not.

Alcohol has been with us for millennia.[37] Beer, wine, and whiskey are excellent analgesics. When intoxicated, people forget about their troubles—at least temporarily. Although there have been eras when drinking was more widespread than it is in our own, the ready availability of spirits today provides an easy release for those who assume that they are entitled to imbibe. So does a panoply of other palliatives. Consider marijuana.[38] It too has an ancient lineage; nonetheless it was seldom the drug of choice for Europeans. Nowadays, however, getting stoned has become a rite of passage. Even high-school students indulge. Nor is this epidemic likely to abate. With more states legalizing pot, its usage is apt to expand. Furthermore, because the culture has legitimized it, the stigma that once restricted its spread has dissipated. Time and again, we hear that pot is less dangerous than alcohol and therefore not a menace. Why then not anesthetize our troubles by hiding behind curtain of smoke?

Nor can there be an objection to legal medications. Antidepressants and antianxiety agents have become standard parts of life.[39] Ever since the introduction of tranquilizers, it has been considered legitimate to suppress unwanted feelings.[40] Why should these be tolerated when a pill can banish them from consciousness? Indeed, not long ago we were told that Prozac would make us better than normal. It would sharpen our thinking and bestow emotional maturity. This was all so easy—and so scientific. No longer would moderns have to struggle with internal demons. A magic bullet could make them go away without people having to exercise courage.

Too often nowadays when we experience fear, we attribute it to a mental defect.[41] We describe ourselves as in the grip of anxiety or as having been traumatized. Instead of owning up to our terrors, we depersonalize them by converting them into medical symptoms. They are not something we personally control, but something that happens to us. Yes, we are hurting, but we do not have to confront the hurt—or even acknowledge it. Rather than recognize dangers that might put us in jeopardy or seek to overcome them, we prefer to blot them out. Let our therapists or physicians deal with them; we have better things to do. This applies to depression as well. Why should we feel sad when sadness can be chemically controlled? That it might take courage to identify the source of our sadness or surmount its discomfort is excluded from our calculations.[42] Why seek emotional bravery when the cause of our distress is so simple to circumvent?

Likewise soldiers are not expected to have to deal with the traumas inherent in battle—at least not directly. Shell shock and battle fatigue, which were once stigmatized, have now come out of the shadows as something entirely different. Post-traumatic stress has been recognized as a medical condition.[43] No doubt exposure to death is harrowing. It is extremely frightening to any normal person. It also leaves scars. But now this intense fear has been deemed too painful to be acknowledged and confronted. After World War II millions of service men and women returned home following years of unremitting danger. Nonetheless, the vast majority of them adjusted to civilian life without much trouble. Contemporary soldiers are apparently more fragile. Their pain needs to be "understood." They have to be excused from the demands of ordinary life because they have endured extraordinary trials. This is true; they have indeed experienced horrendous ordeals. But in telling people they are too frail to deal with their fears, they are also being told that they do not have the courage to overcome them. Being provided help is not itself problematic. Nevertheless, the pervasive excuse-making that accompanies it often is.

In general, people are being provided a cushion against the pain of living. This includes the sting of interpersonal relationships. The advent of the computer, for example, provided a barrier that has been employed to separate people from the distress of interacting too closely with others. Now they can sit down by a keyboard without having to endure the agony of face-to-face rejection. Love, of course, has always been challenging.[44] Finding an appropriate partner and navigating the shoals of courtship is difficult. It is therefore not surprising that an electronic buffer is used to control the resultant vicissitudes. By enabling people to network indirectly, each party is thus able to deflect the rigors of rejection in private. Furthermore, the impersonality of the machine is less painful, and hence less bravery is required to explore potential liaisons.

None of this is objectionable per se. People have always used intermediaries to buffer inconvenient interactions. The difficulty comes with their more pervasive use. People must learn to deal with the hazards of interpersonal relationships by participating in interpersonal relationships. When they are relieved of the associated stresses, they are thereby deprived of an opportunity to discover how to manage them. They may also have difficulty dealing with the challenges inherent in intimacy. Close relationships entail perils. People can be hurt—and hurt badly. Nonetheless, if they are prevented from learning how to survive these bruises, they are less likely to find enduring love.

Genuine love requires courage. When it is lacking, the tenuous linkages that characterize the modern scene proliferate.[45] People who are unable to endure the demands and counterdemands of emotional closeness are also deprived of its blessings. And, importantly, so are their children. We humans were designed to be social creatures. Nonetheless our relationships are fraught with heartaches. They are painful to acquire; painful to sustain; and painful to lose. Yet despite their uncertainties, without them most lives are unfulfilling. And so, if we are to be happy, we need the bravery to tolerate this pain. Palliatives, whatever their form, are destructive when overused.

NO FAILURES

In a nation that perceives itself as all-conquering, most of those associated with its glory assume that they also have a right to be victorious. A majority of Americans expect to be winners—irrespective of what they personally do. They insist on coming out on top: period. On the other hand, in theory at least, everyone is to be equal. Not only that, but their equality is to be at an exceedingly high level. All must live in the luxury and security procured by sustained victories; all are to be surrounded by sycophantic respect. Remember: no one is to judge anyone else. All are deserving of unconditional positive regard. Merely by virtue of being American, they are special. Anything less would be unjust. In a nation of all kings and no commoners, prominence is to be theirs without exertion or contradiction. Personal distinction is an *entitlement*.

Nor need Americans compete for elevated status. Were this demanded of them, they might lose. They could . . . *gasp!* . . . fail. No, all must be awarded the laurel wreath. In the traditional Olympic Games there was only one winner per contest, whereas in today's Little League every participant receives a trophy. Merely taking part is considered the equivalent of triumphing. Besides, competition is gauche. Cooperation is obviously more fulfilling.[46] Working together without anyone feeling the sting of defeat enables all to do better than they could on their own.

As a consequence, courage is no longer needed. With failure banned, all can participate in the spectacle without fear of stumbling. No one need experience the shame of being exposed as less skilled than others. None need worry about appearing incompetent. Because no one's self-esteem will ever be placed in jeopardy, no one's abilities will ever be questioned.[47] This way everyone can feel good about themselves. And, needless to say, if they feel good about themselves, their subsequent performances will be superior. Treated as winners, they will surely perform as winners.

This, however, is juvenile thinking. But then again, millions of Americans do not want to grow up. They enjoy being pampered children. Growing up might saddle them with responsibilities that they might not be able to meet. Better, then, to play computer games that provide gratifyingly high scores. Better also to root for sports teams and participate in fantasy sports leagues. With so little at stake, the pain of loss will never be severe enough to require authentic bravery.

Many American children grow up in permissive households.[48] Their desires are never thwarted and their achievements never denigrated. They get their way almost all of the time. If, perchance, they receive a bad grade in school, Mom or Dad will surely confront the misguided teacher. And if battalions of helicopter parents complain of low grades, these will later be inflated. Or, if sonny boy finds the pain of being hit by a soccer ball unbearable, dodgeball will be barred from the curriculum. Only nonviolent games are to be permitted. Worse still, if junior's accomplishments are so meager that he cannot gain college admission, standards must be lowered so that everyone is eligible to attend. Why should just the most intelligent succeed? This is discriminatory. Only a school system that produces totally equal results can be considered fair.[49] Tracking by ability must thus be forbidden. This would stigmatize the losers and condemn them to inferiority.[50]

Nor should failure be allowed on the job. Everyone is entitled to good pay and lifetime security.[51] Hence bosses who impose rigid standards based on measurable results need to be constrained from inflicting this sort of abuse by obliging government regulators. Employers must not be allowed to promote people based on alleged merit. Unless jobs are distributed according to statistical probabilities, this imbalance demonstrates that judgments of worth were unfairly manipulated.[52] The tests were in all likelihood rigged. Lawsuits for discrimination must therefore be encouraged and minimum wages substantially raised. No one should be allowed to feel the pain of subservience. No one should be forced to engage in work that is not fully satisfying.

But if, through some unavoidable circumstance, a person does not become a boss, he or she is nevertheless entitled to live like one. Government transfer payments must be generous, otherwise their recipients might feel like failures. Welfare benefits need to be such that people receive more than they would from an entry-level job. Likewise, food stamps must cover alcoholic beverages, as well as lobster-tail dinners. Social Security, Medicare, and Medicaid must be liberal, irrespective of whether they bankrupt the nation. Obviously, to do less might subject some individuals to the humiliation of having less. Their inability to keep up would be visible for all to see, which would make their failure more galling.

In a just society, no one should be better than anyone else. People must therefore be responsible for one another. Each must be each other's keeper, rather than their competitor.[53] Pride in one's superiority must be discouraged on the grounds that it rubs others' noses in their inferiority. Losing hurts, so there must be no losing. Even the appearance of losing is upsetting. Universal success may be an impossible goal; nevertheless its pretense has to permeate our political and social institutions.

MORAL COURAGE

Life is hard—even in rich countries. Personal slights, pain, and failure are part of our human heritage. To pretend that they are not does not relieve us of their discomfort. Nor does it excuse us of having to confront their possibility. People can run away and hide; they can also make believe that they are living in a totally benign universe. But this does not make it so. Life is replete with sorrow and loss.[54] As a result, those living in denial escalate their chances of failure. This is true on a social level; it is true on a personal level. An old saw has it that cowards experience a thousand deaths, whereas the brave die but once. No society, no matter how generous, can protect us from this fate.

The good life is one that is fortified by moral courage.[55] This is especially so in rich and powerful societies. Their very success magnifies the dangers of an unwillingness to deal with fear. Individually and collectively, their members need to be honest about their apprehensions. As a result, they require the courage to be candid with themselves and each other. If they are not, they will make regrettable decisions from which they will suffer. This is all the more so because their power makes their choices more consequential.

Consider the implications of refusing to be offended. People who have the ability to fend off unwelcome information also have the ability to fend off unwelcome truths. When an uncomfortable reality, or even a potentially uncomfortable reality, is banned from consciousness, fictions inevitably fill the void. When these fabrications become extensive, the subsequent errors also become extensive. People who live in a truth-free bubble are prone to dreadful blunders. We all make mistakes. These cannot be avoided. But when we refuse to entertain perspectives other than our own, we ensure that our errors are not corrected. The truth can be harsh. It can collide with our fondest dreams. By the same token, others' opinions might be wrong. What they believe, including about us, can be off the mark. Nevertheless, they might be right—if only partially. Should we refuse to admit this merely because we have the capacity to do so, we may be the ones who go astray.

Likewise consider the implications of blocking out all pain. People who never feel pain are in far more danger than those who do. To never endure pain is never to be alerted to what might be harmful.[56] Fire burns. If its touch were not excruciating, we might thoughtlessly put our hands into flames. Thanks to the pain, we draw away and save ourselves from injury. The same is true of fear. Fear warns us when something might be dangerous. Nevertheless fear is painful. Most of us would rather not undergo the emotion. Yet if we have the power to enforce this desire, we are apt to exclude vital information. People who live in a drug-induced haze reside in a fool's paradise. They never see the train that is barreling down the tracks and hence they get crushed under its wheels. Similarly those who never permit themselves to endure the pain of personal rejection also never enjoy the pleasures of genuine love. Sealed off from frightening experiences, they are closed off from endearing ones. The lure of a painless life may be enticing, whereas its reality is dull and/or devastating.

Or consider the implications of a failure-free life. People who never fail never win. If they never compete, they never secure genuine victories. A placid life, where everyone is completely equal, is also one in which no one is special. Indeed, a life in which no one is better than anyone else is one that is less than mediocre. The only way for everyone to be on the same level is for everyone to be as low as the lowest common denominator. Nor would such a world be enlivened by innovation. If no one is allowed to be better than others, then there is no incentive to be different. But if no one can be different, there can be no fresh ideas. All must forever remain stuck in a common rut. Nor would there be the thrill of victory or the agony of defeat, even in sports. In a world without losers, no one is allowed to beat others on the playing field—or in politics, business, and love.

Unless we are prepared to deal with our fears regarding defeat, offence, and pain, we cannot protect ourselves from life's hazards. In addition, only if we master our fears can we fulfill our potentials. Forever holding back is a prescription for ruin. This is particularly true in a market-oriented democracy. The freedom and wealth derived from capitalism and a republican form of government would be dissipated if not protected. The courage of our ancestors bequeathed us remarkable opportunities. Nonetheless, these are not automatic. Each succeeding generation must find the courage to defend them.

A free and powerful society enables its members to make free and consequential decisions. To a historically great extent, they get to decide how to live their own lives. But if they cannot make good decisions, they will have to endure the penalties of bad ones. Accordingly, if they do not possess the courage to make sound choices, they will probably make unsound ones. Unaware of the truth, never alerted to potential dangers, and unwilling to contend for victory, they must settle for the dregs. Good decisions are informed decisions. Courageous people enter the fray with their eyes open and their loins girded for whatever is to come. Meanwhile, the faint-hearted slink away even before they are defeated. They never try to win, in the belief that they never can.

People who lack courage almost never risk the perils of intimate relationships. They rarely find love because they avoid the vulnerabilities entailed in choosing an appropriate mate or in developing a shared life-space. Nor are they likely to experience the joys of effective parenthood if they fear the demands made of them by their own offspring. The opposite of everlasting loneliness is not stress-free romance. Romance is never stress-free. True love can always go wrong. It can be derailed by the unresolved conflicts of individuals who are not prepared to meet each other honestly and forthrightly. Indeed, only the courageous have the capacity to fix love when it goes off course. In a free society, where people choose their mates, this is an ever-present challenge.

Correspondingly, people short of courage almost never live up to their occupational potential. In a middle-class society, we influence the kind of work we do. No longer do we automatically follow in our parent's footsteps. The sons of farmers do not need to be farmers, nor the daughters of homemakers, homemakers. What we grow up to be is not a given. As a result, if we do not discover who we are, explore the work available to us, or put in the effort to develop the requisite skills, we are apt to be burdened by occupational frustration. Social mobility is possible in a market-oriented community, but only for those who take advantage of its options. If they do not—perhaps for fear that they may not succeed—they will probably fail. Very few of us completely fulfill our dreams. Even so, the greatest fulfillment goes to those who take chances. Individuals with the fortitude to try, and then if they stumble, to try again, are likely to achieve at least the satisfaction of knowing they did what they could. Those who do not do so almost never feel the pleasures of achievement. Theirs are lives of brittle disappointment and bitter resignation.

Nor is life free of distress. We all get sick. We all die. We all have loved ones who perish. It is impossible for us, no matter how brave, to control every contingency. Even winners lose some of the time. For many, their religious beliefs assuage this anguish. Belief in a deity can provide comfort in moments of doubt. Here too we must be free to make our own choices. Thus, if we decide to believe, we must have the courage of our convictions. After all, only we can choose to live in accord with the dictates of faith. Or if we are nonbelievers, we must possess the nerve to face an uncertain universe. This too is up to us. Either way, we also need the equanimity to allow others to believe or not believe as they do.

Nor, in a democracy, is good governance certain. People who choose their leaders require the courage to choose good ones. Demagogues, who make promises they cannot keep, must not be allowed to lead them astray. Unless voters are willing to look behind the curtain to ascertain what is true, undemanding, albeit misleading, answers are apt to seduce them into misery. Because life is hard, no politician can make it trouble-free. It is therefore necessary for a free people to recognize when they are being sold a bill of goods. Reality may not always be congenial, whereas alluring unrealities can be fatal.

Many Americans are not certain about whether they have the courage to love, work, or be governed in accord with reality. They opt for fairytales on the assumption that temporarily feeling good is the best they can manage. This is unfortunate; it is also unnecessary. Most of us are capable of more bravery than we realize. Yes, we have limitations and doubts. But these can be managed. Perfection is not within our reach; but then again it has never been within anyone's. Those of us who are aware of our flaws may hesitate. Nonetheless, we are usually capable of more than we imagine. In the following pages, we will investigate how cowardice can be overcome. As a semi-recovered coward, I will try to share what I have learned.

Chapter 3

INTEGRATED FEAR MANAGEMENT

EMOTIONS

Courage is not binary. It is not an either/or proposition; that is, it is not that you either have it or do not. Courage is multifaceted; it has many dimensions. It is therefore possible to be strong in some areas and weak in others. Moreover, these facets can be put together in different ways. In other words, there is more than one way that a person can be courageous. What matters is how the pieces are combined. The following chapters will elaborate upon what I call "Integrated Fear Management." They address our fears head-on and seek to fit the components of overcoming them into a cohesive whole. Moreover, because these pieces interact, it is important to recognize how they do so. Among other things, this provides clues about how to sequence our efforts to grow tougher.

We must begin with our emotions.[1] We humans are not merely cognitive animals; we are emotional ones. We not only figure things out logically; we respond in terms of our feelings. Indeed, absent our emotions we could not understand or react appropriately to our environment. Although these affects are often regarded as irrational, they are, in fact, a critical element of our rationality. Without them we would be at sea, unable to make sense of the multiple options available to us. The world is so complicated, with so many moving parts, that the most super of supercomputers cannot make all of the necessary calculations.[2] We therefore need a shortcut—and that shortcut is our emotions. These utilize our biological heritage, as well as our personal experience, to sort the beneficial from the detrimental; the safe from the unsafe.

We have many emotions.[3] Among these are anger, guilt, shame, disgust, happiness, sadness, surprise—and fear. And of these, fear is probably the single most crucial.[4] All are essential for our survival, but none more so than fear. Without it we would perish; with it we may prosper or stagnate. Which will be the case depends on how we use our fear, and how we achieve this depends on understanding how the emotion operates. Some people operate instinctively. They use their emotions skillfully by essentially flying by the seat of their pants. While they may not be able to explain what they do, they tend to make appropriate choices. Others, comparative cowards such as me (and perhaps you), find it helpful to understand what is happening. We are more apt to make suitable adjustments once we recognize what is going on.

Fortunately, the major emotions operate according to a common template.[5] Each provides us with information and motivates us to action. On the communication dimension, they send messages to us and those with whom we interact. Then, on the motivation dimension, they stimulate both us and those with whom we are in contact, to behave in particular ways. The various emotions do this in distinctive ways depending on what may be thought of as their *goals*. Anger, for instance, helps us deal with major frustrations. When important needs are thwarted, our indignation informs us of this. We are now alerted to the need to overcome whatever may be disrupting our progress. But not only are we alerted, so are other persons in our vicinity. Our anger is attention-grabbing. When we experience it, it is difficult for us to ignore. Likewise when we display it, it is hard for others to disregard. Our faces turn red, our voices rise, and our teeth clench. Others immediately realize that something is wrong. They may not recognize why we are frustrated, but they know that something is afoot.

But anger does not stop there. It motivates us to do something. Merely recognizing that we were frustrated would do little to assuage our distress. We must act—and act in ways that achieve our objective. Anger energizes these actions. It provides us with the strength to pursue our goals both vigorously and persistently. When we are angry, we are prepared to fight for what we want, often over long periods. Conversely, without it, we might give up too easily. Anger also shapes the form of our response. For instance, angry demands are readily identifiable. They are seldom confused with gentle requests. Likewise, anger-based actions possess a characteristic intensity. They have a fighting quality that makes them intimidating. And because they are compelling, they may motivate others to help us overcome our frustrations. Individuals who are impeding our progress are more likely to comply with angry mandates than with gentle requests. Because they know, perhaps unconsciously, that angry people can be dangerous, they furnish what is desired. To put it simply, they are frightened into submission. Of course, they could also respond with counter-anger. If so, this might produce additional frustration. It is consequently useful to understand how to deploy our anger so that it achieves what is desired. Otherwise the outcome could be lamentable.

Sadness too has communication and motivation components that influence us and others.[6] This emotion's goal, however, is to cut ties with significant losses. Often in life, we do not obtain what we want. Not all frustrations are overcome. Some relationships, for example, never come to fruition. Other attachments are ruptured despite our strongest longings. Thus, people die; romances fracture; and parents abuse their children. In each of these cases, what is lost may be agonizing. Indeed, the mere thought of its absence may be difficult to endure. Nor is what is gone always recoverable. When this occurs, holding tightly to what has vanished is usually a miscalculation. That which is truly gone cannot satisfy our needs; hence clamoring for it merely prolongs our misery. It is therefore important to let go so that we can participate in more satisfying relationships.

Sadness thus communicates to us that we have experienced a critical loss, while it also alerts others of this loss. Even more crucially, sadness enables us to let go. We come to realize that what is gone cannot be retrieved and, therefore, step-by-excruciating-step we cut our ties to it. The emotional attachments that kept us linked are thereby severed so as to make room for new attachments. As for others who are aware of our sadness, they are motivated to give us space. People stay away from individuals who are depressed and in the process provide them with the room to work through their losses.

Which brings us back to fear. It too has goals that communicate and motivate—and which do so for the self and others. To begin with, the function of fear is to help us deal with dangers.[7] But not all dangers. Fear is primarily concerned meaningful dangers. In other words, it deals in dangers that could be cause grievous injuries. As a result, fear is modulated. It comes not in one size but is regulated according to the gravity of the threat. In general, the more dangerous the hazard, the more frightened we become. Fear essentially communicates danger by degrees. We experience everything from moderate anxieties to outright terrors depending on the nature of the peril. Moreover, as we shall see, the accuracy of these messages is not exact. They can be distorted by a variety of defense mechanisms. Precisely because we are afraid, we may not allow ourselves to gauge the extent, or the nature, of a danger.

Fear also communicates to others. When we are afraid, those around us become aware of our fear.[8] They see it in our eyes; they notice it in how we carry our bodies; they hear it in our voices. And when they do, they can respond in several ways. First, they may suspect that this danger also threatens them. Like deer on a hair trigger, they too are alerted that something in the neighborhood might be harmful. Second, they may realize that our fear makes us vulnerable. Because frightened people may not adequately defend themselves, predatory humans recognize that now might be the time to swoop in and take advantage. These bullies love the idea of intimidating people who are stressed. Third, this same message of vulnerability can notify our friends that we need protection. Rather than exploiting our plight, their nurturing instincts might come to the fore and they could rush to our defense.

As to the motivational aspects of fear, the psychologist Walter Cannon brought them to our attention almost a century ago.[9] He identified these as contained in a fight/flight instinct. Few today quarrel with his assessment. When people are afraid, they either try to extinguish whatever is causing the danger or they seek to evade it. Suddenly they experience a strength and an aggressiveness that they did not know they possessed. For example, a rush of adrenaline may provide the stimulus to take on an intimidating foe. This same hormone, however, can also impel people to run away as fast as they are able. Under the best of circumstances, this dual approach works well in reducing significant perils. These impulses complement each other and enable us to take the appropriate course. When misapplied, however, they can make things worse. This is largely because our fears can also motivate others. Predators, for instance, are emboldened by a potential victim's fears. They are inspired to cash in because they assume that they can easily prevail. The nurturers, in contrast, are stirred to be protective. They hope to assuage a friend's fears and revive his spirits.

Nonetheless, the above scenario is too simple in a number of respects. For starters, we humans experience many more than one type of danger. We are capable of being injured in a multitude of ways, each of which calls for a different type of fight or flight. What is protective therefore differs depending on the hazard. Most of the time when we conjure with dangers, we imagine physical dangers. As we all know, we are vulnerable to corporeal injury. Our thin skins and brittle bones are no match for many hazards of the natural world. Thus, we cannot run away fast enough to escape a hungry lion, nor bite hard enough to discourage a bear protecting her cub. Similarly, if we are dropped from a substantial height, we do not bounce the way that a beetle might. Because we lack a tough exoskeleton, not only would our outsides be pierced, but our insides could turn to mush. Merely falling down, we can skin our knees; and when wielding a knife, we bleed if cut. We are all well aware of these possibilities. Actually, we are mindful of such threats from infancy. Even a loving pinch delivered by a doting aunt can set a neonate reeling.

We also know that not everyone responds to physical dangers the same way. Some individuals are more risk averse than others are.[10] From birth, many of us are temperamentally designed to steer clear of physical harm. Others, in contrast, are energized by physical challenges. They come alive when jumping out of an airplane or skiing down a vertical slope. There are also persons who are so altruistic that they will voluntarily sacrifice their bodies to save others. These folks rush into the teeth of machine guns or fall on hand grenades in order to defend those they care about. Meanwhile, some players engage in heroics during sporting events. Desirous of acclaim, they butt heads with monstrous linemen despite the risk of a concussion, or they leap through the air to score a touchdown despite the pain they will experience upon landing. This kind of recklessness can be inspirational. It can make us aware of the marvelous things of which humans are capable. Nevertheless not all of us are made that way— nor do we have to be.

This, in fact, is not the kind of reckless courage we will be exploring in most of what follows. Paradoxically, physical rashness is not always an indicator of genuine bravery. Many physically fearless people actually crave the stimulation of danger. They pursue it for its own sake because they enjoy it. It literally wakes them up. For them, it is the opposite of threatening. Surprisingly, they regard safety and inaction as enervating. These people seek out danger precisely because it is in combatting it that they feel whole. Such persons often become adept in dealing with risk. They develop into accomplished deep-sea divers and expert auto racers. Moreover, in doing so, they learn to master grave dangers. This is admirable. Such persons deserve our respect. Even so, their audacity is not the norm. Nor need it be. Although they often provide useful services, other sorts of courage are generally more valuable.

Among these is *social courage*. Many people find human interactions dangerous. These folks are shy and/or diffident. They experience human contact as alarming. Ask a group of strangers what frightens them most and a surprising number will respond that they find speaking before an audience terrifying. When confronted by a crowd of unfamiliar eyes, they panic. Suddenly they choke up and wish to run away. I have had students who were so alarmed at making a class presentation that they preferred to receive a failing grade. Some were so petrified that the only way they could proceed was by delivering their report into a tape recorder. Even then, some insisted that only I be allowed to hear their efforts. Somehow the prospect of being judged by others, including persons they knew, was more than they could bear.

Life is fraught with all sorts of fears—some large and some small. As we shall shortly see, obtaining honest love and locating satisfactory employment can be problematic.[11] People fear that they may not be able to manage either. Part of the reason is that these entail dealing with intense emotions. This too can be extremely frightening. People lose control and worry lest they might do something they will regret. Rage and panic are especially troublesome; hence these are assiduously avoided. Many individuals are emotion-phobic. Like the behaviorist psychologist John B. Watson,[12] they will leave a room rather than expose themselves to heated interactions. For them, logical computations and distracting activities help blot out overwhelming passions. Like Theodore Roosevelt,[13] when both his wife and mother died on the same day, the only way they are able to survive is to divert their attention. Roosevelt achieved this by immersing himself in legislative business. *Emotional courage* too is therefore desirable. People who can deal with powerful feelings have a leg up on those who cannot. They do not have to run away.

Moral courage is similarly vital to leading a fulfilling life.[14] A derivative of social and emotional courage, this faculty enables us to make ethical choices. Sadly, the temptations of depravity are all around us. The mere idea of breaking moral rules can be exhilarating. Nevertheless, this can be a dangerous invitation. It is easy to be seduced into conduct that injures us and/or others. What looks like it might feel good often entices us into ignoring latent pitfalls. As a result, rather than follow social guidelines, we are lured into flouting them. This then is another sort of danger to which we must be alert and another sort of courage that ought to be cultivated.

Whatever the perceived danger, the next step is liable to be action. Yet here too there are complexities. The question is not merely whether to fight or flee, but how to do either. There are many ways we might respond, depending on the nature of the threat and the resources available to us. We humans are a plastic species. Unlike skunks that have one principal way of dealing with danger, we have many. This means we can make mistakes. We can decide to fight in a way that exposes us to greater dangers or we can flee into the arms of a deadly peril. Fortunately, the fruits of such errors are customarily learned early in life. To illustrate, challenging the bully down the block could generate a major thrashing, while seeking comfort from an untrustworthy parent might produce yet another betrayal. Such outcomes increase our anxieties. As a consequence, it is essential to learn when and how to protect ourselves. What works best is complicated and is therefore difficult to master.

Courage, whether physical, social, emotional, or moral, is not unitary. It is not as if we can imbibe a dose of all-purpose bravery. What is needed to allay our fears varies with the challenge. Nevertheless, unless we can neutralize most of the dangers we encounter, we are apt to remain fearful. Only genuine safety, which is experienced as safety, is able to return our equanimity. Only then will the communication and motivation set in motion by a danger relent. This is when the messages we receive again assure us that we are secure and hence that the conduct intended to keep us from harm subsides. Major fears never disappear all at once. Indeed, the more potent they are, the longer it takes to trust that a particular menace is truly gone. Still, with time, and continued security, our attitudes can change. What was once frightening may eventually no longer set off alarm bells.

SOCIALIZATION

Although our fears both communicate and motivate, what they communicate and motivate is not fixed. The messages we receive and the actions we take are frequently modified over time. We all begin life with a primitive set of stereotyped emotions, nonetheless these evolve as we mature. We discover new dangers and fresh ways of coping as we grow to adulthood.[15] In short, our emotions are socialized. They are altered in the process of learning how to become a fully social animal.[16] Were this not so, inappropriate reactions would routinely get us into trouble. Both external and internal stimuli would recurrently stimulate unfortunate defenses.

It is sometimes alleged that we humans do not have any instincts, but this is untrue. Were we not born with a propensity to engage in sucking behavior, we would never receive the nourishment needed to survive. Likewise, were we innocent of an ability to gag, when we were overfed we would choke to death. These impulses are not taught. They are hardwired into our brains. The same is true of many emotional reactions. Thus when we hear a loud noise, we have a startle response. We practically jump out of our skins from surprise. And when we are angry, we lash out. As yet uncoordinated infants will strike at the perpetrators when roughly handled. Hence if they are uncomfortably handled, they may bite the aggressor. They will even do this to their mother's breasts when frustrated by not getting enough milk.

Nor do children have to be taught certain fears. A dread of snakes, spiders, and heights seems to be innate. These dangers were so ubiquitous in our environment of evolutionary adaptedness that a horror of them was genetically imprinted. Although we no longer live in an untamed wilderness, reflexive apprehensions still warn us of its hazards. By the same token, infants come equipped with tactics for dealing with these threats. Hence when frightened, they cry. This usually upsets their parents, who come rushing to the rescue. Crying is thus an effective way of eliciting help—for babies.

The pioneering psychiatrist John Bowlby,[17] when writing about attachment behavior, commented on another innate protective mechanism. He highlighted the importance of *home bases*. Because human infants are born unable to walk, they must gradually acquire the motor skills to do so. Unlike deer, whose fawns can stand on their legs within hours of birth, human babies must be carried about before they can crawl and must crawl before they can stand. Furthermore, standing is frightening. So is taking those first few steps. Falling is not only possible; it is likely. As a result, toddlers require reassurance when they venture out on their own. The normal method of achieving this is to use mother as a point of reference. Babies who have learned that she will protect them look to her when in doubt. Before they attempt to walk, they first check to make sure she will be there if needed. Then, when they tumble, they hurry back to her for solace. She is, as it were, a genetically engineered source of courage. Her presence is a potent antidote to fear.

Children who cannot count on their parents to provide dependable protection have another instinctive remedy. They become clingy. Having ascertained that they are liable to be abandoned during moments of need, they hold fast to the very persons who have let them down. This may not be an effective strategy in that parents who are clung to tend to be further alienated by this tactic. But what is the child to do? Is there another recourse? Sadly, some of the remedies children use to manage their fears make them worse.

For the most part, innate responses to fear lose their usefulness over time.[18] The most solicitous parent eventually tires of comforting the child who never ceases crying. Consequently, despite their fears, children are eventually expected to walk on their own. They cannot be carried forever or always rely on the presence of a solicitous adult. They must learn to take care of themselves, which means they need to acquire mechanisms for managing their fears. An inability to do so would leave them physically and socially crippled.

One of the first aspects of socializing our fears is distinguishing what is actually dangerous. Most youngsters are initially afraid of falling and scraping their knees. They scurry to Mommy so that she can kiss it and make the pain go away. Yet they eventually learn that they can endure the pain, which they likewise discover will go away on its own. Falls are still dangerous, but less so than was originally imagined. On the other hand, rushing into the street at first seems no different than rushing anywhere else. Because automobiles were not part of our environment of evolutionary adaptedness, we have to be taught about the harm they can do. Parents typically achieve this by panicking when little Johnny runs out to retrieve an errant ball. They grab him by the shoulders and loudly warn him never to do that again. He is now frightened by this reaction and transfers this fear onto his desire to dart into traffic. Henceforward this alarm bell is added to his repertoire, where it is summoned when needed.

Other acquired fears are subtler. Social shame imparts many of these. Young children are unaware of how they are expected to dress or the proper way to utilize tableware. At first, they may not even realize that they are supposed to be clothed. Unlike Adam and Eve's response after biting into the apple, they are not embarrassed by their nakedness. They must therefore be taught not to take off their panties in public or, later on, not to put their trousers on backward. This knowledge is generally instilled through ridicule. People make fun of deviants by calling them *babies*. So painful is this experience that the young come to fear it, that is, it becomes a learned danger. So is using soup spoon like a shovel. There is, they discover, a right way to transport food to the mouth, which they had best master if they are to avoid censure. Such lessons do not end in childhood. Many an adult has been embarrassed by her lack of understanding how to use the multiple table utensils found in fancy restaurants. Faux pas can seem so treacherous that the uninstructed dread social encounters that might make them look unsophisticated.

We also learn how to respond to dangers. Indeed, we learn that different dangers call for different rejoinders. Always crying when things go wrong is a sure way to be regarded as a superannuated infant. After all, big boys (and girls) don't cry! Neither should all dangers be run from, nor fought against aggressively. In fact, how to run varies with the threat, as does the method of fighting back. Take running away. Many a child has been terrified of her first day of school. Being left alone by Mommy to fend off a room full of strangers is disquieting. Yet can little Mary run home? It is probably too far away and likely separated by a great deal of alien territory. Accordingly, should she cling to her teacher or hide in a corner? Alas, these techniques are apt to be of little avail because they will not make her teacher or classmates disappear. Unlike in a game of peekaboo, these mysterious others will still be there when she again opens her eyes. Even crying will not remove the danger. Mommy won't return to hold her hand, nor will the teacher comfort her in a familiar way. A new way to deal with this danger must therefore be found.

What about fighting back? Crying is a kind of fighting, but it won't work in this case. Nor will Mary obtain relief by hitting the teacher. If anything, she may be punished by this powerful other. Throwing things, of course, would only exacerbate her loss. Hence, for the time being, little Mary may not know how to thwart what she experiences as an assault. Eventually she might discover that she can influence her teacher's conduct by excelling in her studies. This previously mysterious woman, once she becomes better known, might be manipulated by what she finds important. This is a crucial discovery. People differ and consequently the way they are best fought differs. Accordingly, our means of fighting evolves. It is only after Mary learns how to study that she will be able to use her newly acquired academic skills as a tool to keep others friendly.

Because we humans are social generalists,[19] we have multiple ways of accomplishing what we desire. While a capacity to write or deploy verbal elegance is inherited, these abilities are not realized without years of scholarship and practice. The same applies to utilizing literal weapons. Spears, swords, and firearms take time to master. Not everyone becomes equally proficient at employing every form of armament. Socialization is uneven. Given our disparate abilities, what works best at effecting fight or flight differs from person to person. Likewise, which abilities are efficacious depends on the circumstances in which they are employed. Our opponents differ in their abilities and motivations; hence what works with some may not work with others.

Learning how and when to fight or the appropriate moment to run away is a lifelong endeavor. As a consequence, so is acquiring courage. In fact, in the light of the above, we can now ask: What is courage? Surprisingly, the answer depends on what it is not. Courage, it seems, is the opposite of what occurs when socialization fails.

When people become extremely frightened, their fear often mutates into panic.[20] At such moments, they forget everything they have learned about how to defend themselves. Their terror is so intense that their heads empty of all cogent thought. No longer are they able to mobilize their abilities or recognize the nature of a threat. They instead revert to their instinctive, albeit infantile, responses. Primitive fight/flight reactions leap to the fore; hence panicked people act reflexively.

But since primitive emotions are seldom suited to dealing with adult dangers, the outcomes are liable to be unfortunate. People who panic make elementary mistakes. They confuse their friends with their enemies and seek protection from the very people who are intent on harming them. Similarly, they overdo their rage so egregiously that they engage in unfocused tantrums. Although they strike out energetically, they do so in the wrong places with the wrong tactics. And so they lose. They may even be hurt more seriously than if they had done nothing. Panic is the opposite of courage. It is uncontrolled fear raised to unsafe levels.

Courage exists when our fears do not regress to their primitive forms. This has often been described as "grace under pressure." When it is present, people can think and act clearly despite their trepidations. Courageous people accurately assess the nature of a fear and respond appropriately. Although they are fearful, they are in sufficient control to engage in fight or flee in a manner that provides safety. They too, of course, might make mistakes in how they mobilize a suitable rejoinder. Nonetheless, while they do not possess the wherewithal to neutralize every threat, because their heads are not muddled, they improve their chances. They are also likely to be more flexible and therefore more effective.

Meanwhile, exhortation rarely succeeds in implanting this sort of courage. Because people who have reverted to primitive emotions do not hear these appeals, they remain unmoved. With their heads befuddled by fear, even sound advice, perhaps about calming down and recognizing the character of a danger, is ignored. Nor can people implement protective measures when terror prevents them from coordinating their responses. What is necessary is not encouragement, per se, but learning to understand and exploit their fears. They must discover how to interpret the messages of the emotion and effectively deploy the motivation it provides. This is what integrated fear management is all about. Appeals to be brave can be useful, but usually when people already know how to be brave.

SOCIAL COURAGE

None of us like to fail. We all want to be winners.[21] But winning is a social phenomenon. We win relative to others, many of whom are not anxious to see us prevail. This means that we can lose because these others do things that cause us to be defeated. This makes strangers, and even some friends, relatively dangerous. Whatever fairytales we hear about universal love, we soon learn in elementary school and on the playgrounds of our youth that not everyone wishes us well. Some are bullies, others are rivals, and still others are indifferent. Loving relatives are not always available when needed. In fact, our siblings may be among our most dedicated adversaries. If we are to win, we must therefore assert ourselves. Whatever our fears, if we do not play the social game—and play it effectively—we will not succeed.

The requisite social courage is partly physical in that some interpersonal competitions depend on muscle power. Children fight with one another; they also engage in athletic contests. The weak and/or uncoordinated are thus at a disadvantage. If they fear physical injury or humiliation, they are apt to back down. Nevertheless, emotional strengths are often more important than muscular ones. Most contests for social priority are saturated in emotion. Winners usually prevail because they have been able to intimidate their rivals. These others concede defeat as a result of being frightened into submission. It is because they cannot handle their fears that they withdraw from the field—perhaps in a panic.

Other intense emotions must also be dealt with if people are to obtain social gratifications. This includes anger, which, when it spills over into rage, can be self-defeating.[22] It includes guilt, which, when deeply entrenched, can induce self-paralysis. It includes sorrow, which, if transformed into depression, can also be paralyzing. Paradoxically, it likewise includes love, which, when misplaced, can seduce us into vanquishing ourselves. Other emotions, such as extreme shame, are similarly debilitating. It therefore behooves potential winners to develop the emotional aptitudes to contend in our emotionally saturated social environment.

Moral courage,[23] which is partly emotional, is also a component of social courage. Social life depends on the existence of widely respected regulations to keep interpersonal rivalries from becoming violent.[24] Moral rules can nonetheless be restrictive or sometimes debilitating. As a consequence, moral bravery is critical. It enables people to distinguish the valid prescriptions from the invalid. This permits them to stand up for beneficial guidelines while eschewing detrimental ones. Without this, life would be unfair and chaotic. In any event, people can be overwhelmed by other people's values. If they are to win, they must therefore be able to defend their own commitments against this sort of moral aggression. Yet this too takes the personal fortitude. Self-righteous others can be difficult to fend off if one does not possess the mettle to resist their impositions.

What sorts of social courage are most important? Sigmund Freud provided a useful clue. When asked which abilities enable people to avoid neurotic lassitude, he answered succinctly. They must, he said, be able to participate in gratifying love and productive work.[25] They thus require the capacity to take part in the give-and-take of genuine intimacy and an ability to compete for a satisfying occupation. Although these goals sound deceptively simple, they are difficult to achieve. People who are not prepared to risk loss typically hold back. They shun the advice that it is better to have loved and lost, than never to have loved at all. A quiet corner, where nothing disturbs their serenity, suits them better.

Make no mistake: love can be disquieting. After all, intimacy demands that we open up to another human being.[26] But what if this other takes advantage of our defenselessness? If we reveal our deep-seated fears, will these be turned against us? When we divulge our secret aspirations, will we be laughed at for our naïveté? Perhaps this person, upon whom we have mistakenly bestowed our trust, will abuse it. Maybe his or her weaknesses will awaken a deep-seated selfishness. Consequently how can we be sure that when we let down our guard, we will not be hurt? The answer is that sometimes we cannot. It is very easy to be fooled about the character of another person. One of the skills at which we humans excel is concealing our real selves. It thus takes an act of courage to test the waters and determine the truth. It also takes courage to recover from being deceived. People who are terrified by the pain of being misled are unlikely to regain their balance. Having been hurt, they continuously berate themselves for their personal limitations.

Intimacy also requires fairness. If we are to be emotionally close, we must treat this other person as a moral equal. His or her happiness has to count for as much as our own. But this is difficult for creatures as selfish as we are. We want to win. We want to come out better—even than our loved ones. Altruism is fine, but a steady diet of it suits very few of us. We must consequently exercise the restraint to allow this other person his or her fair share. Yet this sort of sacrifice takes resolution. We must be comfortable enough with ourselves to allow this other to obtain what we might also want. This, ironically, ought not detract from our ability to assert our own needs.[27] We must thus have the courage to pursue balance. An awareness of our respective needs, coupled with an ability to blend them in a way that enables both to do well, entails a maturity that is hard to come by.

So difficult is gratifying intimacy that we are currently in the midst of a plague of divorce.[28] Where once couples promised to commit for life, many have come to realize that this may not be their fate. As a result, young adults have become shy of taking the plunge. They have witnessed too much domestic cruelty to assume it can never happen to them. And so, millions put off marriage. They instead cohabit.[29] Sexuality without love has thus become common. Many have even come to believe that the two are identical. Unwilling to explore their relationship phobias, they settle for perpetual loneliness. Unaware that intimacy takes courage, they look for shortcuts that do not exist.

Satisfying work is also a challenge. Just as voluntary intimacy demands that individuals possess the nerve to risk closeness, so voluntary occupations in a competitive marketplace demand the bravery to seek agreeable employments. Where once marriages were arranged and jobs were handed down between the generations, individual choice has become the norm. In a middle-class society, the sons of blacksmiths need not be blacksmiths, nor the daughters of housemaids, housemaids.[30] But what then are they to become? The possibilities are so broad and our knowledge of them so limited that sensible decisions are difficult to come by. Nowadays it is routine for young people to wonder what they will become when they grow up.

As a college professor, I see this all the time. Teenagers (and often those who are no longer in their teens) enter higher education unsure of what field of study in which to major.[31] Many subsequently shop around, looking for a congenial discipline. But then, once graduation looms, their bravado fails them. They have no idea which jobs to pursue or which might satisfy them. And so they dither. Afraid that they will make the wrong choices, they put off making any choice.

Because a lifetime of happiness seems to be at stake, it is natural to fear the worst. Accordingly, vocational decisions require courage. People need to be clear-eyed enough to evaluate what is before them and bold enough to do their best at whatever they select. They also need the courage to change directions if doing so becomes advisable. Indeed, they need the daring to stand up against friends and relatives who disagree with their choices.

Next, work itself demands courage. Success is not a given. Some recent graduates assume that their credentials entitle them to a swift ride to the top. Most are quickly disabused of this fantasy. Hard work and a raft of ambiguous decisions lie ahead. People must be good at what they do or they are unlikely to move up. When most men were farmers, guiding a plow was a difficult, but straightforward endeavor. Muscle power, not subtle choices, filled one's day. The same was true of the homemaker who could simply follow in her mother's footsteps. This is not the case in the complex techno-commercial society that we inhabit. The occupations in which we engage entail far more uncertainty.

Working with things, as our ancestors did, tends to be clear-cut. Routine tasks rarely require discretion. Working with people and data, however, is more demanding.[32] These tasks are too complex to be reduced to stereotyped procedures. As a result, they require a deeper understanding and more flexible implementation. This is why so many contemporary jobs entail a higher education. An assembly-line worker will simply be told to tighten that bolt, whereas an engineer may not know where to begin designing an effective machine. The latter takes greater knowledge and a refined ability to evaluate options. Mistakes will be made; hence the engineer must be able to cope with these. His boss, for he too will have one, may blame this engineer for decisions that were indeed his own. Accordingly, unless he is prepared to assume responsibility and react appropriately, he is unsuited for this sort of work. Courage is a prerequisite for such occupations. Without it, the engineer would not be able to move forward. Without it, he would crumble under the criticism of his superior. In short, he needs the courage to be self-directed.[33] Were he unable to make independent decisions in an environment of uncertainty, he might fold like the proverbial cheap suit.

Those who intend to enter professionalized jobs might never bother with obtaining the necessary schooling if they did not possess the courage to try. Rewarding occupations take intense preparation. Years of study are needed to enter a field the particulars of which are not initially known. Furthermore, every step along the way provides an opportunity for failure. Good jobs are in short supply; hence they are widely sought. Yet not all can succeed, which means that some will be defeated by the competition. To take a chance on being winnowed out thus requires exposing oneself to this painful possibility. Worse still, losing has implications for one's self-esteem. Those who hold back can comfort themselves with visions of what might have been. In their private universes, they can make themselves out to be paladins. In the real world, however, success goes to those with the guts to play the game. They may get bruised, but only they obtain the fruits of victory.

Success neither in work nor in love is free. Both must be earned. Defeat is always a possibility and hence its prospect must be confronted. Individuals who prefer the gratification of computer games or the solipsistic fantasies of romantic novels thereby disqualify themselves. Their needs are no less valid that those of others, but their social strategies are less rewarding. While courageous people can suffer disastrous setbacks, these are less likely to be final. Wallowing in cowardice might seem safe; nonetheless it is the equivalent of a self-chosen prison sentence.

INTEGRATED FEAR MANAGEMENT

With courage so vital to our personal well-being, what are semi-congenital cowards to do? First off, there are very few literally congenital cowards. Some people may be more risk averse than others, but the primary reason that most of us have difficulty being brave has to do with how we were raised. Those who have not been socialized to master their fears often find themselves sabotaged by primitive reactions. Their emotions regress to an infantile state and they are unprepared to defend themselves from physical or social dangers. Unable to fight or flee in an appropriate manner, their work and love lives suffer.

Nonetheless, emotional resocialization is possible.[34] People who consider themselves too weak to cope with their fears can learn to do so—assuming they try. Irreversible cowardice is largely a myth. Most people can become stronger, that is, if they go about toughening up in the right way. Integrated fear management provides a means of doing so. It is a step-by-step approach that deliberately avoids asking people to do more than they can handle. Intended to keep panic at bay, the objective is to leave people clearheaded enough to make effective decisions about how to protect themselves. The program does not require people to lose their fears, merely to tame them.

1. The first step of integrated fear management is to ensure *safety*. People who are in imminent danger may not have the emotional space to modify how they deploy their emotions. Perhaps already overwhelmed, they cannot step back to reflect upon their situation or to alter it. At this first stage, they generally do not know how best to disarm or escape a danger. The measures they take to remain safe may therefore be clumsy. For the moment, however, temporary safety

will be sufficient. More useful methods of prevailing will come later. What initially matters is that these preliminary protective measures do not exacerbate the situation. It is also important that they can be deliberately deployed. Safety does not exist where it is accidental. Unless people can control their emotional reactions, they will remain at the mercy of what may be an unkind fate.

2. The next step is to develop *incremental tolerance* of our intense fears. Unless these can be experienced without panicking, they cannot be understood. And if they cannot be understood, appropriate defenses cannot be deliberately adopted. In any event, such tolerance does not come all at once. A desensitization process must first remove their sting. People must slowly and cautiously expose themselves to fears that might otherwise be unmanageable. This procedure takes time, yet if it is rushed, a panic may ensue, thereby undoing all that has been accomplished. For some, the requisite patience does not come easily. Nonetheless it is essential. Time is the balm that at the outset enables fears to subside.

3. Once people can experience their intense fears without experiencing terror, they are in a position to *evaluate* them. They can look at them straight in the eye to determine the nature of the danger they are confronting. Primitive emotions tend to jumble their messages. Instead of communicating what needs to be understood, they transmit garbled reports. The threat, whatever it is, thus seems amorphous. Lacking a distinct shape, it feels more intimidating than it is. It is therefore necessary to be clear about the prospective injury and its causes. In many cases, this is more complicated than might be assumed. Developing an accurate understanding may accordingly require digging under the surface of impending hazards.

4. After it is possible to understand dangers, these must be

sorted through. How significant is a particular threat? Is it truly imminent? Is the potential injury especially serious? And just as important, can its cause be dealt with? These questions must be answered before deciding whether it makes sense to fight or flee. For instance, can the peril be neutralized? Or is it possible to leave the scene? Maybe this whole business can be sidestepped? Courage does not demand that a person be courageous with respect to every threat. Some hazards can be ignored; some left to others to master; and some pushed into the unconscious. No one wins all of life's battles. Sometimes we must merely sustain a debilitating blow without collapsing. Sometimes we can hide in the basement. The important thing is to be able to come back and fight another day. In the meantime, some losses have to be relinquished. Instead of agonizing over them, we must let them go so as to move on to more pressing issues. Courageous people know how to choose their battles. They realize that they stand a better chance of winning when they concentrate their resources on encounters where they possess the advantages.

5. Finally, our fears must be *used*. Their energy needs to be leveraged to improve our chances of winning. If we decide that putting up a fight makes sense, we want to fight sensibly and vigorously. As athletes know, fear can provide an edge. It heightens our awareness and provides the power to try our best. As long as it does not mutate into panic, it furnishes an advantage over less-motivated adversaries. Fearful people do not need to be docile. Their fear can prepare them to act. Likewise, those who remain lucid are able to plan ahead. They can develop strategies designed to maximize their assets while taking advantage of their opponent's liabilities. Apprehensive people are also better prepared to run away. They do not stand around waiting for an irresistible menace to do them

in. People who panic tend to freeze, whereas those possessed of controlled fear can protect themselves. As a consequence, they are much more likely to win—or at least not to suffer irreparable damage.

These five steps may sound simple; nonetheless they are difficult to put into practice. They do not spontaneously transpire but must be doggedly implemented. The first thing to be done is to appreciate the nature of fear. As long as it remains a mystery, it is more intimidating than it has to be. Next, the logic of integrated fear management must be respected. Each of its steps builds on the preceding one. The objective is therefore to undertake them in an orderly manner. Although it is not always necessary to complete the work of one before moving on to the next, it helps to be systematic. Ultimately how these steps are traversed depends on our unique situations. There is thus no one best way that suits everyone.

Especially difficult to accept is that integrated fear management takes time. Some fears require years to master; some, decades. It all depends upon how acute they are and how deeply they have been thrust into the unconscious. Fears that make us cowards tend not to be trivial. Small potatoes, such as dread of riding a horse, may take weeks to subdue, whereas long-established fears, such as those regarding intimacy, demand more time. Life is a marathon; not a sprint. Those who insist on instant success are sure to be frustrated. Worse still, they diminish their chances of overcoming their fears. People in the grip of ordinary cowardice can become stronger, but only if they are prepared to dedicate themselves to the journey. They do not even have to be optimistic. They must merely persevere. Setbacks are inevitable, while confusions abound. Nonetheless, victory goes to those who, while they may stumble and fall, get up and keep chugging along.

The following five chapters are dedicated to each of the five steps of integrated fear management. They will walk you through how you too can be put them into practice and provide illustrations frequently based on my personal experience. Too often, advice-givers do not follow their own counsel. They assure us that their prescriptions will work even though they have not done so for themselves. The ensuing rubric, however, is derived from a lifetime of dealing with my own fears and those of my clients. But not just that. It stems from the realization that I, and they, frequently succeeded. When these victories are placed in the sociological context of how people deal with middle-class challenges, the reasons we overcame become clear. The mystery of fear dissolves thereby losing its bite.

Testimonials are easy to cobble together. Anyone can say that they have been miraculously healed. Nonetheless, fear management is not a miracle. It is a process, albeit not an unmitigated solution. While it can help, it is only for those who vigorously apply themselves.

Chapter 4

ENSURING SAFETY

A WORLD OF HURT

Ours is a dangerous world. People get hurt, sometimes very badly hurt. Many of these injuries occur when we are children; others, when we are adults. The former can be extremely traumatic and their results can be long-lasting. As small children, we are exceedingly vulnerable. We do not yet possess the mental or physical skills to protect ourselves from a host of threats. More important, we do not possess the personal experiences or the mental acuity to understand them. As a result, we are often blindsided. Suddenly we are wounded, but we do not know why—or what to do about it. This only increases our fears. As a result, these anxieties can become deeply entrenched. Because they are not understood, they are difficult to assuage. And so they linger. Now part of who we are, they lurk just below the surface, ready to instill mysterious terrors at a later date.[1]

Years ago, when I first taught introductory sociology to non-majors, I realized that I had to include a segment on marriage. Most of the students were barely out of high school, yet they were discernably interested in establishing intimate relationships. I was less sure about how much to say about divorce. For the most part unmarried, these undergraduates would not be concerned with an event they had not personally undergone. In fact, I could not have been more wrong. My listeners hung on virtually every word I said. At first

I was puzzled. Then their questions cleared up the mystery. They might not themselves have endured marital separation, but almost half were the children of divorce.[2]

Divorce was once rare.[3] Marriages were torn asunder, but primarily by death or desertion. Legal separations did not become common until about fifty years ago. Since then they have become an epidemic, with roughly half of all marriages ending in divorce. At first, people assumed that such split-ups would be easy. Two rational people would realize that their union had been a mistake and amicably decouple. They might even celebrate their renewed freedom. As for their children, they too would be better off.[4] No longer trapped by their parent's feuds, they would lead a more peaceful existence. What is more, they would be inspired by the positive example of adults who asserted their right to independent happiness. Besides, children were resilient. Whatever their initial surprise, they would quickly recover. Soon enough, they would realize that this new arrangement was to their advantage.

This, however, turned out to be balderdash. Divorce is usually traumatic. It is a serious loss.[5] When people marry, they do not anticipate their union ending in a breakup. The partners assume that they love each other so deeply that they will be able to overcome whatever hurdles might arise. Should this turn out not to be the case, they are bewildered. They may at first deny that anything major has gone wrong, but once the extent of their quarrels sinks in they are liable to be profoundly dismayed. This other, this person who pledged eternal troth, violated a sacred trust. He or she betrayed a solemn promise. How dastardly! He or she is clearly a terrible person who deserves every ounce of venom directed his or her way. Given this attitude, divorce is seldom a comfortable experience. It hurts—and hurts badly. A blow to the ego, it can be experienced as an existential danger.

As for the children of divorce, they are liable to be hurt even more badly.[6] Relatively passive victims of this rupture, they neither initiated the process, nor could they do much to repair it. Because they probably assumed that their parents' union was perpetual, their worldview is shattered. As important, although devastated, they were required to keep their distress to themselves. Adults enduring this ordeal do not relish the added burden of dealing with angry and/ or saddened offspring. Their children are therefore appeased and asked to repress their dismay. Their pain is to be pushed into the unconscious, where it usually simmers until released in adulthood.

This was the point at which I encountered the young victims of divorce. Just beginning to feel emotionally independent, the first blush of romantic stirrings had liberated their long-subdued fears. Now questions flooded in. Why had their parents divorced? Did they, as children, cause their estrangement? Was there something about men, or women, that made intimacy impossible? The girls often resented their mothers for driving their fathers away. Meanwhile, the boys frequently doubted their masculinity in light of their father's defects. Most wondered whether marriage was possible for them at all. Was their inability to establish long-lasting relationships inherited? Was emotional closeness a danger that they would never learn to handle? Theirs were unresolved aches, which they feared might never go away.

Poverty too is source of fear, hurt, and danger.[7] Ours may be a wealthy society, but not all of us share equally in its bounty. Back in the 1960s, it was assumed that the United States possessed sufficient resources to banish destitution. President Lyndon B. Johnson declared a war on poverty in the belief that this battle would shortly be won.[8] Thanks to our affluence, we had more than enough wherewithal to make everyone comfortable. All that was needed was to encourage the poor to be more assertive in advocating on their own behalf, that is, as long as we also increased their welfare, medical, and food benefits. With these in hand, they would not have to live in squalor, nor hang their heads in shame.

But that is not what happened. Having served as a welfare case-worker in Harlem, I was not surprised this outcome did not materialize. One of my duties had been to distribute leaflets informing people that welfare was a *right*. They did not need to feel embarrassed if they applied for services because these were an entitlement. This ploy worked so well that within weeks our welfare offices were besieged by thousands of applicants. The lines literally snaked around the block. Only by decreasing the number of workers assigned to the front desk was the deluge brought under control. This increased the waiting time, which discouraged the less needy—who melted away. Over the long haul, however, the rolls swelled dramatically. For many millions, welfare became a way of life.

As a caseworker, I understood why. My clients lived modestly; nonetheless, most did not reside in utter nastiness. They had decent apartments, ample food, and enough discretionary cash to purchase fancy sneakers for their sons. The primary concern was that they not lose their checks. Consequently, few made plans regarding how to escape their situation. Fewer still had concrete ideas about schooling or employment. Indeed, many of the teenage girls sought to become pregnant so that they could get a check and an apartment of their own. This way they could circumvent parental scrutiny. Meanwhile many of the teenage boys looked to impregnate someone else's daughter. This, not gainful employment, would demonstrate their manhood. As a child of the lower middle class, I had read about the draining effects of dependency. This was it in the flesh.

Years later, as a sociologist, I was introduced to the idea of relative deprivation.[9] Poverty, I discovered, was not an absolute. Poor Americans were much wealthier than their ancestors or than contemporary Africans. Most had indoor plumbing, television sets, and closets full of clothing. About two-thirds owned an automobile. Their distress did not come from an empty belly or from sleeping out in the rain. It came from the realization that they had less than their middle-class peers. They could see this at the movies. They could experience it if they wandered into fancy neighborhoods. Worse yet, they knew that others looked down on them for their destitution.

Sociology also taught me about the culture of poverty.[10] People who grew up needy often developed a way of life that kept them needy.[11] They tended to live disorganized lives that made it difficult to hold down a responsible job. They likewise thought exclusively about the here and now, which made it difficult to formulate a better future. Intent on getting while the getting was good, they had difficulty delaying gratification—which, for instance, made it difficult to obtain a college degree. They were also fatalistic. Having endured years of suffering, in dangerous surroundings, they could not imagine anything better.

More recently, the poor have been devastated by the twin plagues of drugs and marital dissolution.[12] Heroin, crack, and marijuana are everywhere in our inner cities. Even young children use and/or distribute them. Moreover, with so many people unemployed, criminal activity is rampant. Rape, robbery, and mayhem wait around any corner. Many people have "hustles," that is, small-scale corruptions, such as running the numbers or pimping. As for marriage, it has become the icing on the cake.[13] If women want families, the best many can do is to become single parents. Thus serial monogamy and transient cohabitation have become the norm. Among blacks, almost three out of four children are conceived out of wedlock.[14] Poor Hispanics are not far behind. Because unwed parenthood often results in poverty, innocent youngsters suffer, later on only to inflict the same pain on their own offspring.

Although trillions of dollars were spent attempting to eradicate poverty, it remains with us. Its miseries can be found in virtually any inner city and many rural communities. Those born to it know its pains but not necessarily how to evade them. They may curse their fate or blame their distress on an unjust society, but they do not take the measures that might relieve their anguish. Poverty is oppressive. Nonetheless escaping it is also frightening. Despite its dangers, individuals steeped in poverty often find social mobility more intimidating. They fear the prospect of failure and rejection. Confronting these, and the unknown, therefore requires courage. Unfortunately, living in poverty seldom instills this sort of resolution. People may pretend to be brave—for example, to be cool—but that does not mean they are.[15] Most have endured too many losses to be sanguine about their chances.

I also worked in a psychiatric hospital, in a mental-health clinic, as well as in private practice. Having, in addition, personally spent years in psychotherapy, I am acutely aware of the many losses endemic to the human condition.[16] These are so pervasive that popping pills to cope with depression or anxiety has become a national preoccupation. Routinely advertised on television, these drugs would not be big business if millions of people did not suffer from sadness and agitation. Statistics regarding the prevalence of these conditions are unreliable; nevertheless, estimates range up to 85 percent. In some circles, they are alleged to be of epidemic proportions. This, however, is probably an exaggeration. No society could survive with most of its people mentally ill.

One of the most frightening aspects of serious losses is that in their thrall we can become our own worst enemies. Few of us endure such assaults without fighting back. We tend to become furious with our putative attackers. We likewise retaliate against those who desert us. Unfortunately these others are apt to return the favor. When we are young and vulnerable this presents a dilemma. Because these others are liable to be bigger and stronger, they can inflict further damage. And so we attempt to control ourselves. We refrain from talking back. We do not protest when we are abandoned. Perhaps we also feel guilty about resenting this treatment. When we do, we may then punish ourselves more severely than our foes ever would. Or perhaps, in our terrified state, we are so desirous of love that we are prepared to make countless sacrifices. We will do anything, including foregoing our own happiness, to keep things from getting worse.

The children of alcoholics are familiar with this predicament.[17] Thus, some become scapegoats who are continually blamed for their parents' failings. Others become the family's hero. These folks take on the task of saving Mom and Dad from themselves. In either case, the helper's needs come last. What is more dangerous, these victims voluntarily surrender their happiness. Fearing dire consequences if they stand up against oppression, they direct their attacks inward. Hence, when experiencing protective impulses that they find difficult to suppress, they become self-punitive. Although they want to renounce their tormentors, they fear retribution. And so they hate themselves for what they are feeling. They also hate themselves for being cowardly. Unable to drive out these troublesome emotions, they despise who they have become.

Significant losses, and the pain that they produce, are common. Life is not a bed of roses. While some people have it harder than others do, things go wrong even under the best of circumstances. Suffering may ravage the poor, but the rich are damaged as well. For example, Jackie Kennedy's father, "Black Jack" Bouvier, was an alcoholic. So was Teddy Roosevelt's brother, Elliott. Elliott's daughter Eleanor thus inherited more than her share of defeats.[18] Encumbered by a mother who believed she was ugly, deceived by a father who died before he could keep his promises, incorrigibly uncomfortable in social settings, and sexually betrayed by an insensitive husband, she spent a lifetime attempting to overcome these incubi. Sadly she is not alone. Henry David Thoreau wrote that most men lead lives of quiet desperation.[19] This too is an exaggeration. What is not is that most of us experience failures that leave us frightened. For many, these apprehensions never disappear. As a consequence, they deny us the pleasures we could achieve had we had a bit more courage.

BACK ON THE HORSE

You've heard the advice. If you fall off a horse, you must immediately get back on. If you do not, your fears are liable to multiply exponentially. Should this occur, you might never get on another horse ever again. Better therefore to suck up your courage and try once more. Then if this fails, you are asked to climb on again. As long as it takes, and however much you may get bruised, you must never give up. To make a habit of backing down would ensure a lifetime of weakness.

This, however, is faulty counsel. It works in the movies, where the hero, after being tossed off the bucking bronco, persists until the animal is pacified. In real life, it seldom works out that way. First, many fears are justified. The challenge you confront might not be a horse; it could be a tiger. Remounting its back would thus be foolhardy. There are times when caution really is the appropriate response. The difficulty is in telling when.

My father believed in the "get back on" strategy. As a teenager, he learned to swim by being thrown into New York City's East River. Not only did he survive, but he became a powerful swimmer. From this he drew the conclusion that if you are faced with a difficulty, you must muscle it into submission. You have to tackle it head on so as to defeat it. Naturally, he sought to instill this philosophy in me. I was supposed to suck up my fears and conquer whatever obstacles came my way. This was true of riding a bicycle. It was true of learning how to swim.

When I was about seven years old, our family spent the summer at a resort in the Catskill Mountains. It was a modest place that had a small pool to which we kids retreated on hot days. While I could not swim, I enjoyed bobbing up and down in the cool water. This, however, was not sufficient for my father. As his son, I had to be manly enough to swim. And so he demanded that I allow him to teach me how. He would, he reassured me, hold me up while I developed the skill. Yet as his son, I knew better. Just as he had vowed that he would steady the bicycle while I learned to ride, but then let go, he would do the same in the pool. Consequently, I refused. Nonetheless he would not take no for an answer. His face became beet red and through clenched teeth he demanded that I comply. Now too frightened to decline, I followed his directions. Hence, when he held out his arms, I climbed on. Then he took me out to the center of the pool where, after a few instructions on how to move my arms and legs, he promptly released me. At this, I sunk to the bottom of the pool. Although assured I would float, I was so skinny that I did not. Once retrieved from this ordeal, I fled to our family's room where I refused to return to the pool.

For years thereafter, I resisted learning how to swim. I would not do the dead man's float or blow bubbles into the water. No one could induce me to face the prospect of drowning. According to the get-back-on-the-horse theory, this should have been the end of it. I should never have learned to swim. Yet I did. How I did will be described in the next chapter. My approach, though, was totally different from his—and it worked.

Regrettably, in the long run his approach failed him. Although he suffered from a dyslexia that he never overcame, his fear of being found out ultimately overwhelmed him. When young, he used his native intelligence to sidestep this impediment. Yet as he got older, and the work in which he was engaged, that is, electronic engineering, became more complex, he could not keep up. Eventually he refused to take jobs where his lack of a college education might be a handicap. Despite his very real skills (he was, for instance, able to troubleshoot the radars on fighter jets), his embarrassment at not being able to read at the expected level was too much to bear. At this point, he retreated from the challenge. In his final years, he literally sat in the dark, brooding about the accomplishments he never reached. Happily, my sister, who took a different approach to her dyslexia, had a different outcome. How she managed this will also be discussed in the next chapter.

Breaking down doors or trying to wrestle our fears into submission can sometimes succeed, but it has its drawbacks. Among them is an emotional rigidity. The internal controls needed to keep fears in check can take so much energy that they do not allow the flexibility to deal with new opportunities. In such cases, these fears seldom dissipate. They are suppressed, they get diverted, but they are not conquered. Present in an unresolved form, they require constant vigilance to keep in check. In contrast, dangers that are mastered eventually subside. Because they are successfully fought and/or fled, they no longer remain a menace.

Theodore Roosevelt provides a useful illustration.[20] A man of undoubted bravery, he achieved victories that far surpass what most of us manage. While he was courageous enough to charge up San Juan Hill, to trek through uncharted South American jungles, and to browbeat the titans of American industry into submission, he never overcame some of his personal demons. These were of long-standing. Teddy was a small and sickly child. Because he suffered from asthma, his parents feared for his life. Unable to defend himself from larger boys, he despised his weakness and was determined to overcome it. He did so via a mixed strategy that succeeded in some aspects but failed him in others.

Like many of us, Teddy had something to prove. It was not merely that he wanted to be brave; he needed to demonstrate that he was. He had to accomplish frightening objectives that were perceptibly beyond the norm. Part of this entailed building himself up physically and part required that he place himself in jeopardy. Yet when his wife and mother died on the same day, he was devastated. As earlier observed, his first stab at coping consisted of burying himself in his legislative work. When this proved insufficient, he bought a ranch in the Dakotas. There he eschewed being a hands-off owner. He did what the other cowboys did, that is, participating in roundups, hunting big game, and capturing an outlaw. At Harvard he had earlier taken up boxing in order to prove his manhood, and out West he followed a similar course. No work was too strenuous, or dangerous, to disdain. In this, he did, in fact, establish his manhood. No one questioned his physical courage then or later when he spent a year on safari in Africa.

Nonetheless, this headlong approach to surmounting his fears had its limitations. Frantic activity could keep the pain he endured upon his father's, mother's, and wife's deaths from erupting into consciousness. But it could not make it go away. So frightening were these thoughts that he would not allow anyone to discuss the events that precipitated them. Indeed, when he wrote his autobiography, he never mentioned his first wife. Her name, Alice, had been excised from his life. This was the case despite the fact that his first daughter was also named Alice. So rigid were Roosevelt's defenses that he never spoke to Alice about her mother. Although she wanted him to, he would never permit it.

Roosevelt could master his physical fears by facing them down. Yet he could not do the same with his emotional fears. This affected the nature of his relationships. He was widely admired, but he was also widely disdained. Although he was a caring person, he was not always an emotionally supportive one. Teddy managed to have a loving family life and an effective public career, but he is the exception. Most people who try to ride roughshod over their fears fall short. He was smarter, more intense, and more determined than most, but not even he could manage the whole package. Those of us who have less courage require a more indirect approach. We need to deal with our fears incrementally. Not one decisive battle, but many small encounters are needed for us to become more daring. This has the advantage of freeing our energies for other endeavors. Teddy's superior abilities allowed him to keep many, albeit not all, of his balls in the air. Those of us who are less talented must first reduce the challenges. We can achieve this by initially permitting our fears to subside. Not only are we able to dismount the horse, but sometimes we *should* get off of it. This does not imply that we will never get back on, only that we must do so carefully and piecemeal.

SAFE PLACES

Why do we need to get off the horse? Because the ground is a safer place. If we do not know how to ride or if the horse is rambunctious, sitting on its back can be dangerous. Perched upon it, we are all too aware that we might be thrown to the ground. This can be terrifying. It can be so alarming that for the moment there is little hope of calming down or figuring out how to survive. In short, we panic. This is problematic because panic is antithetical to fighting or fleeing dangers in an orderly manner. Most of the time, we become so uncoordinated that we make things worse—which is more frightening. Bluster and intense effort can sometimes overcome panic, but not always. As expert horsemen know, horses are powerful creatures. Few, if any, of us are strong enough to manhandle them into submission. More useful is appreciating their nature and influencing them in accord with it.

Because terror is the principal barrier to behaving bravely, it must be prevented from forestalling our efforts to acquire courage. The starting place for integrated fear management is therefore finding a safe place. Much in the manner of a toddler's home base,[21] this can provide the confidence to tackle new challenges. If we have reliable place to which we can return when our fears are headed off the tracks, we can reestablish control by retreating to it. We must therefore trust in its safety and in our ability to access it as needed. If we cannot intentionally obtain this protection, we will not feel safe in the presence of an unfamiliar danger. Thus if we do not feel secure, we will not risk the perils of a bewildering universe.

There are many sorts of safe places. We can break them down into three categories. The first are literal places. These are physical locations in which we feel safe. When we are at these sites, our anxieties decrease. While they may not make our worries disappear, they keep us from feeling overwhelmed. In other words, we do not panic when there. A comfortable room, a house in the country, or a flower-strewn meadow can all be safe places.

The second sort of safe place is persons. Some human beings are safer than others. When we are in their presence, we draw a sigh of relief. They may not actively protect us from dangers, but we are confident that they will not inflict additional harm. Accordingly, when we feel beleaguered, we turn to them for a respite. These are usually nice people. They are also apt to be stronger than we are. Like a good parent,[22] they are thus capable of repelling significant hazards. Spouses, friends, teachers, and counselors can all furnish such protection.

Next, there are safe states of mind. These are not actual places but mental tricks that enable us to feel safe. Although they do not make dangers go away, because they enable us to avoid perceiving them, it is as if they had. In this case, out of sight can be out of mind—at least temporarily. These states of minds come in two primary varieties. One is diversions. These redirect our attention away from what might be unsafe. The other is the unconscious, which enables us to suppress uncomfortable thoughts. Both can be effective, as long as they are not abused.

Diversions come in many forms. Among the more common are the arts. Many people who suffer lonely childhoods, such as Carol Burnett, use the cinema as an escape. It allows their imaginations to expand into a happier universe than the one they inhabit. Books can do the same thing. They may fly us off to a South Sea Island or include us in a loving family. Music and dance protect us in a slightly different manner. They fill our ears and eyes with rousing stimuli. These are so impactful that they leave little room for threatening phenomena. Meanwhile sports and hobbies divert by engaging us in pleasing activities. Whether we are involved in playing soccer or collecting stamps, when we are immersed in these pursuits, outside events are pushed aside. Even watching a football game can transport us out of our skin into a fast-paced whirlwind where it is others who are hurt—and, just as meaningfully, who usually overcome their hurt.

Work, in general, can be diverting. Whether this is laboring to build a brick wall or to clean a kitchen spick and span, concentrating on a stimulating goal can keep ominous ideas away. This tactic worked for Roosevelt when he buried himself in legislative business; it worked when he was ranching cattle.[23] It is the favored salvation of workaholics, whether they are toiling with people, data, or things. As long as they are engrossed in these activities, external dangers remain external.

For some, religion is the preferred bulwark against looming threats. Belief in an all-knowing, all-protective deity can cushion the blows of an unpredictable universe.[24] Life is uncertain. We can never be entirely sure whether something we cannot handle will arise. A particularly dreadful danger, one rarely foreseeable in its particulars, is death. We all die, but we do not know when or how. Correspondingly, all of our loved ones die, and we are just as impotent in preventing their demise.[25] This is terrifying—as long as we dwell on it. For the most part, however, we don't. Nonetheless, here in the West, when religious folks do, they think in terms of heaven and an eternal life. God, it is assumed, will rescue them, as well as their nearest and dearest. These people do not have to worry because they possess an omnipotent ally. He will win battles that they cannot.

Another comforting diversion is our fantasies and dreams.[26] We humans have active imaginations. In our heads, we can conjure up people and places that never were and never will be. In our mind's eye and guts, they take on a reality that can feel as tangible as the real thing. Although we may not be able to overcome a dangerous foe, we can daydream about a battle in which he is thoroughly humiliated. In our imagination, we know exactly what to say in order to make him look like a fool. We can also envisage becoming rock stars or conquering generals. And when we do, we momentarily become so strong that no threat is able to disturb our well-being.

The unconscious also provides us with admirable mental defense mechanisms.[27] Sigmund Freud had it exactly right when he discovered that his patients thrust unpleasant experiences out of awareness. They did not remember the disconcerting childhood events that left them paralyzed with fear. Nor was it as if they were pretending not to recall. These occasions were pushed so far down into their unconscious that they had no idea that they were there.

This strategy is not confined to neurotics. It is part and parcel of being human. We all begin life as vulnerable children. However loving the family from which we come, there were sure to have been bitter frustrations that we, as infants, toddlers, or schoolchildren, could not manage. These everyday dangers had to be processed. Since they couldn't all be neutralized, many were placed aside. Had they not been, they would have accumulated into a massive barrier that prevented us from moving forward. The unconscious thus became a repository for these threats. Although they did not dissipate, they were kept at bay.

The Freudian defense mechanisms form a palisade that keeps long-buried dangers from breaking into consciousness. One of these techniques is rationalization.[28] Instead of acknowledging unconscious motives, we pretend that we are acting for other reasons. These tend to be socially acceptable explanations; hence we are not questioned and do not have to delve into the actual sources of our dismay. Another technique is denial. We may simply refuse to acknowledge the truth. We essentially lie to ourselves and to others, without ever admitting it. When this succeeds, we too are deceived. A third mechanism is projection. If we fear our own reactions, we may deny them by convincing ourselves that they belong to another person: *I am not angry; he is. My rage is not a danger. His is.* This way we do not have to worry that we will do something that will get us into trouble. A forth mechanism is sublimation. Now we can take our anger and use it for something valuable. Instead of seeking our own advantage, we might, for instance, fight for social justice. This way others will not attack us. In fact, they may join in our cause because they regard it as moral. In our own minds, persuading ourselves that our motives are pure reduces our vulnerability.

These safe places, whether physical locations, persons, or mental states, serve as sanctuaries. They are not perfect refuges in that the threats they control are not eliminated. The dangers are held in abeyance until such time as we can address them more directly. Of course, sometimes we never do. We don't become strong enough to take our courage in hand and confront whatever menace motivated us to seek protection. In these cases, we can wind up imprisoned by our fears. Because we are unable to venture beyond our safe places, there are things we never attempt and satisfactions we never experience. While we remain sheltered from the worst aspects of whatever frightens us, we never live as fully as we might have had we learned to be tougher.

This is why ensuring safety is merely the first step of integrated fear management. It lays the foundation for stepping outside our self-created perimeter. Most fears can be faced. We do not always have to hide from them. Nonetheless, the initial phase in defeating them may be to temporarily hide from them. We must, however, make sure that this is not the last step.

In any event, when we seek safety, we must take care that this actually creates safety. It is easy to repair to a place that seems safe but is not. Regrettably not every location that looks like a sanctuary is. Thus, expatriate Germans who believed Hitler's Germany would provide them with unequaled opportunities made a serious mistake. Returning to their homeland prior to World War II had dire consequences. Nor is every person who promises protection a source of security. Many a demagogue has made enticing promises on which he/she later reneged. Honeyed words may captivate millions of unwary souls, yet they can still be empty. By the same token, not every diversion offers a respite. Some entangle people in activities that are more dangerous than those they fled. Drug use is a prime example. Even the unconscious can be a trap. When it transforms into a more important source of protection than our conscious defenses, people become neurotic. They cease dealing with reality and have difficulty managing day-to-day life. It is therefore essential to use safe places with discrimination and care. We must keep our eyes open, even as we are trying to close them to a terrifying menace.

Old Places

During the course of growing up, most of us create, and or discover, safe places. Without these refuges, life would be more terrifying than we could bear. As a consequence, when we become adults, many of these remain available. If they do, there is no reason that they may not be sought out. Although these must sometimes be modified to suit our present circumstances, their accessibility makes them attractive.

My wife, Linda, grew up on a farm in northern Ohio and was raised by parents who were decent and loving people. Nonetheless the frictions between her Mom and Dad occasionally grew so heated that

Linda needed an escape. She found it by walking the back acres of their farm. There she could be alone with her thoughts and nature. She could also divert herself with unexpected objects, such as arrowheads and igneous rocks. To this day, Linda loves nature. She enjoys being outside and taking long walks. She also feels fulfilled puttering in the garden and watching the flowers bloom. These clear her head.

I did not grow up in the countryside. I am a city boy from Brooklyn. Nevertheless, when I was a child, my family spent our summers at Gerber's farm in the Catskill Mountains. As with many during the 1950s, the polio scare prodded us to seek a refuge. Although Gerber's is associated in my mind with the tribulations of swimming, most of my memories are of a fonder sort. My father, who terrorized me back at home, spent weekdays in the city; hence I was protected from his anger until the weekend. Free to do as I wished, I wandered the woods in search of salamanders; climbed the adjacent hill, picking blueberries; and played Ping-Pong with friends. These were gentle days that I will never forget. Consequently, like my wife, I too appreciate the countryside and enjoy sharing walks through our exurban neighborhood.

My childhood was different from Linda's in another important respect. During the school year, I did not have a farm to meander about. My primary sanctuary was the corner of my parent's bedroom. During the day, I would repair there with a book, usually the encyclopedia, to read about faraway times and places. I liked to imagine myself a warrior conquering strange lands, then ruling them with a light touch. Later on when I walked to school, I daydreamed about becoming a gifted orator. In my mind's eye, I would give speeches that set huge crowds cheering. Here, at least, I was appreciated. To this day, I must admit to having fantasies of success. Although these have been tempered by the realities of adulthood, they remain reassuring.

Memories of people who were important to me also provide solace. My maternal grandmother and my uncle Milton are both gone. Nonetheless, Lizzie loved me as no one else did. I was her first grandchild, for whom she reserved unconditional positive regard. In her eyes, I could do no wrong. I can still see her holding my head in her hands and chanting, "Ah zees a coup." My spelling may be wrong, but her meaning, "is this a head," is indelible. She loved me because I was smart, and I loved her for loving me. As for Milton, her second child, he was among the gentlest of human beings I have ever known. I never heard him say an unkind word about anyone. For fun, the two of us used to discuss politics. In time, however, I became a conservative, while he remained an ardent liberal. Still, upon hearing opinions with which he disagreed, he did not scold me. Instead, he shook his head and exclaimed, "Where did I go wrong!" all the while smiling broadly. Milton loved me, with a tolerance I wish I could emulate. This cherished memory continues to reassure me when others deride my opinions.

New Places

No matter how many trustworthy old places we have, we also need new safe places. Fresh dangers almost always require novel forms of protection. The process of growing up presents hurdles that are bound to arouse additional fears. For virtually all of us, the unknown is threatening. Although it may be benign, we cannot be sure until we get there. This is the case with adulthood. It is a new place for all of us when we arrive at its doorstep. We, therefore, cannot predict all of the demands we will be required to meet. Nor can we know if we will be up to dealing with these challenges. As a result, we require safe harbors from which to sally forth.

Let us return to Teddy Roosevelt. He began his public career assured of his family's support.[29] Loved by both of his parents, educated at Harvard, and endowed with ample financial resources, although politics was a novel vocation for a man of his social class, his multiple advantages enabled him to adjust to its unique circumstances. Yet when his wife and mother died, his comfortable home was no longer a refuge where he could to recharge his batteries. He thus had to find a different place that did not revive painful memories. This he achieved by heading west and engaging in unfamiliar activities.

Most of us do not need so dramatic a break. Let me start with Linda. Like most teenagers she was unsettled by her parent's divorce. She had not anticipated it and did not know how to react. She was even more disconcerted after her parents remarried each other and then divorced for a second time. Accordingly, she had to get away. A good student, Linda always knew that she wanted to go to college. But now she sought to attend a school distant from home. While she remained within the borders of Ohio, the college she chose to attend was more than two hundred miles away. There she befriended people different from those in her rural community. This opened up new vistas, including opportunities to travel to such exotic places as Chicago. Because she continued to do well in her academics, college served as a safe new place. It also provided occupational prospects and lifelong friendships.

Higher education has become a standard method for young adults to leave unsafe places. Described by psychologist Erik Erikson as providing a psychosocial moratorium,[30] higher education offers a socially sanctioned time-out during which the demands of a job and family are held in abeyance. It is therefore an excellent way to separate from old dangers before tackling new ones.

For some of us, however, this is not enough. My sister, Carol, for instance, fell into this latter category. She began by going to college while still residing at home. Uncomfortable with academics because of her dyslexia, she majored in interior design. Then, after graduation, she entered a relationship that led to marriage. A good marriage, it turns out, can be a new safe place. In her case, she and her husband needed an additional getaway. With many painful memories to leave behind, they decided on a more emphatic escape. For a while, they settled in London, which was followed by an interlude in San Francisco, and then a stint in Washington, DC. Each time they moved closer to New York, until they decided it was safe enough to return. Along the way, they had discovered that physically and culturally different places were able to provide safety, although, for them, of a transitional sort.

My brother, Joel, adopted a different strategy. He too found our family of origin a seething cauldron from which is was essential to find relief. Joel was the youngest of us. With a decade separating us, Carol and I functioned as his guardians when he was small. Then, when we left home, all of our father's pent-up rage came crashing down around his head. Although he managed to keep his sanity, he was so distressed that he sought an early exit. His first safe place was a teenage marriage. He and his high-school sweetheart quickly set up a home financed by her parents. For a time, this approach worked. With the aid of his in-laws, he also began a business and went to college part-time at night. This provided the space to find himself. Eventually he established an identity that, as it happened, was incompatible with that of his wife. This demanded another new safe place that he found by moving to a different city and entering a new profession. Now a lawyer, he was no longer a dependent little boy.

My own journey to safety followed yet another path. Like my sister, I lived at home as an undergraduate. Consequently I did not strike out on my own until I graduated. By then, I had established a couple of close friendships. Now in graduate school and barely treading water financially, two of my friends and I decided to share an apartment. For me, this was a revelation. No longer berated for being an idiot, I could engage in conduct that was previously prohibited. My buddies and I cursed if we wanted to, ate pizza for breakfast, and stayed up all hours of the night. The freedom was wonderful. It, rather than our tiny apartment, was the source of our safety. Eating ice cream by the gallon was a declaration of independence. While it was delicious, what made it more sumptuous was that there was no one around to tell us we shouldn't. Eventually my friends and I went our separate ways. Each of us set off for schools in different parts of the country, with each of us ultimately ending up as college professors. Some of this can be attributed to the safety we experienced in speaking our minds in arguments that often lasted till six in the morning. Because we were friends, we disagreed without rancor. This was interpersonal safety of a welcome sort.

Non-Place Places

Sometimes safety is provided by what we do not do or where we choose not to go. In other words, avoiding unsafe places can itself furnish safety. Regrettably, many of us find ourselves in jeopardy because we put ourselves in harm's way. Accustomed to being surrounded by danger, it never occurs to us to step away from it. Worse still, we may be attracted to these familiar perils. Thus, even when we set out on our own, we may find ourselves embroiled in recognizable conflicts with recognizable foes. Its Yogi Berra's déjà vu all over again, for reasons that we seldom comprehend.

When in chapter 8 we investigate effective methods for using our fears in order to win, I will emphasize the need to choose our fights wisely. Because no one has the ability to succeed in every contest that comes along, only some challenges should be taken up. Which of these are selected depends on the issues at hand and the resources available to us. But in the meantime, it is important to stress the necessity of avoiding unwinnable situations. In these cases, the safest thing is often to do nothing. Nonetheless, most of us, when we are afraid, feel impelled to act. Whether we choose to fight or to run, we do not want to remain at the mercy of an unopposed threat. This rush to do something is apparently in our genes. Whether or not it helps, it feels safer than inaction. Except that it frequently is not.

Panicky people make terrible mistakes.[31] Unable to think clearly, they tend to adopt bad choices. When this happens, the best thing to do is often not to do anything. Inaction, however, is a safe place that does not feel safe—and may indeed be insecure. Even so, it can be safer than disjointed action. Rather than stumble into a disaster, it is frequently better to think things through. This may subject us to immediate injury, but the wound is usually easier to repair than is the harm done by intemperate action.

There are other kinds of safe places over which we have no control. The state of the economy and international relations, for instance, are largely out of our hands. Although these may have a huge impact on our prosperity and security, there is little we can do about them. Closer to home is the nature of the relationships in which we are entangled. As is commonly said, we do not choose our families. Who these others are and how they impact our well-being is only partly under our control. We can leave the homes in which we were raised. We can travel across the country. We may also change our occupations and find new friends. But we cannot change our parents or siblings. They are tied to us by blood. Even if we disown them, they are lodged in our heads and guts. How we think and feel is indelibly linked to relationships we share.

This became apparent to me once my father died. For years, we had resided in separate parts of the country. I was living in upstate New York and he in south Florida. Perhaps once a year I visited, then quickly returned to the shelter of my separate existence. Hence, when, after a long illness, he succumbed, I did not expect much of an impact. I was wrong. For years I had been trying to write a book. Nothing came of it because after a few pages I always decided that my effort was not up to my standards. Now I sat down and wrote my first monograph. Why? Because it finally felt safe. With my father gone, I did not have to worry about his rejection. He had never approved any project I attempted. Deep in my unconscious I feared that it would be the same with my writing. Now his absence liberated me from this bugaboo. This safe place had no substance, but it made all the difference in what it permitted me to do.

A tragic example of this kind of liberation not occurring transpired when I was a methadone counselor. One of my clients disclosed that he and his girlfriend were soon to have a baby. He was now afraid that he might not make a good father. Because his own father was a violent man, he feared that he might be the same with his child. And so he conceived of a remedy. He would fly down to Florida where his Dad lived and resolve their differences. Once reconciled, he would be free to love his baby. Although his current bond to his father was largely in his imagination, he could not let go of it without doing so in person. Unfortunately this did not work out. Intending to take a two-week trip, he returned home after one. Totally agitated by what had developed into a brawl, he could barely contain his anxiety. I tried to calm him down, but to no avail. The safe place he had projected in his head was completely gone. As a result, he went to his apartment, got a shotgun from the closet, shot his girlfriend in the head, and then turned the gun on himself. With his father still alive and as accusatory as ever, he was not able to establish a safe place in his mind. And so he took what he saw was the only way out. He fled his fears as definitively as possible.

BAD PLACES

Just as there are safe places in which to find temporary refuge, so there are bad ones that increase our peril. Some locations are inherently dangerous, as are some people, activities, and states of mind.

It is therefore important that these be recognized and avoided. Many sanctuaries are mirages. They look safe from a distance, but their shelter vanishes like mist once we get up close.

Dangerous Locations

Foremost among the dangerous locations that can look safe are those with which we have long experience. Because venturing out into new locales can be intimidating, people often decide to stay where they are merely because it feels familiar. This is especially true for people who are unsure of themselves. The poor, in particular, are notorious for being locally oriented.[32] Although they may live in filthy, crime-infested neighborhoods, they cannot imagine residing elsewhere. They know better than outsiders that drive-by shootings and muggings can occur at any time, yet they choose the devil they know rather than the one they don't. This is not a safe option; nevertheless it seems safer than any conceivable alternative.

Dangerous People

Friends are friends. Or, at least, it can seem that way. People we know are comparable to neighborhoods that we know. Their idiosyncrasies are like familiar street corners, some of whose quirks are more innocuous than others. Since we know the territory, we are confident that we can protect ourselves from accustomed hazards. Even so, some people are truly dangerous. Accordingly, if we do not make distinctions, we are apt to be betrayed by individuals we thought we could trust. This includes potential lovers, street-level buddies, and drinking partners.

Especially treacherous are gangs.[33] Inner-city adolescents often associate with these in order to obtain protection. They learn that non-members are vulnerable to attack, whereas members can call upon each other for assistance. The price for this security is, however, high. Adopting a way of life saturated in violence is an invitation to being injured. Friendship bought at the cost of placing one's life in jeopardy is scarcely a reliable source of safety.

Not in the same league, but as emotionally dangerous, are misplaced love affairs.[34] Romantics tend to believe that love can save them from anything. This is not true, although an intense attachment can provide the courage to fight the good fight. Then again, it cannot do even this, if the wrong person is chosen. Insecure people are often desperate to be loved. And because they are, they tend to make terrible choices. They frequently mistake exploitation for concern and egotism for selflessness. Certain that they are unlovable, they cling to the slightest indication of affection. This makes them vulnerable to unscrupulous manipulation.

My brother Joel's late ex-wife was such a person. Although she too was needy, she was extraordinarily selfish. She fancied herself a princess who deserved everything he could give her. If he did not, she sought revenge, at one point setting him up to be investigated by the police. Only gradually did he realize that her promise of love was a trap. So keen was he on fleeing our father's wrath that it took years to pierce his illusions and recognize her actual character. This inclination, by the way, is one of the reasons that teenage romances so often fail. The naiveté of the very young makes it difficult for them to assess the validity of a relationship.

Dangerous Activities

Drinking and drug use have already been depicted as dangerous.[35] They deserve another mention because they are so routinely embraced in contemporary society. Some substances have been extolled for expanding our consciousness. They supposedly make us more creative and/or mellow. In fact, they do neither. Drugs, such as cocaine, provide the illusion of industriousness. They make their users feel energetic. In the long run, however, they become so addictive that they prevent systematic work. Meanwhile, other drugs, such as marijuana, provide the illusion of tranquility. Their users feel at peace as they surrender any ambition they might once have had. These, therefore, are graveyards of hope rather than bastions against harm.

Alcohol, of course, is the granddaddy of chemical defenses.[36] Despite the alarming example of homeless derelicts, alcohol remains the favored escape of millions of Americans. Why this is so always seemed a mystery to me, that is, until a psychiatric client of mine explained why he continued to get drunk. George was both intelligent and articulate. Nevertheless he periodically imbibed so excessively as to become incoherent. When I asked him the reason for this self-abuse, he told me that people who claimed alcohol did not work were wrong. He insisted that it worked extremely well in that it blotted out every trace of painful thoughts. On the other hand, the aftermath was problematic. For George, and many others, alcoholism felt less dangerous than his inner turmoil. It may have been killing him by rotting out his liver and destroying his brain cells, yet when he was under the influence he felt safe.

For others, sex has the same effect. They experience the ecstasy of the sex act as life-affirming. And so they trek from partner to partner, seeking the ultimate gratification. Someday that moment will surely arrive and they will be liberated. Only they never are. In the grip of a compulsion, their carnal appetite is never appeased. Nor do they ever find love. Intent on using and being used, they are precluded from establishing intimate relations grounded in trust. Like the *Flying Dutchman*, they are on a never-ending voyage that is devoid of fulfillment. Welcoming harbors always seem just beyond the horizon, fated to disappear as they draw near.

Dangerous States of Mind

A remarkably large number of patrons of psychotherapy are obsessed with guilt.[37] They are convinced that they are worthless beings who deserve to be punished. Certain that they have done something that merits eternal torment, they become their own prison guards. This is because they are determined to discipline themselves before others get the chance. As a result, they find safety in imposing their own suffering. This way they know the outcome, even if it will be agonizing. Except that because they are their own jailers, their anguish never ends. Instead of receiving a conditional release, they perpetuate interminable penalties lest others impose more stringent ones.

Others obtain a pseudosafety by sacrificing themselves to the will of bullies. Certain that no one can love them for who they are, they believe that the only way they can be tolerated is if they offer others endless assistance. Dedicated caretakers, they do not expect anything in return—other than minimal acceptance. Habitually selling themselves short, they surrender their happiness in return for survival. This, of course, is a bad bargain, but it is one that depends on confusing the appearance of safety with its reality.

As we can see, there are many ways to find safety and as many ways to circumvent obtaining it. For those in search of courage, it is essential that they are able to tell the difference. This is imperative because they cannot begin the process of overcoming their fears if they do not possess reliable places in which they can allow their terrors to subside. As long as they remain in the grip of uncontrolled panics, they will not be able to proceed to the next phases of integrated fear management. Safety-first therefore applies not just on the job but also in our efforts to become bolder and self-assured.

Chapter 5

INCREMENTAL TOLERANCE

NEAR AND REMOTE MISSES

During World War I, pilots of the newly invented airplanes discovered that they could drop bombs directly on enemy targets. This had several advantages. One was that they could see the target, which improved their chances of hitting it. Another was that they were too high to be effectively shot down. A third was that they could strike objectives more distant than could be reached by other means, such as artillery. By the time of World War II, aerial technology had so improved that each of these benefits was greatly magnified. Now purpose-built bombers could carry tons of explosives many hundreds of miles away to be dropped with greater accuracy. This enabled military planners to envisage air supremacy as a means of achieving victory.

Both the English and German high commands believed that their enemy could be bombed into submission.[1] If sufficiently high concentrations of heavy bombs could be dropped on inner cities, these would devastate their infrastructures. In the process, tens of thousands of inhabitants would be killed. The destruction would be so massive that ordinary mortals could not endure it. As a result, they would put pressure on their government to pursue peace. Because the Germans began the war with a larger air force, they were first to put this theory to the test. Fleets of bombers crossed the English Channel to deliver dozens of lethal assaults on London. In what came to be called the Blitz, the city's center was reduced to rubble. Many thousands were indeed killed, while many thousands more were left homeless. Even those who were untouched had to sleep in subway stations and then walk to work surrounded by burning wreckage.

Ordinary Londoners, who did not have access to bunkers, should have been terrified. They ought to have been trembling with fear from morning to night. Nonetheless, this is not what happened.[2] The Londoners did not surrender. Tired and disheartened, they did not give in to their fears. The question was, why? Why did so many ordinary people put up with such extraordinary dangers? Was there something unique to the English spirit that enabled them to maintain a stiff upper lip throughout these attacks? Evidently not, because when the Germans later came under assault, they reacted the same way. Their urban areas sustained even greater damage, yet they too managed to keep going. How? Where did their courage come from?

Before the war began, English officials worried that so many people would be traumatized by mass bombings that they prepared psychiatric facilities to treat the anticipated mental casualties. Fortunately, these were not needed thanks to a psychological reaction studied by J. T. McCurdy. As described by Malcolm Gladwell in his book *David and Goliath*,[3] McCurdy concluded that there were three types of reactions to the bombing. The first was actually a non-reaction. After all, the bombs did hit some people. Many of these victims failed to survive and hence did not experience fear.

A second group endured near misses. The bombs fell perilously close to them and hence they were frightened. These folks could see the damage and carnage firsthand. Perhaps wounded, their fears were thus reinforced. Often dazed and left mentally off-balance, they became preoccupied by dangers they knew to be real. Now feeling jumpy, they worried about subsequent bombings. For them, a close brush with death had intensified their uncertainties. They survived, whereas their courage was shaken.

A far larger group did not experience near misses. They were too distant from the points of impact. Living in a city under siege, they were nonetheless aware of what was taking place. They could hear the bombs going off and could later see the damage, yet they were not in immediate peril. It was others who had been injured, not them. Whatever their initial qualms, their worst fears had not been realized. Perhaps they were invincible. Perhaps, like a George Washington,[4] who heard the bullets whizzing past his head during battle, they too were convinced they would be spared. Death and destruction might be all about, but it would not visit them. This would not be their fate.

Most of those who experienced remote misses felt liberated. Relieved to have survived, their courage grew. Now the bombing seemed almost normal. It became a background noise that need not concern them. They were free to go about their business as if nothing were happening. To quote an onlooker, "small boys continued to play all over the pavements, shoppers went on haggling, a policeman directed traffic in majestic boredom, and the bicyclists defied death and the traffic laws. No one, so far as I could see, even looked into the sky."[5]

This result surprised McCurdy and the British authorities—as well as it might the rest of us. It did not accord with common sense. Dangers are dangers and hence they should be recognized as such. Just because a bomb did not hit us today does not mean that one will not hit us tomorrow. Rationally, fear should still be present. Theoretically we should calculate our actual chances of being injured and respond accordingly. Only we don't. We make decisions based on our personal experience. As long as we remain safe, we do not make dispassionate investigations into the odds against us. We simply feel secure and it is this that determines our subsequent behavior.

Remote misses are the psychological equivalent of a mental shield. People are so relieved at surviving that their lack of injury feels astonishing. Although miracles do not often happen, when they touch us personally we feel charmed. What had been regarded as a danger thereby losses its terrors. Courage, it seems, can be a product of safety. When we are palpably secure, as demonstrated by not being harmed, we become less afraid. Some dangers, such as fear of snakes, are coded in our genes, whereas many more are learned through living. We thus discover that fire burns by touching fire. We are likewise taught that being run over by an automobile can be lethal by being exposed to parental alarm. We also learn that by not putting our hands in the flame or running into the street, we will be safe. It may take numerous instances of not being harmed to convince us that we are secure, but, in the end, we take fire and automobiles in stride.

How many of us are truly afraid of being consumed by a shark? When we go to the movies and see people being mauled by great whites, we might later have nightmares. More often, while sitting on a veranda, drinking iced tea, it never occurs to us that we are in imminent danger. The threat of great white sharks is too far away. Similarly, how many of us are truly afraid of being in an automobile crash? We know there are tens of thousands of highway fatalities every year, but the victims are usually strangers. Moreover, although we witness the accidents that slow us down on the Interstate, we don't actually see the casualties. The ambulance lights are flashing, yet the blood and gore are screened from view. From where we sit, safely ensconced in our vehicle, the whole business has an antiseptic quality. It might as well be a movie. Hence we are not afraid.

One of the secrets of developing courage is thus exposing ourselves to remote misses. We do not have to hide out in bomb shelters in order to obtain protection. We can venture outside, as long as we steer clear of looming dangers. If the bombs are going off miles away, we soon realize that they will not rent our flesh. They become like fireworks. We see the airbursts. We marvel at their beauty. But we are confident that we will not be harmed.

Why do parents bring their children to fireworks displays? Why do they put them on amusement park thrill rides? Why too do they hold their hands as they marvel at the lightning strikes during a thunderstorm? These all constitute remote hits. No one gets hurt, despite the children's preliminary fears. They can watch the beautiful colors in the sky, hold their breath while going down the roller coaster, and cover their ears when the thunder jolts the house. Yet they survive. And when they do, after perhaps multiple exposures to apparent dangers, they become less apprehensive. They can now pay closer attention to what is happening. Now aware that they are not in peril, they can allow themselves to learn more about what is taking place.

Here then is a mechanism for increasing our courage. We can arrange remote misses. We do not have to wait for nature—or a war—to thrust them upon us. If we have fears that we cannot manage, we can intentionally expose ourselves to safer versions of them. Instead of rushing headlong into a danger, we can start by confronting something less fearsome. Rather than jumping back on the horse, we can begin with a hobbyhorse and then perhaps move on to a donkey. There is no point in allowing ourselves to be blown up just to prove that we are not afraid of dying. Neither do we have to wrap ourselves in cotton batting. Keeping dangers at a reasonable distance is usually sufficient.

DESENSITIZATION

Psychologists have developed a method for exposing their clients to remote misses. The technique is called desensitization.[6] Its objective is to make people less "sensitive" to whatever frightens them. When in the incremental presence of that which is otherwise too terrifying to bear, their clients are expected to lose their terror of it. The feeling is gradually to subside so that it can be experienced without precipitating panic. Step-by-step the subject is thus subjected to instances of fear, but in a manner that enables his dread to diminish. Ultimately that which seemed too formidable to encounter loses its sting. No longer a signal of destruction, the message sent becomes more benign.

The classic use of desensitization has been with phobias.[7] Some people develop apparently irrational fears to nonthreatening stimuli. Other folks may recognize, let us say, that the color blue is not dangerous, yet the victims are convinced it is. How then to persuade them it is not? Of course, fear of a color is not terribly disabling. Agoraphobia, in contrast, is.[8] Some people are terrified by the prospect of leaving their homes. They consider the outside world too dangerous to endure. The *agora* was the ancient Greek marketplace. It was where business was transacted. Today's agoraphobics prevent themselves from doing business by avoiding anything outside their front doors. This so limits their opportunities that it empties their lives of pleasure. No wonder many seek release from this self-imposed incarceration.

The way out—literally—is a slow and steady progression. If agoraphobics are hurried too quickly into an environment they cannot manage, their fear escalates. For them, this is the equivalent of a near miss. Remote misses, however, are more difficult to arrange. Nevertheless, they can be created by not rushing headlong into danger. The client is thus first taken to the door of his house. It is opened, but he is not asked to go through. The next day, and the day after that, he is brought to the same open door. Eventually, once he is convinced that he will not be forced out, his apprehension declines. His emotion, that is, his fear, weakens. This is not a logical decision on his part. We humans do not control our feelings in a logical manner.[9] Not reason, but direct experience alters their nature. Particular affects warn of danger, not by calculating what hurts, but by establishing a trip wire that has previously been installed via negative practice. Feelings are learned in the doing; not in the thinking.

And so our agoraphobic, after many days of standing at the door's edge, becomes desensitized when doing so. Nothing bad has happened, which amounts to a remote miss. The imaginary perils he had conjured up remain far distant; hence he is less fearful. Next, he is asked to step outside. Nonetheless he is asked to take only one step. If this is too much, he is allowed to retreat. One step, however, can usually be managed. Here too the previous formula is followed for several days, that is, until what had been threatening becomes less so. After this he is asked to step off the porch, to walk down the block, and so on. At each location, he is allowed to develop comfort at his own pace. At none is he forced to go beyond what he can endure.

Another way to describe this procedure is "incremental tolerance."[10] Increments are small additions, whereas tolerance implies the ability to experience a stimulus without running away. As long as the pieces are small enough and the option of a quick getaway remains, over time most of us become less sensitized. Trivial challenges are thus like remote misses. They do not create alarm. Moreover, although each may be tiny, when summed over long periods they can add up to a massive challenges. Incremental tolerance thus works to reduce fears, albeit not overnight. Many people assume that if they cannot become courageous immediately, they never will. This is a huge mistake. The second stage of integrated fear management always takes time. Our emotions, especially if they are intense, change slowly. As a consequence, unless they are not allowed the space to do so, they seldom transform. This is particularly true of fear.

Why do so many of us fail to realize this? Oddly, it is because we are phobic about our fears.[11] We so dread them that we will not permit ourselves to gaze directly upon them. Instead we deny their nature. We pretend that they are something else. We call them anxieties, stresses, pressures, traumas, worries, or apprehensions.[12] Nonetheless, anxieties are no more than fears the source of which is obscure. We feel as if we are in danger, although we do not know why. Meanwhile stresses refer the physiological responses we have to endangerment. They are the fight/flight reaction reduced to the hormonal level. Traumas, in turn, are associated with the injuries we might sustain when a danger is real. They are mental analogs of physical wounds. Lastly, apprehensions are forewarnings of fear. They are the little shock waves that precede the tsunami. In each case, we can fool ourselves, and perhaps others, into believing that we have more courage than we do by essentially repudiating the threat.

In fact, these verbal games are not altogether futile. They can shelter us from fears that we are not yet prepared to handle. As such, they may constitute part of the desensitization process. By providing safe mental places, they are able to confer the breathing room to pause before moving on. As long as we eventually do proceed, they serve a useful purpose. Only when they become habitual do they trap us in cowardice.

In Alcoholics Anonymous, members are taught that they do not have to enter a sober lifestyle all at once.[13] Years of abusive drinking generally deprive people of an opportunity to learn the skills of normal living. Consequently, they don't always know what to say or how to act in a novel situation. At such moments, they can feel overwhelmed. They typically fear that they will be found out and ridiculed for their frailties. AA therefore advises that they should "fake it till they make it." They are told to pretend that they know what to do. Although they may not be entirely comfortable, it is sufficient to get by.

Yet in getting by today, and tomorrow, they eventually feel safer. What had been a pretense ultimately becomes genuine. Hence, when they claim to be able to do a job, they, in time, acquire the grace do it with authentic ease because they *can* do it. Reliable performances that begin as masquerades thus mutate into the real thing. An incremental tolerance of their discomfort eventually eliminates the discomfort. They become desensitized to their dread of failure and consequently are less likely to fail.

Faking it till we make it is part of the normal process of becoming competent. No one is skilled from the first moment they try something new. Likewise few of us are free of trepidations when we enter virgin territory. Our lack of competence and anxieties might be found out. Nonetheless, the newly minted doctor must act as if she had always been a doctor.[14] Not yet settled into her role, she needs to put up the appropriate façade. Her patients expect it and her colleagues will help her to sustain it. Were she, on the other hand, to expect her fears to evaporate the moment she began to practice, they never might. Her anxieties about being afraid would reinforce her fears about being competent; hence these would remain operative longer. The same applies to automobile mechanics, salespersons, and newlyweds. None of them is liable to give a polished performance from the get-go. Happily, this is usually unnecessary. Even when our role partners are distressed by our ineptitude, they seldom call down the curtain on our out-of-town trials. This would also create problems for them, which they see no point in generating.

Years ago, when I had no idea of how to make a living, I decided to become a cab driver. My driver's license was two years old, but I had never owned a car. In fact, the only driving I had done was during the week of lessons I took before passing the test for the license. Still, I was also able to pass the exam for a hack license and soon found myself employed. Not surprisingly, my first night out I had no idea of what to do or where to go. As long as I stayed in Manhattan, with its grid street plan, I was okay. As luck would have it, however, one of my first fares took me to the Bronx. But having grown up in Brooklyn, this was terra incognita. And so I careened from street to street, completely dependent upon my customers to show me the way.

I was terrified. Nonetheless I pretended to keep my cool, albeit imperfectly. Besides being a hapless driver, my anxieties made it difficult to pay close attention to the confusing traffic. The result:

I got into four accidents. Count them: *four*. None was significant. Not a single one caused me to have to exchange information with the other drivers. Then, when I got back to the garage, the mechanic who welcomed me commented on the dents I had accrued during my first day on the road. I, however, waved him off with a smile, irreverently asking what he was talking about. My cab was already so banged up that he could not have detected additional damage. After a while, he merely gestured me to move ahead.

I was afraid, but not so afraid that I could not take out a cab again. The one accommodation I made was to drive during the day. Oh, and to try to remain in Manhattan. I was still pretending to be a cab driver. I did not, for instance, warn my customers about my lack of skills. Nonetheless, as might be expected, after many weeks behind the wheel, I got to know my way around. I understood the traffic patterns and learned the best routes to get where I was headed. Soon enough I was a genuine New York City cab driver. I did not have to pretend and was not scared. Out-of-towners were uneasy on our crowded streets, but I had become part of the hair-raising ambience. I was completely desensitized.

A COMMON PROCESS

Incremental tolerance is not confined to the therapeutic couch. It has been used from time immemorial to develop the strength to confront our fears. Again, consider Theodore Roosevelt. As a weak and timid boy, Teddy was determined to overcome his doubts. Nonetheless, this ability did not come all at once. Ashamed of being "timid," years later he admitted that "there were all kinds of things of which I was afraid at first."[15] Yet "by acting as if I was not afraid, I gradually ceased to be afraid." According to biographer Doris Kearns Goodwin, a childhood friend of his also noted that, "by forcing himself to do the difficult or even dangerous things, [courage] became a matter of habit."[16] Still, Roosevelt did not begin by confronting his worst fears. Years passed by as he built up his physical strength and attempted new activities. What at first he counterfeited eventually became the real thing. Although he forced himself into more challenging pursuits than most of us would attempt, the resultant fears subsided only "gradually." They did not instantly disappear.

People differ in how they engage in incremental tolerance. Because we have temperamental differences, what works for some will not work for others.[17] This means that some of us can proceed through the desensitization process more quickly than others can. Each of us, accordingly, ought do so at a pace comfortable for us. If we do not, panic will intervene to stop us in our tracks. For some, excessive speed can even throw them into reverse gear. The dissimilarities between my brother, Joel, and me are instructive in this respect.

When living in upstate New York, I took up skiing. Never very good at it, I disliked the cold and falling down. In any event, I developed the ability to proceed down a slope by means of slow turns that kept me upright. Since Joel had never been on skis before, when he visited me one year, I decided to expose him to the sport. How we comported ourselves was a study in contrasts. Joel was much more daring. A veteran of skydiving and deep-sea diving, he enjoyed the thrill of physical danger. I did not. This disparity was apparent in how we tackled the ski lift. Before jumping on, as was my wont, I stood quietly by observing how it was done. Then after I was satisfied I knew what to expect, I gingerly moved ahead. Joel simply got on without any fanfare.

Once we got on the slope, our inherent differences also made themselves felt. I proceeded to head down the hill in my accustomed slow arcs. Joel, however, pointed his skis straight ahead. Then, after ten yards, he fell. At this, he got up and headed down again. After another fifteen yards, there was another cloud of snow and another inglorious tumble. He continued this way until he got to the bottom. But then he immediately got on the lift so as to repeat the sequence. Joel did this all day, at the end of which he was skiing more confidently than I was. Because he was much more tolerant of failure than me, his learning curve was faster. Nevertheless, although his tempo for coping with fear was swifter, one approach was not better than the other. Both styles were successful. The important thing is to match our desensitization efforts with who we are. It is the mismatches that cause trouble.

One of my customary techniques for tackling frightening activities is to carefully examine novel territories before I proceed. I want to understand what I am up against prior to facing my fears. Others utilize different safe places as a backup when they engage in incremental tolerance. For example, my sister devised an ingenious procedure for coping with her dyslexia. Carol was two years behind me in grade school. Our teachers therefore expected her to live up to my academic standards. Because of her reading problems, however, she could not. This exacerbated her fears in that she also had to cope with their disapproval. By the conclusion of her school career, Carol could read—but just barely. This was enough to get by in most cases; nevertheless, she was so uncomfortable that she avoided reading when she could.

Others might have limped along in this condition, but for Carol being second-rate was anathema. Because it made her feel intellectually inferior, her pride compelled her to seek a worthier solution. She found one after she became a mother. When we were young, the conventional wisdom had it that children should learn to read in school. The teachers, as professionals, would presumably do a better job. By the time Carol had her daughters, this conviction had changed. It was now recognized that children who start school with an ability to read do better later on. Thus, my sister did not want her little girls to be left behind the way she had been. There was no question but that she would attempt to teach them herself.

It was in attempting this that Carol discovered a means of dealing with her dyslexia. She found that by teaching her children, she could reteach herself. As preschoolers, they had no idea of who was a good or bad reader. This made them a tolerant audience. They did not condemn their mother for mistakes they did not realize were mistakes. As a result, they provided a safe place. Carol could therefore go over the lessons as slowly as she needed to. Whatever fears she encountered along the way, she had the time to master. They were desensitized in seriatim as she confronted more advanced lessons. In the end, she found the means to become a competent reader.

As for me and swimming, I too inadvertently engaged in incremental tolerance. Just as Carol found it excruciating to be an ineffectual reader, I felt the same with respect to swimming. My friends could all swim. My little sister could swim. Why couldn't I? Was I somehow so cowardly that I could not master a skill everyone else did? This was intolerable! As a consequence, when I entered my teens I sought an answer. It was then that I realized my grandfather used the sidestroke. He was able to swim long distances without immersing his head in the water. Here was the solution. As long as I could keep my head from getting wet, I did not have to fear drowning.

Even so, I could not permit others to watch me endeavoring to learn this peculiar stroke. Their potential laughter would have added to my fears. And so when my family went on outings to Zach's Bay at Jones Beach I found an opportunity. The bay was wave-free; hence I did not have to worry about an angry surf. Its beach was also large enough to find a place away from prying eyes. Under these conditions, I could allow myself to try new things. In the safety of a private space, I could contend with a series of fears at my own pace. Hence, like an agoraphobic slowly becoming accustomed to the terrors of the outside world, I mastered the terrors of swimming. As long as I did the sidestroke, I was okay. In fact, I became so proficient that years later when working as a camp counselor, I was able to swim across the lake with ease.

This, however, was not good enough. Others might not realize I was afraid of using different techniques, but I did. My father was a strong swimmer who specialized in the Australian crawl. I, sadly, was not in his league. Still afraid of putting my head under water, I refused to contemplate the trauma. Eventually my shame became more than I could bear. Then living on the Upper West Side of Manhattan, I decided to take advantage of the local YMCA. It had an excellent pool and hence I became a member. Week after week I attended that pool. With no one around to chide me, I could blow bubbles in the water just as years earlier I had been instructed to do. I could also attempt the dead man's float. Lo and behold, with more flesh on my bones, I floated. Unlike when I was seven, I did not sink to the bottom of the pool. This was a confidence booster.

But I was far from done. Step-by-step, I taught myself the Australian crawl. Eventually I became good enough to do fifty laps of the pool at a time. Then I went on to the breaststroke and the backstroke. Now one more challenge remained. Could I learn to dive? Others around me did so beautifully. Could I? My strategy here was the same as with swimming. I took on my fears one by one. Starting with the easy things, like jumping in feet first, I gradually moved on to headfirst plunges off the diving board. Although I never became truly proficient, these were real dives. That's when I quit. I was not swimming and diving because I enjoyed the activity. My goal was proving to myself that I could do it. Once I had accomplished this to my own satisfaction, the motivation to continue evaporated. This campaign had taken over a year; yet once it was won, it was won. Having utilized self-identified safe places to learn to tolerate my fears, I no longer feared swimming. That was enough.

Earlier I wrote that I began writing books after my father died. Once he was gone, I felt safe from his perpetual criticism. Nonetheless, that was not the only fear I had to overcome. Ever since I published my first monograph, people have asked for advice about how to do the same. Apparently a great many folks have a book in them that they hope to get out. Yet few do. Of all those I have coached, only one has published books of his own. The rest were too intimidated to get started. After all, books are long. They require sustained effort. Many of my colleagues are, in fact, able to produce articles. Yet these are short. Books, in contrast, contain so much material that most people fear that they will run out of things to say. They also fear that they will not say it well.

I too had such trepidations. Once my father was gone, I set up an office in my home and began to write. Then I ran into a familiar roadblock. Those first few pages did not meet my expectations. They were no match for the quality of the books I had been reading. What to do? In the past, I would have stopped. My fears of not being good enough would have immobilized me. This time things were different. I kept writing despite my misgivings. Allowing myself as much time as I needed to get the job done, I did not rush. I learned to tolerate my discomfort and kept going. Once I finished that first chapter, I made another discovery. The computer made it possible to go back and edit my work. Although much of what I read displeased me, I could improve it. Indeed, I could go back as often as I desired. Soon it became clear that writing (at least for me) was more about rewriting. I did not require the courage to do a perfect job from the outset. All I needed was the courage to deal with one small part of the book at a time.

Thanks to allowing myself to develop incremental tolerance in the safety of my home office, I had developed a kind of courage that most people never attain. A majority never realize that books are not composed in one fell swoop. They are, in fact, written chapter by chapter, paragraph by paragraph, and sentence by sentence. Few of us have the personal fortitude to confront an entire volume all at once. That, happily, turns out to be unnecessary. Nor do we require perfection. Manuscripts can be amended chapter by chapter. They can also be upgraded years after they were first conceived. Even then flaws must be tolerated. These are inevitable. Many of us magnify our fears by expecting more of ourselves than is humanly possible. Yet, as long as we chip away at challenges little by little, we can achieve far more than we imagine. Reality never lives up to our fantasies. Still, if we allow ourselves to cope with our fears gradually, and safely, we usually can get farther than we dreamed. But first, we must learn to live with our fears so that we can determine their extent.

GETTING STARTED

Incremental tolerance is a process. Desensitization never happens all at once. It is a step-by-step enterprise that requires patience and perseverance. We encountered the first step in the last chapter. Reliable safe places are the starting point. If we do not have them, we must create them. The objective is to make these available before we require them. Then, when we begin to confront our fears, we can retreat to them as necessary. This will slow us down. Nonetheless that should be of little concern. One of my father's mistakes was the belief that his fears had to be mastered quickly. He assumed that they were so dangerous that if they were not speedily conquered, he would never be able to control them. For most of us, this turns out not to be true. If we move too rapidly, we are apt to panic and not just retreat, but leave the scene entirely. Nor does having braved a fear mean that our courage has been fully consolidated. Successfully dealing with a terror all at once does not ensure that we will be prepared to deal with it a second time.

The slow-and-steady approach is more satisfactory. While it

takes longer, the achievements are more durable. Hence once we are confident we have access to a safe place that can be used as a shield, we must decide which fears to confront. This is not easy because significant fears tend to be repressed. Both our unconscious and a host of diversions keep us from recognizing their existence.[18] How then can we decide what these are or which should be tackled? We can begin by asking what we are not currently allowing ourselves to do. Which goals would we like to accomplish that we are not permitting ourselves to pursue? In these cases, we are almost invariably holding back because we are afraid of something. What is it?

In most instances, we have multiple fears. Life is a minefield littered with dangers lurking in a myriad of places. Obviously, we cannot deal with them all. There are too many. Nor can we deal with them all at once. This would overwhelm the stoutest of hearts. Instead we must engage in what amounts to triage. We can think of our fears as divided into three categories. The first contains our absolute terrors. These are so horrifying that we cannot bring ourselves to look upon them even from behind the strongest barricades. The second group includes a set of significant fears. These are salient because they have a powerful impact on our welfare. They are usually so potent as to prevent us from accomplishing important tasks. Were they mastered, however, we would be free to lead more fulfilling lives. The third group comprises our less noteworthy fears. These are neither terrifying nor devastating in their impact. Consequently, were they to remain in place, we would not experience acute difficulties.

As with those wounded in battle, it makes most sense to deal initially with the middle group.[19] In war, the first category consists of victims who are unlikely to survive. No matter how much effort we put into saving them, this is apt to be wasted. With respect to our terrors, if they are extremely severe, we may never have the strength to tolerate them. At least, at the outset, they are too much to bear. Better therefore to set them aside—or rather to keep our defenses against them in place. In the mental-health field not all patients are regarded as suitable for psychotherapy. Some, such as schizophrenics, are so fragile that "covering" therapies are recommended.[20] The objective is to strengthen their defenses so that they can cope with daily life. Only the stronger clients are candidates for a deep analysis. Only they have the power to tolerate it.

The third cluster of fears, that is, the trivial ones, can be safely neglected. In battle, these casualties are likely to survive without immediate attention. The same applies to our modest fears. Because the dangers of which they warn are less devastating, they can be ignored without causing a great deal of harm. None of us needs the courage to deal with every fear; hence these can be sidetracked.

The middle group of fears, those that signal important dangers but are not too horrifying to tolerate, should be our focus. These can be dealt with; hence overcoming them makes a constructive difference. Such distinctions improve our chances of acquiring courage that is worth having. They also enable those of us who fear that we are cowards to restrict our efforts to a manageable range. Just as in military hospitals, few of us have the resources to do everything we would like.

What sort of fears lie within this zone? If we revert back to Freud's suggestion that normality consists of being successful at love and work,[21] we have a convenient starting place. As most of us learn, both of these objectives are difficult to attain. The paths toward their achievement are strewn with obstacles. As a teenager, I, for instance, was terrified that no one would ever love me. I was such a peculiar person that no self-respecting woman would lower herself to be attracted to me. Cowardly, incompetent, and, as I thought, ugly, no decent female would want me. Besides, any woman who would was clearly not good enough for me. Like Groucho Marx, who averred that he did not wish to join any club that was willing to admit him, I had boxed myself in. I had established a wonderful excuse for failures in any relationship that I might enter. Perhaps it was best not to try.

At the time, I thought I was unique. In the movies, the male and female leads always seemed fated for each other. Whatever misadventures intervened, by the last reel they found eternal happiness. In stark contrast, I had met with numerous rejections. The girls I fancied never seemed to fancy me. And the pain was excruciating. Why then should I subject myself to it? The mere thought was terrifying. At the time, it did not occur to me that so many of the songs on the radio were about frustrated love. According to the lyrics, either romance never came or if it did, it was ripped apart by a cruel betrayal. Clearly, my fears were not exclusive. Others were also comforted by these melodies. Like it or not, love was not easy then; it is not now. Rejection is part of the means through which we find a suitable partner in a society where marital partnerships are voluntary. Nevertheless, almost no one enjoys this. Most tremble at the prospect. Still, it is part of the courtship process.[22]

But our fears of intimacy do not stop there. Dating is supposed to be fun—and can be. Yet it is also frightening to make discoveries about how others perceive us. While our mothers may hold us in high esteem, strangers don't always agree. Even if we are not rejected, we are apt to suffer unwelcome lessons. First, we soon realize that not every potential partner values the same things. Some may like us, whereas others do not. Second, we might not be the persons we thought we were. Our self-perceptions can be distorted. How others see us thus helps us to understand who we are and what we want. Then, when we find someone who is compatible, we must go about the business of establishing a stable relationship. This invariably entails a give-and-take that is filled with unanticipated discord. Both standing up for ourselves and giving in to another's desires turn out to be scary. Will a fight over what we, as a couple, should do ever end, or if it does, will we have to submerge our egos in order to gain acceptance? No wonder people are afraid of commitment.

How then are we to begin desensitizing our reservations about intimacy? The easy answer is slowly. It we are to tolerate our fears about closeness, we must start somewhere. This first step, however, should be small. Diving into the social whorl with both feet suits only a tiny fraction of us. Nowadays, for many, the best place to commence is group dating. Sometimes referred to as "hanging out," this enables people to interact without having to endure a tinge of obligation. Facebook too can provide a nonthreatening venue. This provides interpersonal learning with the possibility of a hasty retreat readily at hand. Rejection still hurts, but these innovations make it easier to disguise.

Actual face-to-face intimacy, especially when accompanied by commitment, is more difficult to manage.[23] Its terrors ought, therefore, be put off until they can be handled. Voluntary intimacy is for adults who have previously mastered many of their social fears. Because closeness is inherently intimidating, unless the partners are capable of tolerating its uncertainties, they are apt to do something foolish.[24] As a consequence, cementing an interpersonal bond depends on slowly and carefully developing the capacity to experience fear of it without going overboard. Another name for this capacity is emotional maturity.

Equilibrating our fears so that we do not attempt to tolerate more than we are able to is a delicate operation. Knowing when too much is too much is generally discovered in the doing. At such moments, that is to say, when we reach our limits, an orderly retreat to a safe place is typically called for. There is no dishonor in recognizing when a retrograde step is needed. This too takes courage. Should a false bravado intervene, the upshot is liable to be panic. This then sets the clock back even further. It must be remembered that a pause in desensitization can facilitate it. We all have boundaries. These must be respected. If they are, forward progress can be resumed. Self-protection is not the equivalent of giving up. It is a full stop only if we allow it to be.

As for developing incremental tolerance of our fears regarding work, a similar sequence is appropriate. When I was young, my father warned me that I was impractical. Although I got good grades, this merely entailed book learning. Bereft of hands-on experience, when I encountered the demands of actual jobs, I would falter. How then would I earn a living? Obviously no employer would take a chance on someone as unskilled and ignorant as me. Worse yet, I knew better than anyone how little I understood about the real world. Why then would a sensible boss hire me for anything but a menial job? Such an outcome would shatter any pretense I had about deserving to be respected for my intelligence and would cast me into a nether-world of failure. But there it was. This was who I was.

Again, I assumed that I stood alone in such doubts. After years of unsatisfying jobs, I would joke that I was still trying to figure out what I wanted to be when I grew up. Little did I suspect that millions of my peers felt the same. This insight finally dawned on me when I worked as an employment counselor. Most of my clients were also confused about what they should do. Nonetheless, it was in becoming a college professor that I realized the full extent of these fears. Most college freshmen have no inkling about what would constitute an appropriate major. Acutely aware of what their parents want, they are unsure of their own desires or abilities. And why not? When have they had the ability to test themselves against the competition? When have they had an opportunity to peruse the sorts of employment available in a techno-commercial society?

Our young people know something about what their parents and close relatives do for a living, yet they seldom see them doing it.[25] Because home and work are physically separated, they are not like farm children who can absorb the skills of farming by modeling themselves after their parents. Although they can read books, watch television, and take part in computer simulations, this is not the same as being there and witnessing it firsthand. When I was a kid, I played at cowboys and Indians, and, even though I grew up in the city, I wanted to be a cowboy. When my relatives urged me to be an engineer, I thought they meant that I should drive a train. Today's youngsters are not quite as naïve, yet what do they actually know about what engineers do? Nor do they understand much about policing, despite what they see on TV. They don't even understand the realities of what their rock-and-roll idols do. All they get to witness is what is done on stage.

Many college freshmen are not even aware of the nature of the subjects available for study at their schools.[26] At mine, we therefore offer an orientation for incoming undergraduates. Professors from the various departments describe the nature of their programs to students who believe that they might be interested in them. The number of potential psychology majors invariably dwarfs those of sociology. Most teenagers assume that they understand what psychology is about, whereas they have few notions about sociology. Our majors thus come from students who have taken an introductory course and realized they prefer it to the alternatives. I, by the same token, began college intent on majoring in physics. Then, when I found that I hated this subject, I changed to chemistry. After this too proved a disappointment, I flirted with psychology before settling on philosophy. Sociology did not arrive on the scene until more than a decade later.

In fact, *major-shopping* has become a college staple.[27] Here too my confusions were a foretaste of what has developed into a common phenomenon. Many parents are discomfited by their children's presumed lack of practicality. Nevertheless, this is an indicator of their offspring's lack of self-awareness or occupational awareness. Those involved understandably find this ambiguity disconcerting. What may come is not merely seen through a glass darkly; it might not be seen at all. The solution? Patience. Frightening uncertainties must be endured. If they are, it becomes possible to explore unanticipated options. The same goes for identifying a promising career after graduation. This too requires a level head, which begins with tolerating the anxieties about not knowing what the future holds. The fact is that contemporary Americans go through an average of seven different jobs before they find a congenial match.[28]

For most people, learning to bear these ordinary fears is a good starting point in developing incremental tolerance. These challenges are so widespread that a majority of us experience them. For others, more idiosyncratic fears will suggest themselves. Whatever the case, it is up to each of us to decide where to begin. Then, if we make a mistake along the way, we can shift gears. There is no single pattern that fits everyone. Moreover, there is no shame in making adjustments as they are needed. Taking a step sideward, or backward, is not evidence of an ineradicable defect.

But word of caution. What has been said thus far might be misleading. It may sound as if all of our fears must be tolerated before we can move on to eliminating them. Not only is this untrue, but in most cases it is impossible. The situation is more like that encountered when people enter psychotherapy. Therapists talk about peeling back the onion. They ask their clients to begin with the problems they find relatively easy to manage and then, as each is solved, they will be better prepared to dig deeper into the unconscious. With each small victory, their clients can expect to grow a bit stronger. This makes it possible to deal with more alarming issues as they go along. These become less intimidating because more resources are available to master them. Ultimately it is possible to go far back in time so as to face down problems that in the beginning might not even be recognized.

The same sort of sequence occurs in developing incremental

tolerance to our fears. It is not necessary—or even advisable—to wait to desensitize every anxiety before going on to evaluate, sort through, and use already-tolerated terrors so as to fight or flee significant dangers. Not only is it possible to jump back and forth in integrated fear management, it is the norm. Fears are typically handled as they come up and as our capacity to confront them emerges. People need not follow an officially prescribed schedule. Indeed, there is no such thing. How attaining courage progresses is unique to each of us. Integrated fear management, in short, first asks that we be true to ourselves.

There is a good reason for this. Our fears are chained. Intolerable fears are not of one kind. Nor is there a single central fear that once desensitized opens the way to coping with all of our other fears. This is because fears do not come upon us all at once. We start out as infants in a world that for many holds significant terrors. Furthermore, before these have been conquered, they may serve as an anteroom for additional fears. These new fears rest, as it were, on a foundation of the old. Yet these too may precipitate further fears—and so on and so on. Eventually a sort of layer cake of fears builds up, with those at the top more readily available for inspection than those at the bottom. This is where triage comes in.

Let me be more specific. Imagine an infant who has been beaten by his father. He does not know why he has been struck or how to cope. Nonetheless, because he is afraid, his fight/flight impulse prompts him to fight back. Now his father assaults him more severely. As a result, he comes to fear his own urge to resist. Therefore, he seeks to suppress this desire. Yet this is usually difficult; hence he fears that he will lose control. At this point, his fear of losing control interferes when he begins playing with other children. Apprehensive about the possibility of striking out against them and thus inviting their wrath, in holding back he inadvertently gives the impression of being fearful of social interactions. His peers become aware of this, which they perceive as weakness. This then becomes a signal for them to take advantage of his difficulties, which only exacerbates his social misgivings. As the years go by, additional social fears arise as he encounters novel social settings. School, dating, and work all contribute further anxieties that rest upon a base that goes back to his earliest years. Now he is disquieted because he does not know why his fears are so extensive. Because most of them have been repressed, they remain mysterious. In any event, they are there and can be debilitating.

In cases like this, and they are quite common, especially among people who assume that they are cowards, it makes no sense to dive to the bottom of the pile. In fact, this is usually impossible. Since our oldest fears are associated with a time when we had the fewest resources to cope, they feel the most threatening. We must thus acquire the strengths to deal with our less intimidating concerns first. Incremental tolerance is, if nothing else, incremental. Of necessity, it begins where people are able to begin. Booker T. Washington[29] advised his black brethren to begin their assent out of slavery from their current situation. He asked them to cast down their buckets where they were. As eager as they might be to mount to the highest peaks, they were to start by acquiring the skills that they lacked. Reading and writing needed to precede a college education. It is the same with people whose fears are holding them back. They too need to start where they are. This means tackling their conscious fears first. Although these may be less pervasive than their ancient terrors, they are more accessible and thus less apt to induce panic.

Although the resources needed to deal with our prehistoric fears are many and potentially robust, they take time to develop. Before overcoming our childhood fears, our adult fears must be put to work in making our adult selves strong enough to face down these long-buried worries. Oddly, our antique worries probably derive from near misses, whereas we need to utilize newly constructed remote misses to provide the armor to go back in time. This protective shield derives only in part from incremental tolerance. It also comes from learning how and when to fight against our anxieties. Ultimately it is victories that increase our strength. With these in hand, we acquire the tools, and the confidence, to tackle deeper-seated fears.

With this in mind, we can consider the next step in integrated fear management. Once important fears are tolerated, they can be inspected to determine their nature and extent. What danger does a particular fear communicate? How serous is it? Before we can eliminate a hazard, we must first understand it. Whether to fight or to flee, and how to do so, depends upon what we are up against. What is entailed must therefore be evaluated. We need to examine it so as to decide how best to proceed.

Chapter 6

EVALUATING OUR FEARS

PSYCHOTHERAPY?

Why should people who want to become more courageous engage in incremental tolerance of their fears? After all, doing so is not an agreeable exercise. Why not just let sleeping dogs lie? The reason is that for fears to be overcome, they generally need to be understood. The question therefore is: What is making us fearful? Just as important: Why is this making us afraid? Can impending dangers, whatever they may be, be managed? How are we to tell? Our fears must, in short, be evaluated before they can be adequately dealt with. If not, we will be operating blindly—which is itself a source of fear.

Incremental tolerance allows us to experience problematic fears directly. We can now feel them without automatically doing something untoward. As it happens, openly experiencing an emotion is essential if we are to appraise it accurately. Less direct methods are apt to be distorted by a desire to bury what is unpleasant. Later on, reliving such repugnant emotions will also assist us in modifying them. Freud, when he invented psychoanalysis, believed that understanding what had been repressed was sufficient to remove obstacles to our well-being.[1] He thought that an intellectual grasp would be satisfactory. In time, he discovered that returning traumatic emotions to consciousness likewise required that they be experienced. They needed to be felt. Otherwise, delving into the past was merely an academic exercise. The pioneering psychoanalyst Franz Alexander summarized this insight by describing what was involved as a "corrective emotional experience."[2] This depiction was so on target that it remains central to the therapeutic enterprise to this day.

Nonetheless, re-experiencing grave fears usually begins by trying to understand what has gone wrong. It helps to know what we are looking for before we plunge in. There is no need, however, to flesh out what we dread in its entirety. Nor do we have to do so all at once. A stepwise exposure is satisfactory. The next question is: Do we need to engage in psychotherapy in order to achieve this? The short answer is no. There are alternatives. But to understand these, we need to take a brief excursion into what psychotherapy accomplishes and how it accomplishes it.

Most people fear psychotherapy.[3] I certainly did. They equate it with madness. It is assumed that only people who have serious mental issues are candidates for the couch. My father unquestionably agreed with this assessment. The mere thought of seeing a psychologist was anathema to him. Doing so would have been tantamount to admitting that he was crazy. As his son, I was not going to be drawn into this trap either. Had I done so, this would have furnished him with the proof that I was as irrational as he claimed I was. It was therefore better to soldier on than to admit I had weaknesses that others might exploit.

Had I been honest with myself, I would have realized I too was afraid of what might be dredged up. Secretly convinced that I was as brittle as Dad alleged, I did not want to discover the full extent of my flaws. I did not know, as most people who fear psychotherapy do not, that a person's strengths are just as likely to be uncovered. People who dig into their past generally learn that what they suspect may be too terrifying to confront is so because they were children when these fears arose. Had adult resources been available to them back then, they would have felt less so.

I got lucky. After dropping out of graduate school, going into the army, taking a series of dead-end jobs, and entering a disastrous live-in relationship, I was at my wits' end. So badly had I messed up that I had even come to question my intelligence. How could someone who once did so well in school make so many boneheaded mistakes? Perhaps I was mentally defective. At this point, I sought the advice of the professor I had earlier considered a mentor. Martin Lean was exceptionally bright and articulate. Confident in his intellectual abilities, he was unruffled by my immature attempts to demonstrate my superior aptitudes. By taking my juvenile superciliousness in stride, he gently helped me understand that there was much I did not know. Unlike my father's defensive hostility, his self-assured sanity permitted him to remain even-tempered.

Dr. Lean's emotional maturity was so obvious that it came as a surprise when he asked me if I had ever contemplated psychotherapy. He then went on to explain that he had undergone an analysis when he was younger and it had done him a world of good. At first taken aback, I soon regarded this as authorization to go into therapy myself. If someone as sensible as Lean could emerge from the ordeal unscathed, so perhaps could I. Several years of individual and group therapy followed. Indeed, without them, I do not know where I would be today. By encouraging me to engage in introspection, they opened up a universe that had previously been closed to me. Later, after I became a clinician, I was able to provide a similar service for my clients. As a result, not all, but many, were able to explore their inner selves.

How does psychotherapy achieve this? It does so by providing a safe place and a knowledgeable guide.[4] Freud required his patients to lie down on a couch. This settee was covered with pillows so as to make it comfortable. Meanwhile he sat in a chair behind the client and out of sight.[5] The goal was to provide a benign ambience free from the therapist's critical input. Client-centered therapists attempt to do the same by being nonjudgmental.[6] Rather than be as interpretive as Freud was, they allow their clients to make independent discoveries. The aim is to provide "unconditional positive regard."[7] In this way, clients learn that they do not have to be defensive. They are thus free to express embarrassing details without fear of ridicule. Freud sought to encourage this attitude by instructing his patients not to censure their inner thoughts. They were told to bring up whatever occurred to them so that it could be examined in detail.[8]

Neither of these approaches is, however, necessary.[9] What frequently is necessary is the presence of a trustworthy helper. The psychotherapist Jerome Frank emphasized the centrality of what he called the "therapeutic alliance."[10] Our fears are, by definition, frightening. Digging into them, as counseling endeavors invariably do, is therefore disturbing. It is consequently essential that a helper not insert further doubts. People excavating old fears are vulnerable. Their defenses are down: hence they are exposed to additional injury. This makes it crucial that a helper be dependable. He or she must be someone who will not take advantage of the situation. Competent helpers thus have to be emotionally mature individuals who do not need to boost their egos at the expense of others.[11] This assurance must come from who they are and not from an artificial effort to maintain personal control. A suitable helper must be genuinely caring and fundamentally trustworthy. Furthermore, the client has to be aware of this. This other's dependability must be so real that when tested—and it will be—he or she passes inspection.

A reliable constancy is the *sine qua non* of providing a safe place. Without it, all else is window dressing. Nonetheless a competent therapist (or resocializer) should also be an expert cicerone. Exploring one's fears can benefit from the input of someone who knows the territory. Because we humans experience similar dangers, it is possible for a stranger to point us in useful directions. As long as a helpee is not coerced into agreeing with the guide, he or she can eventually make unique discoveries. People also get to talk about what they find with this other human being. It is amazing how much doing this can clarify our thoughts and sharpen our perceptions. When allowed to be ourselves, and to reveal ourselves, without fear of censure, we are typically set on the road to getting in touch with who we are.[12] Most of us, for the sake of self-protection, accumulate disguises that, while fooling others, also fool us. Penetrating these can therefore be liberating. It is much easier to be oneself than to invent a doppelganger who is designed to prevent our fears from being exposed.

Therapy is not magic. It cannot eliminate fears. While it can soften the blows and provide an ally who augments our courage, it cannot make terrible feelings disappear. When I was in therapy, not lying on a couch, but sitting in a chair across from my therapist, she asked me to imagine that I was confronting my father. By then we both knew how often he had beaten me. We were also aware of how terrifying I found this. She now suggested that I conjure up an image of my adult self preventing him from hitting me. This sounded easy, but no matter how hard I tried, I could not do it. The mere thought was petrifying. I could see his eyes bulging out his head and his hand raised to come down on me. He still felt too big and powerful to repel. It would take years of further work before I could confront this horror with a modicum of confidence.

What then of people who do not go into therapy? Do they have any hope of dealing with such terrors? Can they look at painful truths without automatically pushing them into the unconscious? The happy answer is that they can. How do I know? Because both my sister and brother were able to do this. Although we dealt with similar childhood issues and abuses, neither of my siblings required formal therapy. Each came to evaluate major fears during the course of normal living. This takes time and commitment, but safety and quasi-therapeutic allies can be found outside the consulting room.

Joel did this beginning with his teenage marriage. His wife, unfortunately, was not of much assistance. Nor were her parents. These folks had too many problems of their own to provide either useful guidance or a safe haven. Thankfully Joel was able to locate good friends. He could talk to them to unburden his woes. Likewise aware that he had much to learn, he set out to learn it. And so he read and he went back to college. He did not, however, get in touch with family members. The thought of dealing with our parents was unbearable. Neither could he cope with interacting with Carol or myself. Contact with us would have brought back a host of painful memories. It would also have made him feel dependent. No, exploring his past was something he had to do on his own.

Joel, at first, dealt with his fears indirectly. For instance, he learned that he could support himself by running a small business. He did not have to become a supplicant who acceded to the protection of others on the condition that he maintained the fictions they demanded. Thus painful truths did not have to be hidden because these others required that they remain unspoken. Joel was also able to complete his undergraduate and legal studies at night. This too increased his confidence, as did passing the bar exam the first time around. When he subsequently divorced and moved to a new city, he found, while working for another lawyer, that his legal skills were better than most. This provided the impetus for him to set up his own practice, which fairly quickly became prosperous. He also remarried, this time to a woman with whom he could share his emotions. While she too had her fears, in coping with these together, they both grew stronger.

Marriage can be a double-edged sword.[13] For some people it increases their insecurity, while for others it provides a safe haven and a trustworthy partner. Joel got lucky the second time around. His new wife was far less selfish than the first and in helping her he helped himself. Carol's marriage similarly assisted her in coping with her fears. What helped even more was motherhood. Both Joel and she found that in protecting their children, they better understood the perils that they had earlier endured. Moreover, by defending and advising their offspring, they provided the equivalent for their younger selves. Almost by proxy, they re-parented themselves. Because they could feel the anxieties their children felt, they could also re-experience what they had felt. All this was done in safety, which led to insights that had formerly languished. I, in watching their development from afar, was amazed at the patience, and the tenderness, they provided their children. This was so different from what they had endured. Later, when talking to them about what they had done *and* felt, I realized that they had achieved understandings I acquired via therapy. We were now on the same page although we had followed different paths to get there.

It turns out that there is no single best way to evaluate our fears. Whichever route we take, what matters is that it fits us and our circumstances. The important thing is to engage in the business of discovering what we are afraid of—honestly and forthrightly. Style points are irrelevant.

TYPES OF DANGER

What can we expect when we begin the process of examining our fears? One thing is certain: there will be surprises. Some phenomena that once seemed to be extraordinarily dangerous will turn out to be harmless. Conversely, others that looked safe will reveal hidden perils. In still other cases, we will have misperceived the source of a danger or its magnitude. We may also be mistaken about the resources available to deal with particular menaces. Dangers are not unitary, nor are the means of controlling them unidimensional. If we are to protect ourselves effectively, we must be able to make the appropriate distinctions and act accordingly.

Physical Dangers

To repeat what has become a mantra, the world can be a dangerous place. It is littered with hazards that might cause us physical damage. To be unaware of these or to treat them lightly can thus be an invitation to injury. As earlier affirmed, people who are without fear usually wind up in an early grave. After all, fire does burn and falling from great heights can produce broken bones. Furthermore, placing one's head in the lion's mouth is indeed asking to be made its dinner. Courageous people do not ignore such dangers. Nor do they fail to take protective measures. They may, on the other hand, take calculated risks. Jumping from a plane without making sure that one's parachute has been properly packed is foolhardy. Nevertheless, once this has been ascertained, one can go ahead and take the leap.

All of us should be afraid of dying.[14] We are mortal and death is permanent. Poisons should therefore be feared. Similarly, exposure to communicable illnesses needs to be avoided. Nor should knives and guns be carelessly tossed about. Just as our mothers warned, we can poke an eye out if we are not careful. Motorcyclists who do not wear helmets, football players who too vigorously ram their heads into their opponents, and divers who do not check the depth of the water before they take the plunge are asking for trouble. In each of these instances the danger is real and should be recognized as such.

Other physical dangers are less substantial. Some depend on our unique vulnerabilities. Hence, all of us start life as children. This means that we are smaller than most others. Relatively speaking, adults are giants. They may be benign giants—but then again, perhaps they are not. Had I not, for example, been aware that my father's anger was on a hair trigger, I could very well have provoked him to do something neither of us wanted. Ironically, some dangers derive from our own fears. Thus, when I was small, I dreaded large dogs. Many children do not, but my family did not have pets. Hence, when strange canines barked, I jumped. Told that these animals smelled my fear, I could not prevent myself from reeking of it. As a result, I did, in fact, make a tempting target. The same can be said of dealing with bullies. They too represent a material danger to the small and timid.

Abandonment is one of the most significant dangers that small children can face.[15] Comparatively helpless, they are powerless to fend for themselves. Unable to feed, clothe, or protect themselves from the elements, if left on their own, they might perish. Children may not know why they are afraid, but they sense when their parents do not love them. Threats of desertion, whether stated or implied, are therefore profoundly disquieting.[16] The implications are too serious to overlook. Many children are, indeed, neglected and suffer physical harm. Adults must thus be able to look back to ascertain whether they were once in this sort of jeopardy. If they were, they had ample reason to be frightened. All of the previously enumerated dangers are magnified when dependable adult protection is unavailable.

Social Dangers

While abandonment may be construed as a social danger, the potential harm is physical. Other dangers are more patently social. To state the obvious, we humans are social animals. We crave the company and support of other humans.[17] As a consequence, fundamental to becoming a happy adult is establishing satisfactory social niches. Unless we occupy satisfying positions within larger communities, our needs are unlikely to be met. Even though our physical integrity may not be menaced, our social equanimity will.

We humans are, for instance, role-playing animals.[18] We do not all perform the same activities within our communities. Every society creates a division of labor in which some individuals specialize in some tasks, whereas others specialize in other tasks.[19] What we do—what we are expected to do—has a huge impact on our subsequent happiness. Thus, if our jobs are particularly nasty, we are apt to suffer. Despite our wishes, we may be forced into repugnant occupations, such as those formerly required of Hindu untouchables.[20] These folks were once compelled to gather dung or tan hides with urine, irrespective of their abilities or inclinations. Whatever their personal predispositions, this was their socially decreed fate.

Families too have divisions of labor into which their children are recruited.[21] Ergo, before these youngsters understand what is taking place, they may be obliged to be scapegoats or caretakers.[22] A son's assignment may thus be to take the blame for others' mistakes. Or a daughter's duty might be to take care of her parents at the expense of her own needs. Should this occur, these children are apt to rebel. But if they do, they will probably incur severe penalties. These, especially when they entail corporal punishment, are often dangerous. They can inflict personal pain that is difficult to circumvent.

Another social danger derives from the fact that we are hierarchical animals.[23] Despite idealistic professions of the desirability of complete equality, this neither is, nor ever has been, the case. We invariably rank ourselves relative to others. Although we may claim that everyone deserves the equivalent respect, given the opportunity to accumulate greater esteem than our peers, virtually all of us seek it. We all want to be special and hope to bask in the acclaim of becoming star athletes or the glory of being elected class president. Who among us does not relish having greater power than others? Conversely, who strives to be powerless? Don't we all want to be winners, while simultaneously dreading the prospect of being losers? If only in our imaginations, we dream about being better than others.

This is part of the human condition—as, unhappily, is losing.[24] Hierarchies imply the existence of a top and a bottom. Thus, if people compete for preference—and they do—some will do better than others. Moreover, doing worse hurts. Merely to contemplate the possibility is painful. It therefore constitutes a danger. On the social level, this might entail being consigned to a lower social status. After all, some of us are born into poverty.[25] If we are, this imposes hurdles that make it difficult to rise above our station.[26] Just as universally, sibling rivalries are a sign that, whatever their parents say, some children obtain privileges that their brothers and sisters are denied. Worse still, powerless parents tend to be threatened by assertive children and hence protect their own supremacy by depriving their children of dignity.[27] This too is a danger to which, in looking back, many adults realize they were forced to endure. If so, this may explain some of their fears.

We are also relationship animals; that is, we develop emotional bonds with some people, but not with others.[28] All of us require reliable attachments. Stated another way, all of us need to be loved. Unfortunately, not all of us are. Many parents are incapable of selflessly bonding with their children.[29] Perhaps deprived of love when they were young, they have little to give. Perhaps themselves hungry for affection, all they know how to do is to take from others. Such parents may resent the natural demands of their offspring. If they do, they may punish requests for affection. Here too lurks another danger of our sociability. Obviously, if we did not care about being loved, we would not be frightened when it is denied. Furthermore, if such fears were not aroused when we were small, they might not arise as powerfully when we are adults. In other words, adults who appear to be inappropriately fearful of emotional closeness may be reflecting the rejection of a bygone era. In evaluating their current fears, they may discover that these have deep roots.

Sometimes social fears are not what they initially seem. Because our defense mechanisms disguise what is especially painful, we often cover over our most serious fears with less distressing ones.[30] This is why it is frequently important to dig deep into our psyches to determine what we actually dread. As long as we are protecting ourselves from a derivative hazard, our underlying terrors may remain in place to prevent us from realizing our ambitions. Psychotherapy is one of the methods for uncovering these; so is honest, and persistent, introspection.

When I was in therapy, one of the big surprises was that I was as afraid of my mother as I was of my father. My fear of him was easy to exhume. He had beaten and intimidated me from infancy onward. He was always ready to lash out when he was frustrated, and had I not been aware of this propensity, I might not have survived. My mother, on the other hand, was apparently sweet and protective. Quick to affirm her love, she recurrently promised to protect me from my father. She was thus the good parent, whereas he was the bad one.

My therapist, however, was not so sure. With time, she became aware of my difficulty in developing close attachments to women. Strongly heterosexual in my impulses, I nevertheless avoided intimate relationships. My excuse was that women were not attracted to me. Somehow I was not sexually appealing. My therapist, Elaine, found this explanation inadequate. Something else was going on. She concluded that I was projecting my fears outward and converting my need for emotional distance into their putative desire for distance. But why? Where did these fears come from?

Then, during one session, I remembered an incident from when I was a preschooler. My father was angry about something or other. I never discovered what. In any event, he was furious. Determined to give me the thrashing I "deserved," he charged after me. Now terrified, I ran and hid under the bed. This infuriated him further. Gnashing his teeth and calling me a rotten kid, he grabbed a broom and sought to expel me from my hiding place. I, however, scooted from side to side, effectively keeping out of reach. This only increased his rage. It was at this point that my mother intervened. She kneeled down and very softly explained that my father wasn't going to hurt me. It was okay for me to come out because nothing bad would happen. Nonetheless, Dad had not calmed down. He was pacing impatiently just behind her with his face as red and his eyes as distended as ever. I did not come out. Despite being tempted by my mother's promises, I knew what would happen if I did.

Once this memory came back, so did a host of other recollections. It became clear that my mother frequently betrayed me. Deeply concerned with protecting herself against her husband's anger, she habitually sacrificed me for her own needs. Naturally, this too made me angry. Yet she was the most important source of safety I had. I therefore repressed my doubts and allowed her to appease me— if not in this instance, then in many others. When she promised to comfort me, I permitted her to do so. Then when my father tore me from clinging to her lap, I blamed him, not her. The real problem, the one that horrified me, was that I was my own worst enemy. Because I wanted to believe her, because I so desperately craved the tender consolation of her touch, I was vulnerable to being seduced. My Dad, I ran away from; my mother, I required enormous restraint to keep from luring me into danger.

Why was I afraid of women when I was so physically drawn to them? Paradoxically, I was afraid precisely because I was so attracted to them. My sexual desires were a Trojan horse. They pressured me toward an intimacy that my unconscious warned against. What could I do, except to fool myself into believing that I kept my distance for other reasons? Indeed, I convinced myself that it was attractive women who were keeping their distance from me. Had I not, many years later, come to this realization, I would still be protecting myself from a danger that no longer exists. I would not have changed my tactics, nor today be happily married to a woman who is very different from my mother.

I also made a mistake with respect to my father. The danger that he represented extended beyond the very real possibility that he would beat me senseless. My mother was an emotionally distant person. Whatever her declarations of love, she could not express them openly. Extremely self-contained, when asked why she didn't laugh at the television sitcoms the rest of the family found hilarious, she explained that she was "laughing inside." Her defenses never broke down, however genuine her efforts to be a loving mother. Dad, in contrast, was extremely emotional. Not only his rage, but his love routinely burst through to the surface. In the end, he was real in a way she never was.

How much this meant to me did not become apparent until after he died. As I earlier explained, I did not begin writing my first book until he was gone. While it is true that fears of condemnation held me back, something else did as well. For all my anger at the man, I loved him deeply. I knew he cared, despite his rages. I also knew how frustrated he was. When he was young, both he and his family expected great things of him. Everyone was aware of his intelligence and intensity. How then could he not succeed? Yet his dyslexia got in the way. It dissuaded him from going to college or competing for high-level jobs. Unsure of why this was so, his frustration mounted. My successes in school only reminded him of his failures and stoked his envy. Despite his pride in my accomplishments, he could not prevent himself from tearing me down.

Nonetheless, my unconscious love of him did not waver. However angry I was, I did not want to hurt him. Aware that my intelligence and intensity came from him, I identified with his dilemma. Why didn't I write books sooner? Because I knew that this would deepen his distress. Because he was already depressed, I could not bring myself to depress him further. Still, this was a danger I could not allow myself to recognize. Thoroughly conflicted in my attitude toward him, my ambivalence suppressed a desire for success that might have urged me to ignore his pain. This too was frightening.

Perhaps this sounds absurd. If it does, it is because so many of us have repressed ambivalent emotions. Life is filled with contradictions, which, because they are difficult to acknowledge, or to resolve, present us with hidden quandaries. This is all the more reason to root them out and confront them directly.

Emotional Dangers

This book is focused on the intense fears that turn us into apparent cowards. Nevertheless, if we are to become courageous, we must also deal with other intense emotions. They too can be so powerful that we are apt to run away from their reality. As a result, these too need to be evaluated and tolerated. In fact, they too must be utilized effectively if we are to win the battles that keep us anxious. We humans are profoundly emotional creatures. When we are masters of our passions, these can assist us in becoming successful. Yet when we are not, the opposite is liable to be true.[31]

Years ago I wrote a book on anger management. It came out under the profoundly clumsy title *I.A.M.* (which stood for *integrated anger management*).[32] I did so partly to understand my father's anger and partly to gain control over my own. People who are browbeaten invariably experience counter-anger. This, however, is especially dangerous for the young. Not yet in control of powerful feelings, they may inadvertently behave in ways that make their situation worse. I wanted to ensure that this did not happen to me. I also wanted to learn how to deploy my anger so that I could become a winner.

People who are extremely fearful are also liable to have a problem with anger. If fear arises when we are in danger, young children who are under the thumb of an angry parent have reason to fear this external anger. When I scrambled under my parents' bed to escape my father's wrath, I was afraid of him. I knew that he was barely under control. His hands were trembling as he tried to keep himself from doing something he knew he shouldn't. Oftentimes when he caught me out in the open, I would crouch down in the duck-and-cover position recommended during the 1950s nuclear scare. Meanwhile my mother would stand in the background warning him not to hit my head. "Not the head! Not the head!" she recited like a prayer. Fearful that I might be brain-damaged by angry blows that he could not moderate, my mother and I both feared his rage.

But I also feared my own rage. I could not help myself. My desires were so routinely thwarted that I felt compelled to fight back. This meant that every now and then I threw a tantrum. Not surprisingly, the consequences of these outbursts were not favorable. Dad was bigger and stronger and would not abide what he perceived as disrespect. The upshot was generally another beating. This was even more dangerous; hence it was imperative that I get my anger under control. Whether justified or not, expressing it too vigorously was a tactical error.

The only way out was to suppress my anger. I needed to push it out of consciousness, lest I act upon it. Yet it did not go away. Buried deep in my psyche, just as with my fears, it awaited a suitable moment to break through to the surface. Anger, the strength of which I did not understand, continued to haunt me. Suddenly I would find myself arguing for a position more vehemently than was appropriate. Others too were surprised by this—and taken aback. Where did this eruption come from? Was it as alarming as it appeared? Few could tell. What was clear is that this was no way to make friends or influence people.

Here too my dilemma was not idiosyncratic. Other frightened people also fear their submerged anger. And rightly so! Unacknowledged wrath can be deadly. This requires that it be dealt with. A sequence parallel to that for dealing with fear is therefore advisable. It entails of developing a safe place where anger does not flare up, where it can be tolerated step-by-step and then evaluated to determine its source.[33] This helps bring it under control. Anger can also be used to overcome our frustrations. Despite the fact that rage is treacherous, its total absence is even more perilous. People who are unable to get angry, despite having been mistreated, invite further mistreatment. Others regard them as so harmless that there is no downside to abusing them.

Fearful people must be able to use their anger as well as their fear. If they are to win the victories that enable them to defuse dangers, they must be able to deploy their anger so as to overcome significant obstacles. Without this ability, others will force them into a cowardly crouch. While anger can be frightening, this is primarily when it is not understood or mastered. As part of our normal social equipment, it has to be tamed and exploited.

This includes evaluating our anger. Why are we angry? What frustration caused it to erupt? And how are we fighting back? Is our anger so intense that it has gone rogue? Has primitive rage prompted us to behave destructively? Perhaps our anger needs to be resocialized so that we can learn to deploy it more effectively. If so, then this is another ability we must work on acquiring. Emotional maturity is a complicated phenomenon that entails the effective control over many different affects.

Closely related to anger is guilt.[34] As an internalized version of anger, it too can go rogue. And when it does, it can also be extremely frightening. Guilt converts external anger into potent internal controls. Ironically, we may get angry with ourselves so as to stop ourselves from getting angry. The trouble is that we can overdo this tactic. Everyone needs to feel guilt about some things.[35] We all engage in conduct that we should personally prevent. In this respect, guilt is a civilizing emotion. When, however, it becomes habitual and suppresses the normal impulses that enable us to be happy, it is a threat. All of us have the right, if not the duty, to pursue our desires. Although we can go too far, we may also not go far enough. We therefore need to balance our desires against those of others in a way that is fair and does not imprison us in a jail of our own making.

Excessive guilt is thus legitimately frightening. The question we must ask in evaluating it is therefore: Is it valid? Have we done something that warrants intense self-anger? Perhaps we have internalized anger that derives from the excessive demands of other people. My dad was more than penny-wise. As a survivor of the Great Depression, he did not believe in spending money on anything that could be regarded as frivolous. This included eating out at restaurants or purchasing new clothing. The mere acquisition of a hamburger would send him into a towering rage. No wonder I learned to feel guilty about expending funds merely because this gave me pleasure.

In retrospect, this seems absurd. At the time, it was not. By my teen years, when my friends were going to the movies or traveling into downtown Manhattan on a lark, I was frightened by my desire to follow suit. Nonetheless, appearing to be a cheapskate also frightened me. What was I to do? Years of adult living were subsequently required to put this guilt in perspective. What is more, a sense of scale was needed if I were not to torture myself for overstepping unrealistic standards. Others who are afraid to take chances also need to reassess their guilty impulses if they are to escape from a self-imposed cowardice.

Shame too can be excessive and terrifying.[36] When youngsters are ridiculed for the way that they look or for a lack of sophistication, they can convert their embarrassment into a punitive shame that is as debilitating as unwarranted guilt. When we feel ashamed, we want to hide from view. We aim to separate ourselves from social interaction so that we are no longer the center of bemused attention. As with guilt, this is sometimes necessary, for instance, when be behave selfishly. Oftentimes, however, the derision that causes us to conceal our humiliation is misplaced. The problem may not be ours, but that of our tormentors. Just as another's anger can derive from self-interest, so can his mockery. There may thus be no reason to feel ashamed.

Once again this requires frightened people to step back and evaluate their shame. If incremental tolerance enables them to endure the fear of being embarrassed, they can obtain a more balanced assessment of their shame. In many cases they will realize that they have little reason to feel ashamed and even less to fear those who would impose it. It is remarkable how often distorted perceptions inflict emotional reactions that prevent us from recognizing that we are not in danger. We become like teenagers who fear wearing the unfashionable clothing or saying the wrong thing. Rather than become the target of bemused gossip, we hasten to conform with what might be a temporary fad.

Disproportionate love can likewise be a source of unnecessary fear.[37] People who have experienced emotional abandonment as children invariably retain a need to be loved.[38] Sadly, the less affection they have received, the greater the deficit they need to make up. Among the young, neglect leads to clinginess. Meanwhile for adults, it can produce desperation. Lonely people crave love so frantically that they look for it in all the wrong places and when they think they have found it they may hold on with a death grip. Desperation, however, is not a sound foundation for affection. Far from generating stable relationships, a reckless desire to be saved usually generates the reverse. Emotionally mature adults are turned off by demands for instant commitment. They recoil at intense demands for salvation they know they cannot satisfy. As a consequence, desperation provides fertile ground for abusers. It invites these venal persons to take advantage of a forlorn person's desolation. A fanatical quest for love is therefore self-defeating. In most cases, it generates either exploitation or further loneliness.

As a consequence, an exorbitant desire for love and an unremitting fear of never obtaining it cry out for a clear-eyed assessment. Why were we not loved? Was it something about us? Or was it about those who rejected us? Did we do something that repelled them?

Maybe there was something we could have done to change their attitude? Perhaps we are now trapped in a desperation that we ought to discard. Perhaps like me, we are more afraid of being loved than of being rejected. I did not understand that my mother's inability to love was tied to the circumstances of her birth. I could not, as a child, realize that her own mother's terrors when she was born might have afflicted her. If I was manipulatively appeased, it might therefore have had little to do with my own deficiencies. Once more, an ability to tolerate our fears can enable us to understand how our other emotions, in this case, love, place us in danger. Although this may require additional work in learning to tolerate and master these affects, in the end it is usually worth our while.

The last extreme emotion we may need to reevaluate is sadness. Our fears are so often grounded in losses that it is essential we be able to cope with these defeats.[39] If we cannot let go of that which we cannot have, then we are unlikely to obtain what we can. The difficulty is partly in telling which losses are irreversible. This requires that we not be so terrified of our sadness that we will not allow ourselves to examine it. Grief is scary. It can feel like a portal to death. With joy banished from our experience, there may seem to be no reason to hold on to life. We may therefore be intent on preventing ourselves from being engulfed in an inky blackness. Unfortunately, if we are, we cannot let go of what is lost. What is worse, this is tantamount to cleaving onto that which places us in jeopardy. Rather than relinquish bonds to our abusers, we may keep them, and their nefarious conduct, close at hand.

One of the most important aspects of evaluating our fears is thus determining what is irredeemably lost. Thus, with respect to my mother's inability to express love, I needed to recognize that her unalloyed affection was something I would never obtain. However much I deserved it, I did not possess the power to eliminate her fears. Of course, this made me feel sad. But it was a sadness I needed to experience if I were to move on to relationships with women who could love me. None of us likes losing; even through it can be a prelude to winning. Those of us who have had fewer satisfactions than we should have are often reluctant to give up the little we acquire. Convinced by bitter experience that hope is an illusion, we are terrified by the prospect of having nothing. Nonetheless, emotional toughness is a boon. Whether the affect to be conquered is fear, anger, guilt, shame, love, or sadness, once we develop the capacity to endure these without flinching, we can convert them into allies. Controlled feelings make us stronger and therefore better able to deal with dangers that might otherwise be overpowering.

THE DEGREE OF DANGER

Once we are aware of the nature of the dangers we face, whether these be physical, social, or emotional, we need to assess their extent. How dangerous are they? Will they result in death? Perhaps we might be crippled. Maybe our social reputation will be ruined such that we will never again be respected. Or maybe we are destined to remain unloved—forever. Our careers and health could likewise be ruined, and our happiness irreparably lost. Depending upon the seriousness of the danger, it might be impossible to win. Or this could just be a microscopic bump on the road to wherever we are actually headed.

When we are blinded by an inability to recognize perils for what they are, we have a tendency to overestimate them. Oppressive parents, in retrospect, seem to be gigantic ogres. In our imaginations, they loom over us as implacable threats. Our efforts to get them to relent therefore seem destined to be ineffectual. The same goes for the school-yard bullies or the demands of learning calculus. Most of us, when we return to the neighborhoods in which we grew up, are shocked by how much smaller things look than we remember. Our vantage point has changed, and they are no longer as intimidating. On the other hand, that which has been out of sight tends to encourage lively fantasies. Indeed, the longer we are removed from childhood bugaboos, the more ominous they may feel. Our imaginations embroider upon their impact; ergo the danger feels greater than it was.

Most of the fears that condemn us to cowardice arose when we were small. We then resided in a world filled with mysteries. Not only did we not understand physical, social, or emotional dangers, there was no way we could have done so.[40] Our limited mental capacities and restricted experience prevented us from obtaining an accurate perspective. Youngsters believe, for instance, that they are the center of their own universe. Whatever punishments befall them seem to be the product of something that they did. Almost completely unable to assess the motivations of those around them, they assume that they have more influence than they do. When this distortion is combined with their manifold weaknesses, it swells their apparent peril. Life itself seems to be at stake—even when it isn't.

Do you remember your nighttime terrors? Do you recall your fears of the darkness? I do. What was out there? Were monsters lurking under the bed or hiding in the closet? You did not know; therefore you required adult reassurance. Do you remember how scary it was to fall asleep and to lose control? Maybe you would never wake up. These were outsize fears born of defenselessness and ignorance. Unfortunately, if these fears were never mastered, perhaps because we did not receive reliable protection, they possess the potential of fermenting into a witch's brew. But if they do, they can garble the magnitude of our adult challenges. Unless these are reevaluated without being twisted by fears we are unable to tolerate, they can remain—at least in our imaginations—too massive to be managed. Fortunately, when we are able to tolerate them, we can modify our viewpoint so as better to judge their scale.

Fears that have been thrust from consciousness also acquire an unwarranted universality. If Dad was a merciless bully, then all men may seem to be bullies. The mere fact that they are male imbues them with his qualities. Or if Mom was emotionally withdrawn, this may seem the authentic nature of all women. Females may feign heartfelt love, but this is an illusion to be guarded against. Childhood understandings tend to be simplified. Dependent upon a lack of refined insights, they ignore crucial differences. Unless applying our adult acumen later rectifies this error, we are liable to misconstrue the depth of a current peril. If so, we may prevent ourselves from embarking upon satisfying enterprises.

Distortions regarding the enormity of various dangers also arise from underestimating our adult abilities. Now able to control hazards that were once life-threatening, we are capable of cutting these risks down to size. Dad is no longer as physically prepossessing as he previously was nor Mom as heartless as she seemed. Having grown older and more sensitive, we are better judges of reality. Now we can hold back his blows or understand the fears that made her defensive. As a result, they are not as unsafe as formerly. No longer vulnerable to perils we could not then curtail, we are now able to neutralize them. When this ability is factored into our evaluation of contemporary dangers, we are better prepared to estimate their impact. Currently controllable, they both feel, and are, less dangerous. In short, as "big people," we have joined the ranks of the giants.

AVAILABLE RESOURCES

An accurate evaluation of the dangers we confront clearly includes their nature and extent. How we ought to handle a particular hazard depends upon what it is and how serious its implications are. For example, the appropriate fight or flight response depends on whether we can escape or neutralize a threat. The manner in which we might be injured and the extent of the potential damage enable us to determine the best way to respond. Yet so do the resources available to us. Are we able to deploy a response that successfully implements a fight or flight strategy? Are we, for instance, strong enough to defeat this particular foe? Perhaps we are not fast enough to run away from him. However accurately we assess a danger, unless we possess the means to counterbalance it, we remain in danger.

While an accurate evaluation of a peril improves the likelihood of determining how to counteract it, if we do not have the horses to do the job, we are still in trouble. We must therefore evaluate who we are and what we can do. The nature and magnitude of a danger helps govern what happens, but so do our strengths, weaknesses, and tactics. If we cannot bring the appropriate weapon to bear at the appropriate moment, we are liable to be harmed. As a consequence, we must look inward, as well as outward, before deciding what to do.

The good news is that we are no longer children. Whatever our liabilities, we are bigger and stronger than we once were. We are also more knowledgeable. Although we may feel small, weak, and confused, many more options are available to us. Dad's blows are less likely to be fatal because we are better equipped to ward them off. Mom's blandishments are apt to be less seductive because we can obtain love from other sources. It may take time for these advantages to sink in, but when they do, they alter the safety/danger equation.

Consider our anger. Young children have few alternatives for making it known. They can kick and scream, and perhaps curse their parents, but these responses are unfocused. Adults, in contrast, can be more articulate.[41] They can state in words what they desire, thereby making is easier for others to provide what is needed. Given my current abilities I could tell my father that the forced feedings he once administered were frightening. I do not have to howl in rage-filled terror. Similarly better equipped to recognize my mother's fears, I could comfort rather than hate her. This, in turn, would likely elicit more helpful responses.

Adults are also more dangerous. They can back up their threats more effectively. As long as they can control their impulses, they may respond in ways that cause damage to those who thwart them. These others know this and are therefore more inclined to do what is demanded. Hence, when the antipathy of my department chair jeopardized my being granted tenure at my college, I did not need to cower in a corner. I was able to go on the offensive. At one point I threatened a lawsuit—because I now understood what a lawsuit could do. I was also able to contact a high-powered attorney. This made me a far more intimidating foe that I ever had been with respect to my father.

Adults also have broader alliances at their disposal.[42] Children are isolated within their families of origin; hence if potent coalitions are arrayed against them, they have little wiggle room. Adults, in contrast, can operate outside their families. One of the reasons I was able to obtain tenure at my university is that I had enlisted a bevy of allies. As a consequence, when I was threatened, they came to my defense. Together we were far more potent than I would have been on my own. Both socially and occupationally, adults have access to people who might agree with them. As long as they are socially adept, they have places to go when they are endangered. Cowards don't always realize this. Hobbled by their fears, they assume that they are isolated when they are not. This places a premium on accurate social evaluations. The availability of suitable networks can make all the difference to the outcome of an interpersonal clash.

Personal talents can also make a difference. When I lived with my parents, I assumed that I could not support myself. Utterly convinced that I did not possess marketable skills, I imagined that I was at the mercy of their demands. Thus, if my father threatened to disown me, I quaked at the possibility. Going out and obtaining employment changed this. Learning that I had genuine counseling skills ensured that I would be hired somewhere. This took the sting out of Dad's warnings. I would not starve. Nothing he could do guaranteed that this would happen. Given my abilities, I possessed controls that I previously lacked. These could protect me, if not from everything, then from a host of dangers.

Many of us who regard ourselves as cowards are trapped in an out-of-date worldview. We misunderstand why we are afraid or what we can do about it. This is unfortunate. Life is never without hazards. None of us is entirely safe. Even so, we are not completely at the mercy of an unyielding fate. We can do something about it if we scrutinize potential dangers and evaluate their implications. Next we must decide what to do. Should we fight or should we flee? Maybe we should do a bit of both—or nothing at all. We must therefore sort through our options before swinging into action.

Chapter 7
SORTING POTENTIAL RESPONSES

After we identify the safe places from which we are able to incrementally tolerate our fears so that we can accurately evaluate their nature and extent, we must decide what, if anything, to do. How can our resources best be deployed to ensure continued safety? Courageous people know that they can be harmed, but they do not panic because they are also aware that, most of the time, they are capable of protecting themselves. Less apt to overestimate their perils or to underestimate their ability to respond effectively, they do not dread concealed dangers. Nor do they revert to primitive responses when the unexpected arises. Able to keep their heads while others about them are losing theirs, they usually make better decisions about how to safeguard themselves. As a consequence, they endure fewer injuries, while at the same time attaining greater successes.

DOING NOTHING

Figuring out what to fear, and what not to fear, begins with sorting the sheep from the goats. Not everything that seems dangerous is unsafe. Accordingly, not everything we initially dread needs to arouse our fight/flight instinct. If some of what we once thought might hurt us will not, it can simply be endured. Having learned to tolerate false signals of jeopardy, we do not have to act as if they were valid. We can, in short, do nothing without having to fret about things going wrong.

Of course, we probably will begin by fretting. That which once felt physically, socially, and/or emotionally threatening generally retains an aura of menace. It may, therefore, be difficult to sit still in the presence of a long-standing fear. Merely assessing it as safe does not automatically alter the affective message we receive. Although we might be able to tolerate this false alarm without adopting an inappropriate response, we may continue to feel as if we should do something. It can thus take energy to prevent ourselves from swinging into action. While a desire to act will eventually weaken; we must nonetheless guard against it creating a hazard where none exists.

Let us consider some physical dangers. Children often experience thunder and lightning as frightening. The flash of brightness and the bone-shaking sound seem to prefigure bodily injury. In fact, were we struck by lightning, this might prove fatal. It thus takes time to learn that this is unlikely. Indeed, as adults, we describe an improbable event as comparable to being hit by lightning. As long as we stay away from places that attract such strikes, we are apt to be safe. Hence most of us, most of the time, do little to protect ourselves. Our adult understanding is often a sufficient buffer against terror.

The same applies to a host of other physical dangers, some of which have genetic roots. Snakes and spiders can be poisonous, yet most pose no immediate threat. Heights can be treacherous, but only if we venture onto unsecured precipices. Airplanes crash, automobiles get into accidents, and ships sink; still in none of these cases is the chance of harm very great. Years ago, when I moved to Georgia from up north, I was surprised to discover that there were scorpions living in my neighborhood. In fact, I frequently encountered them scurrying along the floor of my living room. At first, the prospect of stepping into a slipper and being stung was alarming. Then after I came to realize how slow these creatures were and how easy it was to squish them with a paper towel, my anxiety subsided. Now I don't feel a need to run. I don't have to do anything, if I so choose. Scorpions have become a harmless, easily disposed of nuisance rather than an insidious menace.

Social fears, in contrast, tend to be more troubling. Although some of these also turn out to be harmless, they are more difficult to ignore. These fears, while less definitively unsafe than many physical dangers, can elicit an obsessive desire to do something. Although our parents may be residing hundreds of miles away, their specters often seem to be hovering just over our shoulders. Even though they are not present to criticize us, it is as if they were. We know exactly what they would say, and how they would say it, because we carry their facsimiles around in our minds and guts. They thus constitute a dangerous element of our consciousness, which can badger us with negative judgments—just as if Mom and Dad could reach out and punish us in the here and now.

Nevertheless, they are not in the here and now. As adults, we may have long since moved out from under their thumbs. On one level, therefore, it does not matter what they think. We have the option of deciding what to do even if they disagree. Nor are they able to administer meaningful sanctions. They cannot take away an allowance or forbid us to go to the movies. Moreover, we can have as much dessert as our bellies can hold. So why are we worried? Why did I care that my father would have found fault with anything I wrote? I knew full well that he could not do anything about it.

The difficulty is that our social relationships are often as much in us as between us and others. The manner in which we perceive these folks, the ways we feel about them, and how we are prepared to act are all internalized. These interpersonal relationships are hardly ever entirely spontaneous. Indeed, we carry around mental templates that tell us how to respond to Mom, Dad, and the milkman. If we didn't, life would be chaotic. Our roles, ranks, and attachments are therefore difficult to change. Inscribed in our understandings, emotions, and action strategies, these are not available to be modified at will.

As a consequence, they can linger even when they are no longer applicable. Mom will always be Mom and Dad will always be Dad, no matter how many miles—or years—separate us.

This said, when there is a separation, we may, in fact, be safer than our guts tell us. Dad will not yell at us and Mom will not betray us, because they are not here to do so. Whatever our inner experience, it is we who are enforcing these anticipated punishments. Except that we do not have to do so if we do not wish to. Despite the inner voice that warns us of the terrible implications of defying them, they now exist primarily in our imaginations. We do not need to do anything because no harm will befall us. While it may be difficult to keep from erecting defenses that are no longer necessary, we can, in most cases, restrain ourselves. In this sense, doing nothing is a form of doing something, in that it takes effort to inhibit misplaced action. Actually, in many cases, an iron will is required. Still, the rewards for refraining from inappropriate rejoinders are worth it.

Often the shades of social dangers come cleverly disguised. It is not Mom and Dad we fear, but strangers who somehow possess motives not unlike those of our parents. The sociologist George Herbert Mead introduced the idea of the "generalized other."[1] He argued that we summarize the people we know and convert them into a disembodied "they." *They* then tell us the right way to dress. *They* condemn us when we use the wrong fork in a fancy restaurant. *They* have ideas about the kind of person we should marry or the sort of occupation we should enter. Oddly enough, *they* tend to make demands similar to ones we once heard from our friends and relatives. What is more, *they* are powerful because they are everywhere. There is no hope of escaping their censure.

Only there is no "they." *They* are a figment of our imaginations and guts. Built up over many years of experience, they reflect our interactions with hundreds of people. Coded into our beliefs, affects, and normative behavior, we are their conservators. We keep their antique judgments alive by honoring them. In the real world, people are not terribly consistent. They contradict each other with disconcerting regularity. As a result, whom we cram into our composite *they* depends on our choices. Not surprisingly, this usually depends upon which powerful others we have encountered. The ones that mattered most are therefore likely to be over-represented. Except that like Mom and Dad, these folks are probably no longer around. A different cast of characters is apt to surround us today. This, for instance, occurs when people who are born poor engage in upward mobility.[2] Although the judgments of their former neighbors may not have changed, their opinions are less operative in this new social universe. Despite the fact that the home folks would disapprove of fancy patterns of speech, their condemnation can be safely discounted.

Another fictitious social danger derives from our tendency to project power where it does not belong. One of life's biggest secrets is that no one is in total control. Not kings, not presidents, not bishops, not generals, not business tycoons; no one. Each of these, not merely us, discovers that when he or she rises to a position of prominence this entails less power than was originally supposed. Thus Harry Truman opined that when Dwight Eisenhower replaced him has president, Ike would be in for a big surprise.[3] Eisenhower would expect his subordinates to follow orders the way that they did in the military only to discover that civilians are more contrary. The general, of course, already knew this. He had long since learned that Patton possessed a mind of his own. But so too did the privates that both of them commanded. These underlings might say yes, then do as they pleased.

Many people take this a step further and assume that a nefarious cabal is in charge. Not one person, but a mysterious set of controllers lurks behind the scenes, making all of the important decisions.[4] Whether these are commercial, religious, or social leaders, they secretly ensure a predetermined goal. This sort of conspiratorial thinking is common among people who exercise little power. They consequently blame the Jews or the Masons for their own mistakes. In fact, although some individuals and groups have more influence than others, the world is too complex for anyone to be in complete control. The evidence? The Soviet planners believed that they possessed the intelligence and the information to rationalize their economic system, yet they failed miserably.[5] They could not see, never mind dictate, what went on in a factory in Siberia. Just as important, no faction, however sinister, can maintain impeccable consistency. Even the Nazi hierarchy had its fallings out. Hermann Goering and Heinrich Himmler were not close friends.[6] The closest of collaborators disagree. Once more the communists provide a wonderful example of schemers at each other's throats. Joseph Stalin's erstwhile allies despised him so much that they happily allowed him to perish without medical attention.[7] When he had his fatal heart attack, they could have called in the doctors. They did not because they wanted him gone. Sooner or later the most cohesive conspiracies unravel.

Imaginary conspiracies are thus another excuse for keeping obsolete fears alive. Millions of people attribute their personal disappointments to these shadowy dangers. They insist on fighting illusionary threats so as to explain their current failures. They thus remain on guard against space aliens and zombies. Yet were they to do nothing to counter these stand-ins for past hazards, they would have more energy to pursue tangible success. Likewise, converting Mom and Dad into monstrous conspirators does nothing to help win fights that can be won. It merely diverts attention from unpleasant truths.

Nor does holding on to emotional dragons promote real-world victories. Dangerous feelings can be set aside without untoward consequences if they are, in fact, no longer perilous. Guilt and shame that have haunted us from early childhood do not have to survive into adulthood.[8] No matter how often we were chided for being selfish, we do not have to keep reproaching ourselves for this if it is not true. Indeed, we do not have to do anything. If an evaluation of frightening feelings reveals that they are sending dubious messages, we do not have to listen. Even though Dad scolded us for wasteful spending, if we are not wasteful, there is no need to resurrect our guilt. Nor do we have to change his mind or convince others he was wrong. All we have to do is stop blaming ourselves.[9] Likewise if we were shamed because we supposedly had big ears, since this assessment probably revealed more about the assessor than us, we do not have to be embarrassed. We can let go of the feeling. While this is easier said than done, the doing is essentially a not doing.

Inappropriate love may similarly need to be relinquished.[10] Our craving for love might be such that it is directed toward someone who is unable to reciprocate. If, as adults, we make this discovery, it is time to direct our affection elsewhere. No matter how much we wanted Mom's love, if her defensive needs precluded her from offering it, we should stop clamoring for it. This may not be fair. It may be hurtful. All of this, however, is irrelevant. What cannot be had is a waste of time to seek. Although love is crucially important, it is too important to squander. Love should be shared; ergo it must be shared with those who are capable of doing so. Desperation is counterproductive. It is far better to cease pursuing love where it cannot be found. While this is painful to acknowledge, it is essential for our happiness. Furthermore, by not seeking love where it is absent, we make it possible to pursue it where it is. This ultimately happened to me with respect to my wife.

Nonetheless, remaining calm when we are afraid of physical, social, or emotional dangers may be more demanding than we allow ourselves to do. If so, we can permit ourselves to feel afraid—as long as we do not act on this fear. Inappropriate action is our worst enemy. The good news, however, is that time is an ally. The longer a fear is sustained without being confirmed by actual harm, the more likely it is to lose its potency. Eventually, even without our realizing it, it may disappear. Once upon a time, I was painfully shy. Because I feared people, I was timid when I met strangers. This response was so habitual that I was convinced it was part of who I was. Then, and I don't remember why, I asked one of my classes if they considered me an introvert or an extrovert. I always assumed I was the former and therefore expected this answer.

Much to my surprise, it wasn't. The overwhelming majority regarded me as an extrovert. At first, I couldn't imagine why. Then it dawned on me that in the classroom I was a bit of a showman. My students were merely reflecting what they saw. Soon I also realized that my wife was sometimes embarrassed by my public behavior. Nowadays I often strike up conversations with complete strangers. If I see something funny, I comment on it out loud. This, I realized, was not the behavior of someone who is preternaturally shy. Nor was it something I would have done when I was younger. Amazingly, I was not as fearful of social interactions as I once was. Now more comfortable with myself, I was perfectly happy to have others judge me as they wished. My fears of what they might think had eroded so appreciably that they were essentially gone. Nonetheless, at no time along the way did I force myself not to be afraid. I merely ceased being so after years of not worrying about it.

FIGHTING BACK

Sometimes, however, we do want to do something about our fears. They are not such that they can be safely disregarded. The question is: What should we do? Which sorts of responses would reduce our concerns? The answer depends on the nature of a fear and the means available to reduce it. Physical, social, and emotional dangers generally require different responses. The fight/flight instinct does not apply in the same ways to all. Thus physical dangers rarely succumb to a pugnacious mentality. How, after all, does one fight a fear of falling off a cliff? Physical dangers are thus best dealt with either by avoiding or arranging to neutralize them. We won't fall off a mountain, if we never climb one. Similarly, we are unlikely to be hit by a car if we look both ways before crossing the street. Being in the right place, with the appropriate equipment, attitude, and skills, enables most physical perils to be managed. Moreover, as adults, these become less threatening because we understand more about their sources and the means of evading them.

Nevertheless, there is an equivalent to fighting off a physical danger. The fight/flight mechanism floods our bodies with adrenaline when we are in jeopardy.[11] This increases our strength and fosters an alertness that makes it possible to accomplish feats that might otherwise be impossible. Mothers who are afraid that their children might be crushed under a car have been known to summon the strength to lift it off of them. Mountain climbers who dread falling off a cliff routinely find the muscle power to maintain a vice-like grip. These folks are not literally fighting, but they are employing the same abilities that they would if they were.

Nor do we literally fight to keep intense emotions under control. Although we describe ourselves as wrestling with a potent affect, we do not literally force it to the ground. Our muscles may tense as we seek to prevent a panicky response, but this is not quite the same. Thus, my dad often fought with himself when his rage threatened to go ballistic. I could see him clenching his teeth and fists in an effort not be beat me too severely. His adult self was, as it were, at war with his immature self, struggling to see which would gain the upper hand. Fortunately for me, his adult self often won the battle. While this fight was not literal, it probably did pit some of his muscles against others.

We likewise allude to fighting temptation. The alcoholic who has vowed never to take another drink[12] and the spouse who was sworn not to give in to an unfair demand have a lot in common. Both are beset by impulses they know might be harmful. And so they resist. They too may clench their teeth in an effort to maintain control. They too may employ an inner dialogue to talk themselves out of doing what they know they shouldn't. These internal battles can take as much energy as external ones. They may also require tactical skill to win. Most people develop tricks to keep their emotions under wraps, be this by going for long walks or writing poetry.

Normally, however, we do not battle frightening emotions so much as allow them to dissipate.[13] We humans experience all sorts of impulses upon which we do not act. As emotional creatures, we are swept by passions, many of which never fully rise to the surface. Thus, most of us are moved by films that depict tragic love affairs, yet tears do not literally roll down our cheeks. Or we are told about how a girl was viciously raped and we fantasize about punching out her attacker, but we never do. If we acted on every impulse that we had, we would do little else. Moreover if we did, we would get into so much trouble that we could never extricate ourselves. In fact, most of the time we are perfectly able to allow intemperate emotions to subside. Rather than fight them, we tolerate them long enough for them to lose their potency. Once this occurs, we are safe.

No, literally *fighting* against potential dangers is generally confined to warding off social threats. Once upon a time we fought against intimidating carnivores in order to survive. When confronted with an angry lion, fear mobilized us for the coming encounter. Nowadays, however, few of us venture into the forest to hunt down large game. Since our food comes prepackaged, the closest we get to the chase is in our imaginations. As for live animals, the ones with which we interact are usually pets. People roughhouse with their dogs, but seldom because they are afraid of them.

For better or worse, most of our battles are with other people. While the majority of these are not physical, nonphysical encounters can be equally alarming. Although armed warfare has not been banished from the modern scene, most of the combat civilians experience is less corporeal. Generally speaking, our biggest social fear is of losing.[14] Conflict is endemic to the human condition.[15] We are a truculent lot who fight one another over all sorts of things. Most of the time, however, these are not bodily confrontations. Even though children, especially boys, get into punching matches and criminals employ brute force to intimidate their victims, adult skirmishes are usually less material. We more frequently use words, emotions, and threats to coerce our opponents.

Most of our social battles revolve around social roles, hierarchies, and relationships.[16] Because where we fit in our communities can dictate our well-being, we aspire to win these fights. As important, we do not want to be vanquished. The fact that we might be provokes many of our fears. Because none of us win all of the time, we are aware that we could be defeated. Regrettably, for some of us, these setbacks have been so constant that we can barely imagine a different outcome. When this is the case, we may dread the clashes that we assume lie just over the horizon. Sadly, we may not know how to ward them off.

Winning such clashes reduces the fear of social losses. Yet winning is not ensured. Furthermore, the anxieties over doing so cannot be entirely eliminated because even habitual winners remain vulnerable. How then are we to improve our chances of winning? What works depends on the nature of a fight and the relative advantages of those involved. To be more specific, contests over social roles depend on which roles are at stake, as well as who possesses the requisite skills to perform them. By the same token, the starting points of the protagonists and their relative access to powerful allies can influence the outcomes of disputes over social rank.[17] Last, the dependability of our personal relationships can hinge on the attachment histories of the parties and their emotional maturity.[18] These are complex equations, which means that there is no simple formula for determining who will prevail. This uncertainty adds to the apprehension that most people experience.

This said, the probabilities of victory can frequently be calculated in advance. The disparities in power between the contestants can be such that an upset is unlikely. Consider a fight between a parent and a child.[19] Unless the parent has emotional difficulties, the child may have no recourse but to go to bed at the appointed hour. Although he cannot be forced to go to sleep, he can be compelled to lie down. Even more certain is the defeat of a child who is seeking love from a parent who cannot give it. No matter how accommodating a little girl is, no matter how sweetly she begs, she does not have the power to melt a frozen heart. An extreme example is the double bind. Years ago, the anthropologist Gregory Bateson[20] observed that some parents make demands that cannot be met. Thus, if a child comes too close, she is pushed away. But if she stays away, she is reprimanded for keeping her distance. In these cases, winning was impossible, whereas losing is wholly predictable.

So is the economic failure of poor persons who are stuck in the culture of poverty. If they lead disorganized lives, are both present- and local-oriented, and have a fatalistic attitude toward life, their chances of holding down a good job are minimal.[21] They may be good people, and their bosses might be stinkers, but they will lose anyway. So will habitual drunks and the mentally disabled. Social mobility is not about niceness. It is about being able to exercise greater power than the competition. For this reason, children who are raised in intact families and taught to be emotionally mature have an advantage over those who aren't.[22] Because they are likely to be competently self-directed, they have an advantage over those who are not. Their moral standing is largely irrelevant. What counts is that they possess abilities that are useful in a middle-class society.

Given these disparities, how can people fearful of losing improve their odds? What can they do to make it more likely that they will prevail in disputes over roles, ranks, or relationships? Although no one can win every battle, it is possible to increase one's batting average. The first thing to know is that not all battles have to be fought—being challenged does not dictate that we must pick up the gauntlet. Furthermore, just because a victory would provide significant benefits does not require that it be joined. People who elect to fight whenever a fight is in the offing are destined to lose. No one has that much energy. This may not be fair, but when we are exhausted, our chances of being defeated increase. Likewise no one has the time to prepare battle plans in every direction, which ensures that haphazard organization provides openings for our foes.

The key to winning is selectivity. Potential fights must be sorted through before they are joined. Lamentably, a penchant for promiscuous conflict is apt to increase our fears rather than reduce them. So which battles should we fight? There are two criteria. The first is: Can we win? Who holds the advantages in a potential contest? Are we stronger or is our foe? What counts as stronger, however, varies. Sometimes physical prowess matters. If we are playing a game of football or arm wrestling, this can be crucial. If, on the other hand, we are engaged in an academic contest, who is smarter or has studied harder can make the difference. Should we switch to the commercial arena, which vendor has the better product or the more dependable financing? Marketing skills are also important. Or, if the competition is political, what is the mood of the electorate? Are the votes there for one policy or another? And how will the media portray a particular initiative? This can decide where viewers cast their lot.[23]

Because abilities and resources are not evenly distributed, it is important to choose battles where one has the advantage. Children are often lured into a conflict merely by a dare. Adults should know better. If they are thinking clearly, they should not be goaded into confrontations where the other guy is stronger. Like many of us, I learned this lesson the hard way. I am short of stature and not accomplished in the pugilistic arts. Accordingly, getting into a fistfight with one of my students would be foolish. Conversely, I am articulate and reasonably well read. As a result, I do fairly well in public debates. Which then should I choose if I have a disagreement with someone? The answer is obvious.

The same considerations apply to the territory in which a battle is fought. When we are on familiar ground, our confidence rises. Meanwhile that of our opponent falls. This is why executives prefer to schedule disagreeable encounters in their own offices. It is why athletic teams appreciate a home-field advantage. This is also why it is unwise to jump into a fray without considering the lay of the land. Are allies close by? Is there a fallback position? Are surprises apt to occur? As imperative as commanding superior resources is knowing when and where to deploy them. This, however, may be contingent on our familiarity with particular surroundings. Confederate General Nathan Bedford Forrest advised his subordinates to get to a battle "firstest with the mostest."[24] This usually depended on understanding how the armies were positioned and the impediments that might hinder moving troops to where they were needed.

The second criterion for deciding when to fight is the significance of the issue. Some losing battles are worth entering. Few people voluntarily give up their freedom without a struggle. A fairly large number, albeit reluctantly, will sustain injuries in order to promote social justice. Winning is not the only thing that can make us feel good about ourselves. Going down to defeat for an honorable cause can also reduce our fears. If we are comfortable with an objective, losing does not necessarily hurt that badly. Honor turns out to be a condign cure for fear. If we truly believe in the value of what we are defending, we can accept some concurrent anxieties without giving in to them.

Fighting some losing battles has another benefit. As I say, I am a physically small person. Back in grammar school I was always the second or third shortest boy in line. This made me a tempting target for bullies. Although I was scared, and did my best to avoid them, I learned another lesson. There were times when I had to fight even though I knew I would get pummeled. Had I not, things would have been worse. Thus, were I perceived as defenseless, the drubbings would have been endless. If, however, I got in a few good licks, I was no longer a free ride. I did not have to beat up the bullies; I merely had to make them pay a price. Technically I lost, whereas in changing their attitude, I won.

Reputations matter.[25] Who wins or loses often hinges on how people are perceived. Fighting the good fight can produce a reputation as someone who ought not be attacked. Hence, as an adult, while I have lost political battles, I have not lost them all. Decisions about which courses should be taught in my department or who should be hired have frequently gone against me. Nonetheless, I am deemed someone to be reckoned with. I am not a pushover; and because others know it, I am seldom challenged. The upshot is that I have less need to be fearful. No longer considered a coward, I am in less jeopardy than I was in the past. As a result, I do not have to be as defensive because I have less to defend.

On the negative side of the ledger there is another sort of battle that should not be fought. Many of us are obsessed with losses incurred when we were young. Still seething at the injustices we endured, we long to reverse the tables. If Dad beat us for no reason or Mom unfairly withheld her love, we want to reverse history. In our imaginations, we play out scenes of pummeling him or being embraced by her. The problem is that we cannot turn back the clock. What is past is past. Defeats sustained decades ago cannot be undone.[26] On the emotional level, our anger and fear can diminish, whereas on the corporeal level what happened, happened.

Unfortunately for many of us this is not the end of the matter. So fixated are we at snatching victory from the jaws of defeat that we attempt to do the impossible. How we go about this is often by means of proxies. If Mom and Dad, in their historical incarnations, are no longer available to be challenged, we resort to stand-ins. We choose our friends and spouses, not for who they are, but for whom we can make-believe they are.[27] A wife, for example, can be regarded as a substitute for a mother. Irrespective of her personal faults, her husband may punish for the sins of a person she never met. In an effort to nullify previous losses, we may basically seek a compensatory victory in the here and now. Unfortunately, this does not work because the here and now is not the then and there. Whatever we achieve today cannot undo yesterday's failures. Old fears will linger despite our having subdued their proxies. Mom, as she was, remains unchanged.

Worse yet, inflicting damage on innocents is unfair. A woman who had nothing to do with our mother's coldness does not deserve to be punished for what she did not do. Nor can she be expected to alter what she did not perpetrate. On top of this, if we select our friends and spouses because they resemble historic foes, we deprive ourselves of satisfying relationships in the present. Instead of seeking out people who can satisfy our needs, we cleave to individuals who cannot.[28] How can this assuage our fears? If we intentionally expose ourselves to people who present dangers similar to the ones we earlier encountered, won't this perpetuate our jeopardy?

WALKING AWAY

Actually, we do not always have to fight. Sometimes we don't need to. In many instances, the best option is flight. If we can evade a danger, we may be just as safe as if we beat it into submission. But when should we do which? How can we decide on the superior strategy? Moreover, are some ways to flee better than others? A panicked rout is usually worse than an orderly retreat. Are there, in fact, viable alternatives to utter disarray? In ancient wars, the decision in battle often occurred when one side lost its nerve and ran away.[29] The losers would then be cut down from behind, thereby denying them the opportunity to defend themselves. Does flight always have to be this inglorious?

There are two major reasons for running away. The first is that defeat is inevitable. The odds are so stacked against us that no matter how commendably we struggle, a negative outcome is assured. Moreover, this loss will be so disastrous that we might not be able to recover. Far from being able to fight another day, we will be so crippled that a rematch would result in another defeat. As a child, I was in this situation vis-à-vis my father. He was so much more powerful that when he was out of control, had I resisted, my life would have ended then and there. I consequently needed to scoot under the bed or retreat to a corner where I could kneel down and cover my head. What other options did I have? Had I punched him, he would have done far worse to me. Although I did not win, at least I survived.

A second motive to flee springs from less onerous defeats. If the costs of losing a battle are minor, it can make more sense to sustain them than to divert our limited supplies of energy into a fight where the gains are insubstantial. Thus, when as children my sister and I fought over who got more soda, backing off and allowing her to win would have cost me very little. The small advantage she derived was trivial compared with the explosion that might have ensued if I insisted on cosmic justice.[30] Perhaps I could have won. Perhaps Mom might have been persuaded to fill my glass a bit higher. But what about the next go round? Would there ever be an end to the escalation of hostilities? Laying down a marker to let others know that they will not have a walkover has limits. There often comes a time when it makes more sense the stop resisting than to keep up the struggle.

Years ago, when working as a vocational counselor, I got into a row with my supervisor. He failed to back me up when I got into a disagreement with a client's psychiatrist. I did not appreciate his unwillingness to provide support, nor did he appreciate my resentment. After a number of such incidents, he decided to teach me a lesson. Whereas I had been out-stationed at a psychiatric hospital, he transferred me to the main office so that he could supervise me more closely. From my perspective, this represented a danger. It would limit my freedom to do my job as I saw fit. Besides, it would probably become a source of additional friction. And so I decided to fight. I had broken no rules and my transfer would not improve my ability to serve my clients; hence I disputed his decision.

My method was to engage in the memo war to which I earlier alluded. I bombarded his supervisors, and then their supervisors, with missives explaining why what happened was against organizational policy. I knew that my supervisor was not well liked, therefore I expected a sympathetic hearing. In reality, the opposite occurred. The administrators closed ranks. Aware that if his authority were successfully challenged, their own might be in jeopardy, they defended actions I knew they deplored. This prompted me to up the ante and send ever more vigorous protests. The response, however, was more forceful rejection. What then was I to do? Reason and articulate argument had failed to reverse a dreadful decision. What recourse did I have?

I am a stubborn person and thus it took months for me to realize that I could not succeed. Lacking the ammunition to win a long campaign, I had to capitulate. Leaving the scene of battle in this case simply meant discontinuing my memos. I did not apologize; I did not openly admit defeat. I merely stopped fighting. In essence, I fled the dangerous confrontations I had provoked. What was the result?

At first nothing happened. No one said a word. I was not punished: I was not even reprimanded. I merely kept doing my job. Then, months later, without my asking for relief, I was out-stationed to a different clinic. This was only for three days a week; nevertheless it provided me the space I sought. After my having made my case, my supervisor's superiors no longer felt a need to put me in my place, that is, once they did not feel attacked. All of us had proved our willingness to stand up and fight; therefore none felt compelled to do so to the death. We could all walk away from the confrontation with our dignity intact. The dangers we experienced—I of close supervision, and they of disobedience—had been quelled. If I had not won a victory, at least I had not been crushed. None of us, including me, behaved cowardly. While in the end I backed down, I did so in an orderly manner.

Flight can be the appropriate response to danger if retreat is achieved methodically. Whether the hazard is life-threatening or trivial, refusing to take on a fight depends on a cost/benefit analysis and the consequences of escape. If leaving the scene will be less harmful than remaining, staying to fight can be foolish. Coming out ahead is not always the best gauge of what to do. Doing less badly may be the appropriate criterion for selecting the optimum recourse. The verdict between fight and flight is thus a relative matter, with a definitive choice frequently unattainable. Often the best we can manage is to think things through as coherently as we can. With this done, the outcome is in the lap of the gods.

We can also make sure to leave the scene prudently. Instead of running, we can walk away. Running tends to be headlong, whereas walking is deliberate enough to peruse the surrounding territory as we fall back. A calm retreat enables us to make adjustments if additional hazards arise. Then we can plot a new course should the initial one turn perilous. If we walk, we can also put up a competent rearguard action. Rather than be handicapped by a head stuffed with mush, we can coordinate our actions so as to improve the chances of finding a safe haven.

Accordingly, with respect to dangerous social roles, we can leave them. A bad job does not have to be a lifelong trap.[31] If our abilities do not match an occupational niche, or if a boss is a monster, fighting to overcome these difficulties may be futile. So why not change jobs? Or seek a transfer? Precipitous changes can propel us from the frying pan to the fire, but why do these have to be precipitous? Exiting an unwinnable position is not always evidence of cowardice. Moving elsewhere, perhaps by obtaining the training for a different job, can be the best answer. I, for one, left my counselor job. I did not do so hastily, but only after I explored the feasibility to college teaching. Once I realized my options were blocked where I was, I needed an escape hatch. Fortunately, becoming professor was a wonderful fit. Indeed, moving from New York to Georgia was a significant improvement. Far from being an admission of weakness, making this change took courage. And I got lucky. Of course, in going from one situation to another, we can never be completely certain that it will work. Nonetheless, if we keep calm and honestly assess where we are headed, we can often do better. I did!

The same is true for social status. People who are born into poverty do not have to remain there if they plan a prudent getaway. A local orientation and a fatalistic outlook do not have to preclude a systematic departure. People surrounded by failure and disrespect frequently thrash about in wild disregard of the outcome. Distressed by their condition, they lash out indiscriminately. Unable to recognize what leads to success, they fight whatever person or organization seems to be impeding their progress.[32] This, however, generally produces further losses.

Blaming the teacher for one's bad grades might, for instance, have merit, but this is probably of less import than one's own decision not to study. We have control over some things, but not everything. The police, politicians, and corporate executives each, upon occasion, behave badly, yet they, in toto, constitute a target that is too immense for any individual to depose. Those who hope to be rescued by a social revolution must thus gird themselves for a long wait. Bringing down "society" is a fight they are seldom going to win, whatever the virtues of their complaints.[33] On the other hand, if they dedicate themselves to self-improvement, progress is possible. This may entail leaving familiar communities and abandoning hide-bound habits, which, it must be admitted, is daunting. Success rarely comes in one fell swoop, but those who take the time, and possess the courage, to learn can frequently go farther than they imagine. Theirs can be an orderly flight from the dangers of low status, as long as they are pragmatic and tenacious. As a college professor, I often see this in some students.[34] They enroll in college because they were supposed to, but then one day they have an epiphany. They realize that they don't have to be trapped in the lifestyle in which they were raised. If they study, over the long haul they can move up. They can leave the violent neighborhoods of their youth and walk into safer ones.

Treacherous relationships can also be advantageously fled. Once more it is a question of doing so judiciously. Some relationships are inherently hazardous. No matter what modifications we make, they cannot be salvaged. No matter how vigorously we fight to change another person's attitude, he or she may resist.[35] Abusive parents and exploitive spouses are customarily implacable. Their limitations, and not ours, may preclude victory. Should this be the case, it is sensible to admit defeat and move on. Just as alternative jobs are available, so are alternative emotional attachments. Leaving a bitter affiliation is not a death sentence—at least not for competent adults. To the contrary, it can provide opportunity.

My siblings and I offer evidence of what can be achieved. During my college years, I lived at home. Brooklyn College was a commuter school and I did not have the resources to finance an apartment. Deathly afraid that I could not support myself, there seemed to be no choice but to remain at my parent's mercy. Upon entering graduate school, however, I was determined to make a break. Fortunately, I found congenial roommates with whom to share expenses. I also found something more. I obtained freedom. Life without being badgered was a revelation. Here were friendships that were completely different from the oppression I had known. Nor had I run away from home. There was no explosive rupture. Neither had I moved in with people I did not know. My roommates were friends. Their trustworthiness had already been tested. While I was taking a chance, it was not a blind chance. I still remember the three of us worrying about whether we had sufficient funds to buy groceries. Those first trips to the supermarket resulted in purchasing the cheapest cuts of meat we could find. Nonetheless, we proved that we could manage. We had made a break, but not a disastrous one.

Carol and Joel also left our parent's home in quest of less traumatic relationships. Both did so by getting married. Joel's teenage nuptials were a hasty affair, which had unfortunate side effects. Carol's were more carefully considered; hence her marriage lasted. Adulthood, in general, entails forsaking old associations. These may be broken entirely or drastically modified. Nonetheless, to cease being a child requires that one no longer be treated as a child. This is what the storms of adolescence are about.[36] It is why young adults can benefit from moving away to college or obtaining separate living quarters. Our relationships change as we grow older, which may necessitate a separation. The process is rarely painless because new roles and relationships have yet to be proven. Although walking away might be imperative, this does not mean the interruption will be without anxiety.

Divorce too, of course, involves leaving a relationship.[37] In an era of marital instability, this has become a widespread problem.

Intimate commitments should not be taken lightly. Even so, when conjugal battles get out of control, seeking an exit can be the appropriate course. Nonetheless, this is both a loss and a disquieting experience. Some people make the mistake of trying to short-circuit their distress by jumping into another relationship. They run, not walk, ergo they pay a price. The levelheaded strategy is first to figure out what went wrong. Contemplating our mistakes is scary; yet ignoring them paves the way to repeating them. While it can be difficult to endure the pangs of a guarded withdrawal, the sorrows of a hurried exodus are usually worse.

LOSING

Some things are authentically frightening. They are inherently harmful and thus truly dangerous. Notwithstanding this truth, fighting them may not neutralize these perils. Nor can we safely walk away from them all. There are dangers that follow us around. They may be part of our natural condition or stubbornly internalized within us. Either way, they can hurt. In these cases, we may have to absorb the pain. The best that we might be able to achieve is to let go of them—despite our discomfort.

As I have mentioned previously, Theodore Roosevelt was devastated when he lost his wife and mother on the same day.[38] His anguish was so terrifying that he could not remain in the house of death. Accordingly, he sought a getaway in North Dakota, a place he already knew and loved. Throwing himself into the life of a cowboy, he attempted to use intense activity to keep his mind away from his troubles. While he was in the saddle, he was so preoccupied that he did not have to dwell on the past. This was a classic case of walking away from one's fears. Indeed, it was a technique he often used. He also courted fear in order to divert himself from what disturbed him most. His later expedition to the River of Doubt in the farthest reaches of the Amazon epitomized this strategy.[39] That this adventure was life-threatening distracted him from his recent political defeats.

Yet even Roosevelt could not escape some of his fears. People were routinely impressed with his zest for life. Always a center of attention, his energy never seemed to flag. On a hunting expedition, he was the first up in the morning; in the office, he handled a crowded schedule with aplomb; and at home, he roughhoused with his children until they tired. Nevertheless, Teddy did go through a period of dejection.[40] Upon venturing into the Dakota Territories, he not only immersed himself in the life of a rancher, he soaked in the beautiful ambiance. Often alone, he regularly went for extended rides and long walks. This enabled him to think his situation through. More particularly, it enabled him to mourn his losses. Roosevelt was depressed in a manner he ordinarily rejected. Although intent in overcoming any hardship that came his way, in this case he required a lengthy period of letting go. This is what sadness achieves.[41] It allows us to relinquish defeats that we can neither overpower nor escape.

For most of us, death is terrifying.[42] We do not want to die or see our loved ones perish. Yet there is little we can do to evade the grim reaper. We can take care of our health and avoid foolish risks, but even so death will come. Nor can we ensure that others will not succumb to accidents or disease. As small children, our fear of the dark is a surrogate for this fear of death. It is part of our biology. Without it, we would not take measures to keep safe. Yet death is a biological imperative. In the end, there is nothing we can do to prevent it.

So what do we do? The answer is that we grieve.[43] If we are seriously ill, we get lethargic. Or, if the doctor tells us that we have weeks to live, we become mortified. Likewise, if we are gravely injured, we feel sorry for ourselves. The paraplegics I interacted with as a vocational counselor characteristically did the latter. Once they realized that they would never get back to normal, they became depressed. A part of them had died, irrespective of how effective their rehabilitation had gone. Paradoxically, those who let go of what they could not recover usually developed viable alternatives. It was those in total denial who had the most trouble moving on.

The same is true for the death of a loved one or divorce.[44] People who do not become depressed when an important relationship is broken have a difficult time establishing new relationships. In failing to cut their ties with what is gone, they are unable to discover other options. When this occurs, a fear of being alone overwhelms their system and traps them in the past. While depression is painful, it is sometimes essential. Although it can feel like death, it is a gateway to the future. Some injuries, whether physical or emotional, must be endured. They cannot be beaten or erased. The best we can accomplish is to survive them.

Coping with significant losses is integral to acquiring courage.[45] Continuously engaging in losing battles is a prescription for perpetual weakness. So are flights that do not leave our terrors behind. These circumstances are the essence of what were once called neuroses.[46] Folks who are everlastingly anxious and/or eternally depressed have not let go of what they have lost. Still perhaps locked in combat with parents who are no longer present, they can neither win, nor disengage. As a result, their antique fears remain in place and their sorrow never cuts their ties with what is gone. Theirs is a limbo of their own making. Instead of admitting the limits of what can be accomplished, false hopes prevent them from seizing the courage to face life on its own terms.

My father is long gone. Nonetheless, he continues to live on in my memory. When he lay dying, I clutched him by the arm and silently promised that I would complete his unfinished business. In writing this book about fear management, I am trying to achieve exactly that. He never managed to control his fears despite herculean efforts. Had I adopted his policy of breaking down doors and denying my anxieties, I would have been as imprisoned in my weaknesses as he was in his. It was in letting go of unwinnable battles, including those with him, that I discovered a different path.

Today I have twinges of sadness when I recall his unrealized potential. I also have spasms of anger when I remember the undeserved beatings I endured. But these are passing tremors. Nowadays my life is satisfying in ways he never achieved. I accomplished this partly by detaching myself from our clashes and partly by entering psychotherapy. The latter provided the guidance, and the support, to re-experience the traumas I had undergone and, as important, the courage to bury them. The sadness this elicited was deep and mortifying. Yet I am here to tell the tale.

My journey in finding a safe place, tolerating intolerable fears, examining their contents, and sorting through the best ways to survive may not be yours. The good news is that it doesn't have to be. There is more than one way to develop courage. The bad news is that this takes time and discomfort. Anyone expecting instant valor will be disappointed. Whether our fears are unwarranted, successfully fought, appropriately fled, or painfully relinquished, personal fortitude does not come easily. There is no magic wand that can make us safe or brave. These are hard-won—but they can be won, if we make a serious effort.

In the next chapter we will deal with winning. Some dangers can, in fact, be overcome by challenging them. If we do so intelligently and with determination, they can be defeated. And who does not want to win? The problem is that winning is a complex business. There is no single method for doing so. Nonetheless, there are general approaches that improve our chances.

Chapter 8

WINNING

GAINING CONFIDENCE

People who think of themselves as losers tend to lose. Conversely those who consider themselves winners are more apt to win. Confidence makes a difference. A history of coming out on the losing end of battles accentuates the danger of being defeated, whereas a history of winning does the opposite. Winners rarely spend hour upon hour fretting about what might go wrong, whereas losers frequently do. Paradoxically, in concentrating how they might lose, they increase the chances that they will.

Winning, and achieving the safety that winning provides, is one of the surest ways to acquire courage. If courage is the ability to stay cool, even when under pressure, then people who expect to be victorious are less likely to panic. Convinced that they will be able to mount a successful defense, either by fighting or fleeing, they are not troubled by visions of annihilation. This makes it easier to evaluate threats more accurately and respond more appropriately. Because they feel safer, they are less apt to be overwhelmed by misfortune.

On the other hand, when things go wrong losers exaggerate their jeopardy. Social fears, whether about roles, ranks, or relationships, are magnified such that potential adversaries seem ten feet tall. Losers generally dwell on the strengths of their opponents while inflating their own weaknesses. Instead of calculating what they might do to win a fight, they are obsessed with how to avoid defeat.

Their eyes are on how they might be injured rather than how they might damage the other guy.

Losers tend to be defensive. They may have heard that the best defense is a good offense, but they assume that this applies to others. Persuaded that if they go on the attack, this will merely provoke their adversaries, they hold back. From their perspective, it makes more sense to propitiate others than to irritate them. In conceiving of themselves as vulnerable children, losers prefer to appease potential aggressors. Like my mother, it never occurs to them that this might have the opposite effect. Because they consider groveling an offer of friendship, they do not recognize it as of evidence of weakness. That this might be perceived as an opportunity to inflict abuse by unprincipled persons never crosses their minds. Or if it does, they assume that they have no alternative.

Such passivity hinges upon the conviction that other people are always stronger than they are. This is a serious mistake. Others also have vulnerabilities. They too are human and hence they have areas of weakness. People who are unsure of themselves generally fail to realize this. Because these others conceal their limitations, they do not see them. Winners, in particular, do not advertise their shortcomings.[1] In putting on a pretense of invincibility, they thereby discourage rivals. Although they may not consciously fake superiority, if they believe that they are powerful, they project a forcefulness despite its absence. The ways they walk, talk, or dress all proclaim that it would be foolish to challenge them. Genuinely persuaded that they will win, this certitude oozes out of every pore.

Cowards allow themselves to be fooled. They would rather skulk off into a corner than risk defeat. Those in pursuit of greater courage must therefore do otherwise. They must seek out the weakness of their adversaries. Although defensiveness is sometimes required, they must also be capable of offense. Even though they are afraid of their foes, they must attempt to make these others fear them. Victories derive from getting the other guy to back down, which usually entails convincing him that he might get hurt.

When generals prepare for battle they seek intelligence about the enemy.[2] They want to know about their numbers and dispositions. If they can determine an adversaries plans, all the better. This enables them to deploy their own assets more effectively. It is the same in ordinary life. When we are in negotiations about roles, ranks, or relationships, information about our rivals is crucial.[3] It should therefore be sought. What is the other guy thinking? What would she find frightening? It is amazing how much can be found out if it is pursued.

During the Civil War, Union General William Tecumseh Sherman, when explaining his friend General Ulysses S. Grant's success, observed that Grant did not give a darn about what the other guy was doing. He concentrated instead on what he was going to do.[4] Thus, after the first day's disastrous encounters at Shiloh, Grant's subordinates assumed a retreat was in order. They were therefore surprised when their leader asserted that he would "whip them tomorrow." And, of course, he did. Aware that the Confederates were overextended, whereas that he had fresh troops available, Grant was meditating on how he would attack. Although he realized that his forces had endured a terrible beating, he never lost sight of the fact that his foes had also been mauled.

Grant's attention was on winning rather than on avoiding defeat. General George McClellan, however, was a study in the opposite. During the Peninsula Campaign in Virginia, he routinely overestimated his enemy's strength. Although his Army of the Potomac often fielded twice the number of troops as the Army of Northern Virginia, he was convinced that the reverse was true. Hence when General John Magruder set out logs to look like canons, McClellan took the bait.[5] He was also tricked into believing that the same companies marching around in circles represented different regiments.

McClellan saw what he wanted to see. Sure of his tactical inferiority, he perceived strength where it was absent. As a consequence, he took tail and ran even after he won battles.

Grant had what Sherman referred to as "four o'clock in the morning" courage.[6] Despite being surprised, he could mentally regroup to assess a tactical situation. Grant knew that the Union possessed greater resources than the Confederacy and was determined to make these felt. While he suffered reverses, he was always mindful of his advantages. The rest of us need to follow this example. Even if we are rattled when things go wrong, we must keep our heads and refuse to give in to defeatism. Pluses can usually to be found, that is, if we are prepared to look for them.

Confidence comes from winning and winning comes from the realization that it is possible. While cowards may assume that they are fated to lose, this attitude ensures that they will. We all have weaknesses; hence we all lose some of the time. But we all have strengths, which means that we can win some of the time. Getting into the fray, and fighting the good fight to the best of our ability, is bound to result in victories—assuming that we are, in fact, fighting to the best of our ability. If we do, our successes will bolster our self-assurance. Winning begets further winning, which provides the foundation for greater courage.

HALF A LOAF

Paradoxically, while cowards expect to lose, they also imagine that if they win, they will never experience another defeat. Having been victorious, they assume this will dictate the results of future encounters. Nevertheless, this attitude can precipitate additional loses. Confidence is a boon to courage, whereas overconfidence undermines it. People who expect to win all of the time, and to do so with finality, set an impossible standard. Their goal is so unrealistic that when reverses come they are devastated. So unexpected are these that their import is overestimated. Courage that is based on the anticipation of constant success is fragile. Even the smallest of setbacks may seem to disconfirm strengths that were conceived of as absolute.

Winners must be able to accept partial victories. If they are never satisfied when they obtain some of that they want, they are likely to press forward until they lose. Like Napoleon, after achieving a string of historic victories, they feel invincible.[7] Then they march into the equivalent of a Russian winter. Although they have amassed the counterpart of an army of six hundred thousand, they miscalculate their opponent's assets. Worse still, by putting their foes in danger of total defeat, they motivate a stouter opposition. Our adversaries should not be overrated, but neither should they be discounted. Even a beaten enemy may have the wherewithal to recover. Leaving others a shred of dignity can thus prevent further conflicts.

Neither should winners demand everything that they might want. However thoroughly an adversary has been vanquished, it may still be impossible to satisfy our every whim. Regardless of how much territory we have gained, or gold we have amassed in our treasury, we might continue to want more. The Buddha warned that desire is at the root of personal suffering.[8] This is true to the degree that we humans can be insatiable. Whatever we acquire, we tend to want more. Yet this frequently motivates unwise objectives. Instead of enjoying what we have, we perseverate upon what we do not have such that we are never happy. In this case, we may be winners, yet feel like losers.

We live in a world filled with other humans who also have ambitions. Although economists agree that we can usually increase the size of the pie that we share, most of us want a bigger piece than the other guy. Nevertheless because not everyone can have the biggest piece, frictions are inevitable. These do not, however, have to get out of control. Ours does not have to be a Hobbesian universe of all against all. Conflicts may be unavoidable, but these need not escalate into war. Misfortune can be avoided if we are willing to make deals with others. When we negotiate our differences, we can arrive at agreements where both sides gain something.[9] These arrangements need not be completely equitable—they seldom are—but if those involved are satisfied, this is usually sufficient.

Deals that keep the peace depend on the party's readiness to settle for half a loaf. They may not get everything they want, but they can obtain more than they would have had they not made a deal. Winning is relative. Getting some of what was desired, and at the same time preventing serious injury, may be the maximum achievable. If so, snatching defeat from the jaws of victory is ill-advised. In fact, in working cooperatively with others, we may obtain more than we would have had we worked alone. Cooperation creates synergies unavailable to loners.[10]

What is the most we can obtain? It is often difficult to tell. This makes it imperative that we assess what is possible in the midst of the action. In short, we must be flexible. We need to recognize fluctuating opportunities as they arise. If we cannot adjust our strategies as conditions change, we will fight when we should stand down, and stand down when victory is in sight. Likewise, how much we should demand, or concede, varies with the state of a negotiation. What people are feeling, the availability of resources, and their respective problem-solving skills can all modify what constitutes a good deal. Hence, those who are unable to roll with the punches are apt to be blindsided by an adversary who can.

Prioritizing our goals can circumvent a negative outcome. Not everything we desire is of equal import. Some objectives are more crucial to our well-being than others are. It is therefore important to recognize which are worth fighting for. The less significant can thus be sacrificed in exchange for the more significant. But this applies to our negotiating partners as well. For which goals will these others go to the mat? Likewise, for which can we expect concessions? Married partners frequently make deals with each other in which they give up something in order to get something.[11] The issue is whether their transactions are balanced. If they are, both sides can feel comfortable. If, however, only one wins, the other is liable to harbor a grievance.

Negotiators typically determine each other's priorities in the course of bargaining.[12] The strength with which each partner defends particular objectives indicates their respective value. Anger is a remarkably accurate measure of personal concern.[13] Because it arises when people are frustrated, the more unfulfilled they feel, the greater their irritation. This applies when assessing a partner's interests, but also our own. It is remarkable how often we learn what is precious to us by observing the intensity of our reactions. These should be heeded because if they are not, we are unlikely to be pleased.

The degree to which we realize our aims is also affected by our skills as problem solvers.[14] Negotiated agreements need not always cut the baby in half. Because priorities differ, it may be possible to come up with a compromise that gives both sides more than half. Consider a married couple. If they engage in problem-solving negotiations, he can get more of what he cares about while she gets more of what she cares about. Perhaps he procures his favorite dish for dinner in exchange for letting her choose the color of the living room couch. Since she doesn't hate what he loves, and vice versa, each gets more of what they individually want. Both make concessions, but fewer than they might have if they had not engaged in logrolling.

Personal maturity comes in here. People who cannot handle strong emotions are at a disadvantage. If they resort to primitive rejoinders in the heat of battle, their judgment is liable to be compromised. Should this be the case, they may not perceive when a settlement is to their advantage. Intent on never losing, they thus lose more than they must. Desperate people, that is, people who feel that they can never concede an inch, wind up trapped in never-ending battles. For them, everything is a priority. As a result, they regard allowing the other to have anything as tantamount to forfeiting everything. So transfixed are they on what they don't have that they overlook what they do. Unable to let go of the slightest desire, they have neither the time, nor the inclination, to maximize what they can.

Individuals who are mature enough to accept half a loaf are also better situated to reverse their defeats. Lost battles do not have to stay lost. The dangers of being left with nothing are multiplied by intransigence. It is often possible to get some of what we want once the dust of combat has settled down. I, for example, lost my bid to remain out-stationed at the psychiatric hospital. Out-gunned by administrative opposition, I was forced to back down. Yet after I did, I was granted three days per week at a community mental-health center. This was less independence than I had had, but it was more than I would have had, had I been unwilling to accept this indulgence. Had I insisted on total victory, I would have lost everything. Happily for me, I realized this was the best I was going to get and therefore acceded to it with as much grace as I could muster.

PLANNING

We humans have big brains. By all accounts we are the cleverest species on this planet. Even so, we do not always use our intelligence. When we are frightened, we have a nasty habit of behaving as if we were stupid. This reduces our chances of winning important battles. If we cannot plan an appropriate strategy, we are apt to be defeated.[15] Opponents who keep their wits about them then gain the upper hand. If they can foresee what is likely to happen, and we cannot, they can stay a move ahead of us. As in a chess match, they are able to take advantage of our blunders so as to wind up in charge of the board.

Regrettably, people who have experienced numerous losses tend not to think. They decline to look into the future because they are afraid of what they might see. Hunkered down in a defensive posture, they do not contemplate potentially winning moves. The poor are often in this situation. Convinced that they cannot be victorious, they remain within the confines of their own neighborhoods. Fearful of sorties into unfamiliar ground, they refuse to reconnoiter possible avenues of attack. This is unfortunate. It ensures that they will not be able to exploit such opportunities as arise. Because they are unaware of them, they never take advantage of them.

Disorganization is the bane of the lower classes.[16] A tendency to value spontaneity encourages them to wallow in failure. Whatever their resources, these remain untapped. Systematic thinking is therefore vital to succeeding in interpersonal conflicts. Although this is unexciting, it lays the foundation for victories. On the other hand, helter-skelter behavior precludes appropriate countermeasures. Doing what momentarily feels right usually interferes with recognizing what is liable to work. Meanwhile, intelligent reflection enables us to decipher what is happening. It also enables us to formulate a suitable defense and/or an effective offense. Undisciplined emotions seldom achieve this. When these prevail, it is generally by accident.

Neutralizing dangers typically entails taking calculated risks. The world is so complicated and our human adversaries so ingenious that it is normally impossible to be certain whether a particular tactic will succeed. Nonetheless, in most cases, we must try to decode what is taking place and compute the best response. If this does not work, we have to be prepared to modify our plans in accord with emerging developments. This requires a clear mind and unclouded foresight. Wishful thinking and childish fantasies are not helpful. Unlike many creatures, we are able to "see" into the future. In our mind's eyes, we can imagine what will happen if we do X.

We can also contemplate how others might respond. Then, assuming that they do, we can envision what we might do in response. We thus calculate how to counter their maneuvers. And so on. We can think multiple steps ahead, along a variety of pathways. But if we don't, if we merely react, we are less likely to find an appropriate rejoinder.

We humans engage in what sociologists call "anticipatory social-ization."[17] We are able to rehearse an assortment of alternatives in our heads before putting them into action. Supposing I take a fancy to Mary. How should I ask her out on a date? What if she says yes? What if she says no? Then if we go out together, where should we go? What might she enjoy? What would I enjoy? This sort of prior thinking makes it less likely that we will stumble about when the time comes. Although we have not yet done what we hope to do, mental practice improves our chances of a skillful performance.

If we are to do so, how should we go about this? Because winning often depends on relative strengths, these can be calculated in advance. What am I good at? What is my potential foe good at? Just as important, what are my weaknesses? What are hers? This will suggest vulnerabilities that require a defense and opportunities that allow for offence. Crucial here is absolute honesty. Those of us who live in fantasy worlds can expect only fantasy victories. While imag-inary triumphs can be comforting, when we confuse them with the real thing, we invite disaster. Honest-to-goodness dangers demand honest-to-goodness rejoinders. Although it is a tautology, if we are to win, we must win. Pretending is not good enough.

We must not only assess relative strengths, but also be cognizant of divergent motives. What do we want? What do others want? Not only must we understand people's priorities, but we must understand the nature of their goals. How can we satisfy ourselves if we do not know what we want? Similarly, how can we get others to back off if we do not know what might satisfy them? This sounds like a ridicu-lously simple requirement, but it is not. Why? Because we humans do not always know what we want. So many of our motives are buried in our unconscious that we do not have access to them.[18]

In the process of tolerating intense fears, we are apt to become aware of long-submerged terrors. Likewise, in the process of evaluating these, we may come to realize their nature. Up until now, we may have been certain that our wife's selfishness was driving us crazy, but now we are aware that she is a stand-in for our mother's egotism. In reality, a desire to protect ourselves from Mom's insatiable demands motivates us to fight about our wife's new dress. If so, then getting her to return the garment will not satisfy our needs. Mother's memory will stay as selfish and intransigent as ever.

Planning victories presupposes that we understand what would constitute a victory. Hence, if our true motives are unconscious, our conscious strategies may be beside the point. People who are afraid often remain afraid because they never overcome their actual bugaboos. They fail to realize that they are fighting the wrong battles and thus they never adjust their tactics. The answer may be looking inward with as much candor as can be managed.

By the same token, other people may be giving us grief because they are not in touch with their unconscious. Perhaps they are fighting us as a substitute for shades of their former role partners. Unfortunately we cannot always help them recognize this. If they cannot summon the courage to engage in honest introspection, we can rarely force the issue. We can, however, take their actual motives into consideration. When we realize, for instance, that complying with their demands will not propitiate them, we may feel less guilty about failing to do so. We may also redirect our energies to achieving something more realizable. If so, we will be less frightened and less frustrated. We will not have won in the way we imagined; nevertheless we may have done our best under the circumstances.

KNOWLEDGE AND SKILLS

Good planning is contingent upon accurate knowledge and competent skills. Dangers are more effectively neutralized when we understand their nature and when we possess the abilities to defeat them. This includes knowledge of both our own and others' strengths and weaknesses. It likewise incorporates an awareness of our own and others' motives. Yet it embraces more. The world in which we operate is enormously complicated. On both the physical and social planes, there are so many variables that they are impossible to identify in every detail. Nonetheless, the better informed we are, the better able we are to protect ourselves.

We live in a mass techno-commercial society.[19] Surrounded by millions of strangers, we are dependent upon their contributions to a marketplace in which we too participate. In addition, the goods and products we create, and trade, often derive from scientific advances of which we are dimly aware. Nonetheless, if we are to counteract dangers emanating from this mélange, we must understand their dimensions. Just as significant, when we compete over roles, ranks, and relationships, the strengths needed to win often derive from an ability to perform more effectively than our rivals. Thus if we are to be better physicians, we must be proficient at practicing medicine. Or if we are to be members of the upper middle class, we must understand how to avoid sliding into lower class. Similarly if we want to be loved, we require knowledge of how love is acquired. In each of these instances, we must also be able to implement what we know. A grasp of the facts is not sufficient. We have to be skilled at what we do, and frequently more skilled than the next guy.

Winning requires us to make choices, yet good choices draw upon accurate information and capable execution. Ignorance is almost as frightening as losing because ignorance tends to produce losses. When we find ourselves adrift in a sea of undifferentiated events, we

become anxious. Then, if we cannot find an exit, we become terrified. This is frequently why children become alarmed. Their mental
immaturity, in conjunction with a lack of experience, collaborates
to place them in an inferior position.[20] They are all too aware that
adults, who have a better grasp of reality, can usually defeat them.
Children are also at a disadvantage in that they are unpracticed in
applying what they know. Even if they understand what is trans-
piring, they may not be able to control events. Loving parents normally seek to compensate for these weaknesses by providing their
children what amounts to a head start. They desist from employing
their strengths so as to give their offspring room to learn.

Sadly, some parents do not.[21] Their youngsters must cope not only
with inexperience, but also with a series of ignominious setbacks.
They thus regard themselves as ignorant losers who are capable of
little else. Afterward, they carry this attitude into adulthood. Positive that they are destined to fail, they do not attempt to increase
their knowledge or augment their skills. Consequently, when they
find themselves in competition with others, they feel inadequate.
Frightened by their deficits, they withdraw into a protective shell.
Their world becomes so narrow that they never allow themselves
to encounter a serious threat or experience a significant success. In
short, they become stuck in a losing position. The way out of this
dilemma is by learning what they don't know and practicing what
they have not yet done.

Sociologists refer to ours as a Gesellschaft world.[22] We reside
in huge societies encircled by countless outsiders. We do not know
most of these people, nor do most of them know us.[23] Starting out
surrounded by our parents and siblings, we have little idea of what
exists beyond them. Indeed, we do not even know the histories
of those closest to us. Only gradually do we expand our personal
frontiers. Little by little we interact with individuals who had been
strangers, but whose nature comes into sharper focus the longer we

deal with them. For some of us, this process is attenuated. Fears of the unknown prevent us from venturing too far into virgin territory. For others, however, learning becomes a lifelong project. They never discover all there is to know because there is so much of it; nonetheless they gain a decided advantage over the stay-at-homes. Less fearful of the unfamiliar, they are better situated to intimidate more apprehensive rivals.

If courage comes from knowledge and skill, where can former cowards begin the process of bulking up? Let us start with some social facts. Not only is ours a Gesellschaft society, it is a multicultural one.[24] Those strangers do not constitute a uniform mass. They differ in important ways. Fortunately, some of these disparities can be categorized. We, for instance, routinely encounter differences in gender, social class, race, ethnicity, and sexual orientation. These are not trivial distinctions that can be waved away by insisting that one day everyone will be equal. Even if this were possible (and it is not), it is not the current state of affairs. While we are all human beings who share a common core of humanity, our biology and interpersonal histories create dissimilarities. We thus ignore these at our peril.

The feminists tell us that men and women differ only in their socialization.[25] Theoretically if boys and girls were raised the same way, only their genitals and musculature would separate them. Otherwise their abilities and inclinations would be indistinguishable. This is nonsense. Women may be as intelligent as men and as desirous of respect; even so, the way the genders think and feel is not identical.[26] To be more specific, there are overlapping normal curves wherein some women are more aggressive than some men; nonetheless, on average, men are more aggressive. Men are also, on average, less nurturing. Socialization can dilute these differences; it cannot scour them away. As a result, if men and women disregard them, heterosexual intimacy becomes difficult. Misunderstandings and conflicts are sure to arise, such that emotional closeness is threatened.

Likewise, although Marxists insist that social class is an artificial construct, it has real consequences. The upper and lower classes do not think or behave alike.[27] Moreover, these differences concern more than a disparity in wealth. They go to fundamental discrepancies in lifestyles. The poor and the rich do not eat the same foods, enjoy the same entertainments, or pray the same way. More important, the rich are liable to be better organized and more cosmopolitan. They tend to perceive themselves as leaders and hence they prepare to be leaders. The poor, on the other hand, are more concerned with avoiding subjugation. As a result, they do not aspire to the sort of education that would groom them for executive positions. This makes it difficult to engage in social mobility. It also explains many of the misgivings they experience when in contact with the rich. Conversely, an awareness of the source of their apprehensions suggests what they must learn if these are to dissipate. Once people focus on gaps in their knowledge and skill sets, they can begin the process of filling them in.

As for race, we Americans are still struggling with the aftermath of slavery.[28] We are all aware of the legacy of racism this left behind. African Americans, in particular, have been handicapped in achieving success because, for generations, they were perceived as intellectually inferior. This is a falsehood that today needs to be rectified. We, as a society, must acknowledge the roots and effects of this canard. From the white perspective, this is not only fair, but it permits the community to utilize the talents of those previously excluded. From the black perspective, it explains many of their anxieties about competing with whites. Other aspects of the culture of slavery explicate the violence, family fragility, and crime so common in inner-city neighborhoods. Although this historical inheritance does not excuse the injustices perpetrated against blacks, it points the way toward understanding and overcoming what went wrong.

Other races and ethnicities likewise possess cultural heritages that make them distinctive. As might be expected, people carry these traditions with them when they enter the marketplace.[29] This can be disconcerting to the uninformed. For instance, individuals who have been immersed in their communities of birth may find strangers threatening. If, however, they are to work together, these fears must be surmounted. This can be achieved by learning how others organize their lives. Once this occurs, what seemed bizarre loses its peculiarity. Odd customs begin to make sense and people are able to make accommodations. In the end, everyone benefits from increased awareness and trust.

Other kinds of social knowledge are also beneficial. As long as economics, politics, and religion are terra incognita, they tend to be unsettling. Why do some people make money whereas others do not? How come some politicians succeed, while others sink into oblivion? Is there a reason that people attend different churches or cleave to outlandish beliefs? In the latter case, we sometimes discount the violence once perpetrated in the name of religion.[30] Religious tolerance has been so securely woven into the fabric of our nation that we are surprised by fanaticism. In fact, the more we learn about each other's faiths, the less alarming they become. Thus, once, not long ago, we were reluctant to select a Catholic president for fear that he would be a tool of the pope. Who today, after the election of John F. Kennedy, believes that? Likewise once Jews were thought to have horns. This too is no longer credible. The upshot is that we are free to believe—or disbelieve—as we choose. We can honor each other's religions without neglecting our own.

Meanwhile, for many, economics remains enigmatic. Wall Street and large corporations are feared as menaces to our well-being.[31] Instead of figuring out how to take advantage of the free market, many people seek to restrain it. While abuses occur, regarding businesspersons as greedy vultures is a caricature. Although some may be, most are not. To be afraid of commercial competition is therefore to reduce our own opportunities. Worse yet, groundless doubts may lay the foundation for socialism. I, like many of my era, grew up believing that socialism was the best antidote to capitalistic avarice. If people looked out for each other's welfare and shared goods and services equitably, all of us would be better off. History, however, does not bear out this optimism. Wherever they have been tried, collectivist economies have failed. Everywhere, from Russia, to Cuba, to Venezuela, they produced scarcity and tyranny. No doubt capitalism has faults, but an unwillingness to understand its nature prevents their rectification.

As for political illiteracy, how many Americans abstain from participating in our democracy? Millions never vote or pay attention to political news. A little over a century ago, progressivism and the good-government movement sought to reduce political corruption.[32] Back then most voters were unaware of the widespread political payoffs or voter fraud. Instead they accepted handouts from political bosses and voted as they were told. Everyone knew that you could not fight city hall. The reformers and the muckrakers who stood up against the political machines thus exhibited real courage. Their jobs and reputations were truly in jeopardy. Today the worst of those battles have been won. Politics is cleaner than it once was. Nevertheless, the specter of demagoguery remains. The emergence of mass media made it possible to manipulate voters.[33] Promises are made that cannot be kept and people believe rather than defy the crowd. Going along to get along as become a way of life. This is easier than being an informed citizen.

Another area of knowledge crucial to becoming winners is health. Although it is a cliché to describe health as vital to success, this is nonetheless true. Curiously, many people neglect their health despite the advances of modern medicine. Afraid about what they might find, they do not go to doctors or buy reference books or consult the Internet. They do not even read the directions on medications they are prescribed. As a result, they suffer. Handicapped by chronic diseases, they have difficulty competing. Although this is a problem of their own making, they thereby compound their fears.

So much knowledge is required of us nowadays that education is more broadly institutionalized than in the past. In most economically advanced nations, instruction is mandatory through high school. A college education has also become prevalent.[34] In fact, post-graduate learning is fairly common. Individuals who hope to become powerful are aware that they need the appropriate credentials. But why? What is there about formal education that enables people to compete more effectively? What sorts of knowledge and/or skills make a difference in providing them confidence?

The former British prime minister Harold Wilson had been a Cambridge Don. He was therefore acquainted with both academe and practical politics. Consequently, when asked about the value of a college education, his reply was unexpected. The chief benefit, he explained, is that it enables people to recognize rubbish when they encounter it. Most who do not attend college are intimidated by those who do. They assume that university graduates acquire an arcane knowledge that allows them to succeed. In truth, those who obtain advanced degrees discover that much of what they are taught is irrelevant. Although acquiring some of this demands superior abilities, much is aimless nonsense. Accordingly, they are not intimidated by pretentious gobbledygook. Now able to see through it, they have the courage to stand their ground when others play the knowledge card.

What then does college teach? What acquired in four, or more, years of classroom lessons is worth knowing?[35] Many parents regard universities as technical institutes. These are thought to impart specialized skills that will make their children employable. To some extent this is true. Doctors, nurses, and engineers are imbued with a professional expertise not available elsewhere. Moreover, the amount of information can be so daunting that it takes years of concentrated effort to master. Unless students apply themselves, they will not make the grade. Likewise, beginners are provided practice in putting what they learn into action. Would-be physicians are exposed to patients and would-be engineers are asked to solve simulated problems. In the end, these students gain the confidence to perform tasks that others cannot. This provides an edge in important endeavors.

Most college students, however, acquire a different sort of advantage. They become generalists, as opposed to specialists. Universities boast about inculcating "critical thinking." Their graduates supposedly learn how to evaluate information so as to make informed choices. Precisely because they have been taught to separate the wheat from the chafe, they make fewer mistakes. This too instills confidence, while simultaneously intimidating those who cannot keep up. Another way to understand this is that college graduates become independent thinkers.[36] Later on, they will not require close supervision because they can figure things out for themselves. In short, they become self-directed decision makers. Personally motivated to do a good job, they know where to look for data, as well as how to put it together.[37] As a consequence, they are competent problem solvers. Aware that they can handle threats, they are less fearful of them.

Learning about history or science widens a person's perspective. Correspondingly, reading literature and studying psychology provide insights into human behavior. On a more general level, becoming a skilled reader opens a universe of possibilities. People who are not overawed by the written word have a place to go when they do not have answers.[38] They thereby take advantage of what others have learned. This enables them to figure out what to do in situations that they have not previously encountered. As a result, they can handle leadership roles. They can be trusted to provide appropriate direction for others. Good leaders are aware of their limitations, yet they are also aware of their comparative strengths. Thus, when confronted with uncertainty and/or determined opposition, they do not turn and run. Buoyed by demonstrable abilities, they are prepared to take on tough challenges.

College teaches another important skill. Undergraduates are required not only to read but also to write.[39] Most academic courses ask students to pass written exams and turn in research papers. Literary proficiency is rarely demanded, whereas organization and clarity are. Practice at meeting these standards instills an ability to engage in effective communication. Leaders must not only make good decisions, they have to make decisions that are understood. If they cannot, then however brilliant their thinking, it will not make a difference. Our techno-commercial society depends on teamwork, whereas teamwork relies on shared information. Indecipherable memos waste everyone's time. Conversely, clarity, whether orally or on paper, is persuasive. As a consequence, collaborative projects are more likely to turn out well.

Of course, no matter how much we know, or how skillful we become, defeat is possible. None of us win all of the time. Courage is about improving the odds. The bravest of us have doubts. Nevertheless knowledge is power because it facilitates effective planning and self-assured action. Our fears don't disappear, yet a record of premeditated success can tame the worst of them.

ALLIANCES

In old-fashioned Westerns, the lone cowboy rode into town in the first reel and rode off in the last after having saved the community. A crack shot who also possessed fists of steel, no villain could stand up against him. On top of this, he could out-think everyone. James Bond was cut from the same cloth. These champions worked alone.

Nothing ruffled their demeanor or deterred them from single-handed heroics. Moreover, they invariably won. Despite a myriad of close calls, they were seldom injured. Without getting a hair out of place, they demonstrated uncanny insights and unsurpassed fighting abilities. Totally self-reliant, except for a fast horse, a trusty six-shooter, or a state-of-the-art sports car, they saved their bacon on their own.

We, in the audience, love these adventures. We marvel at the brazen courage and thrill to the derring-do. Would that we were like that. If only we could be Superman—or perhaps Batman. If we possessed their powers, we too would perform noble deeds. We too would save the world and draw universal acclaim. But, alas, we are not superheroes. Even if we can whip entire armies in computer games, in real life we have trouble handling our bosses and spouses. We just don't measure up. Despite our fantasies, we need help.

In fact, everyone does. The lone hero is a myth. While it is comforting to imagine that we might solve every problem independently, no one can. Happily, courage does not require self-sufficiency. We humans are social creatures. Our greatest achievements result from collective efforts. The same applies when we compete for roles, ranks, and relationships. Tests of strength are not always between individuals.[40] People can contend with each other as members of groups. Indeed, individuals are usually at a disadvantage when arrayed against cohesive alliances. One of the surest ways to become powerful is thus to belong to a successful coalition. With others by our side, we are in much less danger.

People who feel like cowards generally lacked reliable allies while they were growing up. Instead of being able to call on dependable protection, they found themselves alone when dealing with their families and friends. To become winners, they must therefore find a way out of this isolation. The best means of doing so is politics.[41] Politics is the art of assembling and mobilizing coalitions to achieve particular ends. Individuals who are able to bring others together, or who can recruit existing alliances to specific causes, thereby amplify their strengths. Although they may be small and weak, or even less clever than others, they can still achieve victory. As a consequence, politics is ubiquitous. Not just in governments, but in families, economic institutions, and social organizations, they determine who will win and what will be done. It consequently behooves those who aspire to personal confidence to become politically adept.

I learned this the hard way. While I was working as a vocational counselor, I was so convinced of my personal superiority that I assumed I could win every battle. In my estimation, I was smarter and better educated than my colleagues. When it came to writing memos, these would surely be so articulate, so well reasoned, that no one could deny their validity. Imagine my surprise when these missives backfired. Why did my administrators, who should have known the truth, line up against me? It never occurred to me that they might find me arrogant. Yes, I was smart, but there were more of them and they held superior organizational positions. I did not stand a chance.

It took months for me to realize why I could not win. Having grown up on the lone cowboy myth, it never dawned on me that people need allies. For me, depending on others felt like an admission of weakness. Besides, my personal experience argued that other people were unreliable. To place my fate in their hands would therefore have been suicidal. It took time to comprehend that not everyone is the same. Part of being successful is, in fact, being able to distinguish the good guys from the bad ones, the dependable ones from the undependable. Because people differ, it is crucial to ascertain their strengths and weaknesses, and above all their motives. If they are to be recruited to shared causes, it is essential to know what they can and are willing to do. If they are regarded as indistinguishable, it is impossible to inspire them to provide help.

For my own part, I was oblivious of the motives of the administrators I needed as allies. Because discovering their goals seemed irrelevant, I was unaware that they found my memo campaign unsettling. If I had been a smart as I thought I was, I would have realized this. I would not have allowed my fears, or my egotism, to cloud my judgment. Winners are attuned to the needs and aspirations of others. They make adjustments accordingly. If they are to be confident that they can quell social dangers, they need to be socially astute. They must, for instance, be able to make concessions that attract friends. This often entails respecting their weaknesses, exploiting their strengths, and satisfying their aspirations. If this includes giving up something to get something, the bargain may be well worth it.

England's King John did not understand this.[42] Not only did he alienate Robin Hood, but he estranged the aristocrats he needed to survive. Often he was so selfish that he trampled on their rights, and hence they refused to come to his aid when he went to war with the king of France. The upshot was that most of England's continental possessions were lost. John was so humbled that he had to accede to the Magna Carta. In fact, in theory, he was later compelled to forfeit his realm to the pope.

Once I realized the importance of alliances, I changed my attitude toward my colleagues. It was not a question of defeating each in turn, but of creating networks that could be called upon as needed. Thus when I became a college professor I made sure to cultivate congenial associates. If we could establish communities of interest, we could help each other to promote these. As it happened, these associations proved crucial to my organizational survival. When the time came to seek tenure, I made the mortifying discovery that my department chair was an enemy. Despite the fact that I assisted her to obtain her position, she was determined to get me fired.

What was I to do? First off I realized that she was a foe. Even as she was dressing me down, I kept my head and did not share information that she might use against me. Second, I gauged her alliances. Who were her friends and what were they prepared to do on her behalf? Then I looked to my friends and evaluated their attitudes. These were the folks I subsequently consulted. They were the ones with whom I strategized. In the end, it was the strengths they brought to bear in my defense that won me tenure. This was a revelation. It was also an enormous confidence builder. I could protect myself from social aggression as long as I was politically shrewd. What I could not do on my own, I could do if I understood whom I could trust. It was not merely my own abilities, but theirs that mattered.

Neither courage nor winning, derive from superhuman strengths. People who have been cowards are usually unmindful of this. Because they are unable to muster the power to ward off every incursion, they assume that they are personally defective. This is an error. No one is that formidable. It is not necessary to be the most potent person in the neighborhood in order to be safe. Exploiting one's own abilities, while supplementing them with trustworthy allies, is generally sufficient.

SELF-SABOTAGE

Last, but far from least, courageous people must learn not to defeat themselves. Too often, individuals who are accustomed to losing try to soften the expected blows by becoming less intimidating. They assume that if they ask for less, they will be denied less frequently. Meanwhile, if they display their weaknesses, they expect to forestall retaliation—and perhaps generate sympathy. Like lower-status wolves that show their underbellies to alpha animals so as to preclude attack, they believe that if they are subservient, dominant individuals will take pity on them. This way they may not win, but they will lose less badly.

Sadly, this is not the usual denouement. People who believe that they must allow themselves to be defeated in order to avoid being trounced are liable to suffer an unending string of defeats. Not only are the bullies not sated by a perpetually flown flag of surrender, but they usually regard it as a cue to take out their frustrations. The object of their malice is then likely to intensify his self-punitive conduct so that his peaceful intensions cannot be mistaken. This, however, degenerates into a downward spiral of degradation and despair. Losing is not the best avenue toward victory. The price of warding off aggression by preempting it is generally far too high.

Even if people feel like losers, they should not act as if they are. Self-sabotage is self-defeating and unnecessary. AA's "fake it till you make it" admonition pertains here. Pretending to be a winner will not make us one, but it can discourage random aggression. Furthermore, the equivalent of whistling a happy tune while walking past the graveyard may indeed provide courage. Not only might others fail to suspect that we are afraid, we may forget that we are afraid as well. In time, phony confidence can become the real thing. This advice is not new. I did not invent it. I merely repeat it because it has so frequently been verified in practice.

Fear that is not self-sabotaging often provides the energy to win battles. It is a powerful motivator and an unrivaled muse. Moderately frightened people see things that others don't and try things others can't imagine. Determined not to lose, they explore every avenue toward success. As long as they are neither panicked nor unduly conciliatory, they can be persistent and creative. This is why athletes want to be hyped up. It is why warriors need to be alert. Without fear, neither would care about winning. Controlled fear is a weapon. The point of describing courage as "grace under pressure" is to emphasis the value of disciplined anxiety. Conversely, when fears are so deeply repressed that they are not felt, people only go through the motions. It is as if they were anesthetized, with their senses dulled and their responses blunted. Why would we want to do this to ourselves?

This said, there is no need to overcome all of our fears. As long as we are able to deal with those that prevent us from being happy, we can keep some deeply buried. In this case, we can develop work-arounds and security blankets. This will enable us to do what we must, while at the same time avoiding dangers that we prefer to circumvent. Although this may cause discomfort, it can prevent us from attempting more than we have the time or energy to achieve.

John Madden provided the classic example of a work-around. As a Super Bowl–winning football coach and popular television commentator, he had a more productive career than most of us manage. Nevertheless, he was deathly afraid of flying in businesses that require a great deal of travel. His solution was to take the train. This was extremely inconvenient and subtracted valuable time from his busy schedule; nevertheless, the strategy succeeded. It got him where he needed to go. Madden did not have to force himself to overcome his fear of planes; the railroad enabled him to do his job without resorting to an expedient he dreaded.

Other fears can also be sidestepped. People who are afraid of blood do not have to become doctors. They can become lawyers instead. Likewise people who are terrified of speaking in public do not have to be trial lawyers. They can work behind the scenes. Thus, if they live in Britain, they can decide to be solicitors rather than bar-risters. Similarly if they love show business but suffer from debili-tating stage fright, they can take jobs as directors or screenwriters. As the old saw has it, there is more than one way to skin a cat. Per-sonal success is available through a variety of avenues; hence fears that block one sort of approach might be irrelevant to another.

In some cases, we do not have to evade a fear so much as fortify ourselves when we encounter it. We can, as it were, acquire safe places that we carry around with us. These security blankets may provide enough protection to get us through a frightening patch without falling apart. For example, many people need their morning cup of coffee if they are to endure the prospect of an otherwise-intimidating day. For others, they cannot cope without a glass of wine at dinner. Still others find it impossible to calm down if they are unable to munch on a chocolate bar. Although these may be regarded as "crutches," if they allow us to get off the sidelines, they serve a useful purpose. The problem is that they can be overdone. That glass of wine can transform into an alcohol addiction. Security blankets must therefore be employed with care. A lucky rabbit's foot or a quick glance at a fortune cookie will not destroy our future. They might even improve it. On the other hand, littering our homes with thousands of irrelevant mementos could make it impossible to find an important document when we need it. Caution is thus recommended.

Chapter 9

SAVING OURSELVES

THE COLLECTIVIST TRAP

Ａll of us are scared some of the time. Things go wrong and we don't know how to respond. Aware of our weaknesses, we lose confidence in our ability to cope. At such moments, many of us dream of a trustworthy protector coming to our rescue. A father or mother figure of unrivaled compassion and strength will swoop in to protect us from harm. Just as when we were very small, we will be enfolded in caring arms and sheltered from the storm. We will not have to do anything to defend ourselves. We will not even have to understand the threat or mobilize an effective resistance. Everything will be arranged for us.

A desire to be saved is widespread. It is an appealing alternative to courage in a world chockablock full of dangers. In massive societies, such as our own, so much is happening that no one can keep track of all goings-on.[1] Understanding everyone's motives is an impossibility, as is developing alliances with them all. Nor is there any telling where every hazard might lurk. And—it is important to note—our dependence on others heightens our vulnerability. Inhabitants of techno-commercial communities have no choice but to trust others.[2] If we did not, paranoia would shadow us with every bite of food we took and every step we made when crossing the street.

No wonder we question our abilities. After all, they are limited. What then to do? If we can't be James Bond, perhaps we can persuade a James Bond stand-in to act as our bodyguard. This sort of thinking is not novel. When we were hunter-gatherers, we depended on family and friends to protect us. We knew them and trusted their intentions. Even so, we prayed to our ancestors to supplement their assistance. Then too there were the spirits of the forests and streams.[3] Likewise unseen, it was believed that if we could recruit them to our side, they would operate on our behalf behind the scenes.

As societies grew in size, our deities grew in power. Soon an all-powerful God was available to save us.[4] As long as we followed his instructions, he would grant us eternal life and everlasting happiness. Always on call to heed our prayers, in the final analysis he would provide an environment in which harm was not possible. Indeed, a cadre of his earthly minions vouchsafed these assurances. Priests and bishops sanctified to his service guaranteed salvation to the faithful. Specially designed rituals beseeched his intercession and reminded congregations of his power and commandments.

The idea of religious salvation is still with us.[5] Billions of people rely on it to organize their lives. Beset by a myriad of challenges, they find comfort in knowing what lies ahead. Because they are unable to make sense of everything that goes wrong, religion provides them a guidebook. With their faith certified by both the community and prestigious leaders, the devout trust in these assurances. Such promises furnish the courage to deal with tragedies. It is as if they have allies of impeccable strength and unwavering devotion. Whether or not such creeds are true, faith imbues them with enormous power. Religious individuals often display indisputable courage in the face of appalling burdens. After placing their fate in the hands of an unseen being, they feel saved—which to some degree they are. Although the dangers they fear may not be nullified, they acquire the equanimity to act as if they were.

Nonetheless, ever since the first stirrings of the Industrial Revolution,[6] religion has been under siege. Alternate sources of salvation have arisen to compete for preeminence. One of these is the economic marketplace. Throughout most of history people have lived on the brink of disaster. Disease and starvation prowled just around the corner. Then science and commerce came to the rescue. Ways to grow more food and deliver it where it was needed were developed. Medicine too improved so significantly that life expectancy soared. People came to expect improvements in their personal condition. Whatever went wrong today might be fixed tomorrow.

The engine of these hopes was industry and commerce. A new world of possibilities opened up when people were freed to pursue unprecedented innovations. Once the traditionalist hands of the church and the aristocratic state were lifted, a plethora of advances tumbled forth. Individuals in pursuit of their own interests started companies dedicated to fabricating recently invented products. Machine-produced textiles flooded the market, soon to be followed by steel, railroads, and telephones.[7] The possibilities were endless. As long as the free market was kept free, there was no telling what might follow. This perspective, that is, laissez-faire economics, promised a fresh route to salvation. The subsequent progress might one day make every man (or woman) a king.

Nowadays, libertarians champion this outlook. They believe in a pumped-up version of Adam Smith's "invisible hand." Smith argued that the prices of goods and services were set in the give-and-take of the marketplace.[8] As long as these were allowed to operate unfettered, they would keep supply and demand in balance. No superior intelligence, certainly not one coming from the government, was necessary. Libertarians expanded this thesis to include the regularly improved quality of the goods and services. We are now told that we can have the best of all possible worlds if we simply allow social forces to operate unhindered. This then will be our salvation. All of our lives will be enhanced if we simply allow human talents to flourish unimpeded. People merely need the courage to participate in the marketplace.

A third path to salvation is not so sanguine. Its proponents do not trust the motives of businesspeople. They assume that greed invariably gets out of hand. When individuals are allowed to follow their unchecked interests, they tend to accumulate more than their fair share. Wealthy merchants and industrial tycoons care not a fig about the welfare of others. As a result, they are exploiters. Even though they become wealthy, those who work for them are trampled in the dust. The proof of this came once modern corporations arose.[9] Behemoth industrialists, such as John D. Rockefeller,[10] Andrew Carnegie,[11] and J. P. Morgan,[12] crushed the life out of anyone who dared to oppose them. Whether they cornered the market in oil, steel, or finance, they dictated the terms others followed. The notion that the market always arrives at a reasonable balance was demonstrated to be absurd.

Little more than a century ago this distrust of free enterprise coalesced into the Progressive movement.[13] Under the aegis of the muckrakers, the public became aware of the dangers of monopoly. When companies grew to unparalleled proportions, they could rig prices, corrupt public officials, and drive competitors out of business. Although Rockefeller lowered the price of kerosene, Carnegie built lending libraries for the poor, and Morgan prevented financial panics, their power was so great that the potential abuses were terrifying. Something had to be done. Under the leadership of the likes of Teddy Roosevelt, it was. The trusts were split apart, local governments were reformed, and federal regulations ensured that meat and drugs would be safe. Politicians intent on protecting the public interest thereby chained the colossus.

Now the government became the source of salvation. Its ability to rescue ordinary Americans was confirmed by the arrival of the Great Depression.[14] President Herbert Hoover had dithered, whereas his successor, Franklin D. Roosevelt, took decisive action. He closed the banks, instituted price controls, and put the unemployed to work on public projects. FDR stood up against the malefactors of great wealth, while putting a finger on the bargaining scale to favor labor unions. These programs set the stamp for the next generation. Thus, when civil rights were endangered, the federal government stepped in to see that the laws were impartially enforced. And when poverty became an issue, President Lyndon B. Johnson declared war against it.[15] Soon it was taken for granted that whether an evil concerned crime, education, or the environment, federal regulations were essential. In addition, social justice demanded a redistribution of wealth and power. A free marketplace could not be permitted to tread on the rights of women and minorities.

In many quarters, it became an article of faith that any perceived wrong required government rectification. If people could not save themselves, the power of the state must be enlisted to do what they could not. It all made sense. History had established how much the federal authorities could accomplish. Furthermore, because we were a democracy, the people were ultimately in charge. Government power would not be abused because those affected by it controlled it. Events, however, demonstrated that this was naïve.[16] Lord Acton's dictum that power corrupts applied to the government as much as to businesspeople.

As the federal authority expanded, so did the bureaucracies that implemented its regulations. These soon encompassed hundreds of thousands of functionaries who were jealous of their prerogatives. This problem was compounded by the congressional tendency to delegate regulative powers. Because the legislators could not foresee every contingency, they allowed those who enforced the laws to make adjustments at their own discretion. Often overseen by no one but themselves, they erected protective barriers around their baronies. Thus the Veterans Administration could hide long waiting periods by concocting phony waiting lists;[17] the Internal Revenue Service could deny tax protections to organizations that supported political rivals;[18] and the Environmental Protection Agency could put entire industries out of business, even fining family farms for unregulated mud puddles.[19]

Government bureaucracies grew so arrogant that they stone-walled congressional committees, misled internal watchdogs, and told bald-faced lies to journalists. These alleged saviors were evidently more intent on saving themselves than others. No matter how badly they performed their missions, their writ became self-perpetuating. Employees of these agencies were never fired and their incompetence was covered up by additional appropriations.[20] Worse still, in enlarging their mandate, they confiscated power that arguably belonged to ordinary citizens. Millions grew dependent upon government handouts, while millions more were so over-regulated that personal responsibility ceased to have meaning. If people were being saved, it was at the expense of individual discretion.[21] A belief that only bureaucratic experts could make valid choices inspired efforts to remove every vestige of decision making from the public. People could not even determine how much soda to drink or whether to allow their children to walk home unaccompanied from the park.

The irony of this trend was that people were discouraged from saving themselves. Now they were to trust in authorities that neither knew nor cared about them. Of course, these functionaries professed to care, but anyone in contact with them realized that their primary concern was in obtaining more power and security for themselves.[22] Unfortunately, in abdicating responsibility, people failed to do what only they could. They ceased promoting their careers or personal relationships. Local knowledge and motives, exclusive to them, no longer guided efforts to protect them and their loved ones.

Whether our salvation is entrusted solely to the church, the free market, or the government, we are bound to suffer. When we do not do what only we can, we allow others to place their interests above ours. Obviously, when we take charge, we can make mistakes.

Given our limitations, we often succumb to foolishness. The political scientist Cass Sunstein[23] argues that this means we must be protected by external expertise. Nonetheless the government, churches, and businesses also make mistakes; and when they do, these affect more people. Still when we mess up, we are to blame. Dealing with these blunders therefore takes courage. Clearly, if we are to do our best, we must be accountable. If we aren't, whether or not we are rescued becomes a hit-or-miss proposition. In other words, if cowardice impels us to abdicate our responsibilities, we do not have the right to complain after things go wrong. Having ceded control, it is we who have put chance in the saddle.

THE MIDDLE-CLASS FRONTIER

The families to which we belong can often protect us.[24] If we, as adults, are loved, our spouses, siblings, and cousins may rush to our defense. They can provide physical and moral support in times of need. If we are treasured as children, our parents will keep us fed, clothed, and sheltered. They can also provide fundamental guidance. The security that affectionate families afford is not inconsiderable. But neither is it absolute. There are times when we will be on our own and therefore dependent on our own resources. As a consequence, loving parents are wise to prepare their offspring to be self-reliant.

Our religions may also protect us. In making sense of a perplexing universe, they can assist us in deciding how to live. They may also provide consolation in moments of crisis. Believers are able to take comfort even in the face of death; they *know* they are not alone. Market economies may be comparably protective. By facilitating our prosperity, they provide the material resources with which to deal with innumerable hazards. The free market also allows people to make choices about how to support themselves and their families. Governments similarly protect us. They too can provide critical resources. Democracies, in particular, tend to supply a safety net intended to avert personal disaster.

In all of these cases, we can be rescued by external sources. None of them, however, provides unconditional protection. While we may be saved from specific threats, our happiness is not guaranteed. There are always gaps. The rest is therefore up to us. If we do not possess the courage to step into the breach, it will not be closed. The boy who cried wolf did not receive help because he bellowed too many false alarms. Likewise, people who are forever asking to be bailed out are often left in the lurch because others grow tired of defending them. These folks have their own lives. Moreover, if they are sensible, they will not allow clinging vines to suffocate them. That leaves us to take up the slack. We must be able to do for ourselves what our predecessors did for themselves.

Once our ancestors braved the unknown.[25] They crossed a continent strewn with lethal obstacles. They traversed storm-tossed seas to begin a new life among strangers. These people had to count upon themselves. They required sturdy independence, even as the collaborated to build the most powerful nation on Earth. No doubt they were often frightened. No doubt they made serious mistakes. Yet they recovered and moved forward. We can too. We, their descendants, are no less blessed with the stuff of which courage is made. Our challenges may be different, but these too can be overcome.

As earlier noted, we face a middle-class frontier.[26] This is a unique challenge. No other peoples have ever encountered identical difficulties. Nevertheless, our problems are not entirely dissimilar from those our ancestors. They too were dealing with an array of ambiguities. What, for instance, lay over the next mountain? Would there be water to grow crops or grass to pasture cattle? Would outlaws or hostile natives bar the path? They could not be sure. Or if they disembarked at Ellis Island, would they be allowed entrance into the Promised Land? Would the inhabitants be friendly or jobs be available? How could they know? Because they could not, they had to take their chances and adjust as they went along. We are in a similar position. Our society has been changing so rapidly that we cannot be sure of what lies ahead. We too cannot be certain about how we will support ourselves or protect our families.

Ours is the first primarily middle-class society in the history of the world.[27] In former times, there were the rich and the poor—with most people numbered among the latter. Yet ask virtually any American to identify his or her social class and the answer will be: the middle class. This may not always be true. Some people are lower down. Still, their reply confirms the preeminence of the middling order. After all, it is these folks who set the nation's standards. They are the ones who stipulate its values and dictate its fashions. Nowadays the rich dress like the middle class, while the poor aspire to join their ranks. Meanwhile politicians pander to them. The country's prosperity is said to depend on increasing their affluence. Once the yeoman farmer was the social ideal. Today it is the working person—defined not as a laborer, but as a skilled expert.

Even so, how are we to behave as members of the middle class? This is a more difficult question than is often realized. It is not merely a matter of accumulating money. Poor people who win the lottery do not suddenly rise in status. Being middle-class entails a style of life.[28] But what is its character and how is it acquired? The millions of Americans currently engaged in upward mobility are finding out. They are discovering that if they are to be successful they must acquire attitudes and abilities foreign to their ancestors. Indeed, they must become a new sort of person. How they think and behave differs from previous generations. While there were precursors, never before has this orientation been as widespread or influential.

Our mass techno-commercial society could not operate without competent experts. Without millions of people capable of making independent decisions, its factories would stop running and truckloads of goods and services would never arrive at market. If there were no engineers to design bridges, bankers to finance products, doctors to increase life expectancy, computer programmers to systematize assembly lines, and marketers to attract customers, then the grand edifice would collapse. Absent the specialists that maintain our infrastructure, facilitate communications, and organize complex projects, we could not sustain ourselves. We would literally perish. We could surely not live in the same degree of comfort as we now do.

All of this is possible because members of the middle calling are becoming professionalized.[29] More of them than ever are developing into self-motivated experts. As a result, they know how to perform complex tasks autonomously. They can thus modify what they do without a boss telling them how. Still, no one is born an electronic engineer. It takes years of dedicated schooling to master the intricacies of this specialty. A person must also have superior mechanical, mathematical, and practical abilities for these to be learned. He or she likewise needs to put in the effort. Attending classes will make little difference if additional hours are not spent in study. In the end, a newly minted engineer knows what others do not. Furthermore, after years on the job, his or her competence increases. Unlike yesterday's peasants, he or she will be able to design a radar system that prevents airplanes from falling out of the sky.

Even so, this is insufficient to be professional. Professionals must care about what they do. If they don't effectively apply what they know, their knowledge will go for naught. Professionals must therefore be capable of self-supervision. Because they usually know more about their specializations than their bosses do, their assignments won't be done satisfactorily unless they are dedicated to performing them well. Imagine going to the doctor for a major complaint and discovering the she does not care whether you live or die. Imagine that her sole concern is with winning the approval of her superior. Would you want to visit this physician a second time? If she were not personally motivated to help, would you trust her? The same goes for the engineer commissioned to build a bridge. Would we have faith in his designs if he were indifferent to their structural integrity? And how about the police officer on the beat? If he is a bully who is not committed to fair law enforcement, should we allow him on the streets?

In a massive techno-commercial society, where we are dependent on the technical competence of millions of strangers, we must have confidence in their abilities and dedication. Were these in question, we would feel in danger almost every hour of the day. The electricity powering our TVs might go out without warning, automobiles would crash into each other when their tires blew, and our food supply would be so tainted that we would need our stomachs pumped several times a year. Of course, things can go wrong, yet not nearly as often as they would if those upon whom we depend were not professionalized. We trust them because they have been educated in their vocations and certified as proficient in their execution.

We expect professionals and semiprofessionals to make competent decisions and make them unaided. This, however, is not easy. Complexity introduces uncertainties.[30] The more complicated a task is, the easier it is to make a mistake. Those who perform important specialties know this. They are all too aware of their humanity. To illustrate, my wife studies medial error. Many of her investigations concern the medication lapses committed by nurses. Indeed, among her most salient discoveries is how much nurses care about avoiding missteps. Most are consumed with guilt even when their slipups do not have negative consequences. As medical professionals, they realize how serious a blunder could be and hence they tremble at their shortcomings. Still, they keep on working. Surrounded by uncertainties, somehow they find the courage to continue doing their best.

Self-directed decision makers, and this is what professionals are, cannot afford to be cowards. Given their responsibilities, they routinely risk making dreadful miscalculations. They must therefore find the wherewithal to master their fears. Accordingly, they learn that they must be clearheaded if they are to make appropriate choices. Happily, for the most part, they do. Indeed, were this not the case, our mortality rates would soar. The question nevertheless remains: How do they achieve this? Where do they find the equanimity? Nowadays many millions of specialists obviously discover the bravery to forge ahead. Not unlike their pioneer ancestors, they exhibit the gumption to enter unknown territory. As a consequence, were they incapable of conquering their apprehensions, the outcomes might be disastrous. If this were the case, would we allow them to hold a scalpel or to arrest miscreants? Clearly, despite our complaints, for the most part, we trust them.

So again I ask: Where do people find the courage to be self-directed professionals? If they were more concerned with being saved than with serving others, ought they be trusted? Moreover, if they do not have the ability to make competent decisions independently, what enables them cope with the challenges thrown up by a middle-class society? One thing is certain; cowards do not deserve our confidence. If they run away when they are in doubt, they are apt to leave us in the lurch. Any modern society that does not produce enough citizens with the ability to be self-directed will thus not long survive. It must succumb to chaos, ineptitude, and external pressures. Unable to feed its people, protect them from disease, or fend off aggressive neighbors, it would sink into oblivion. The choice is therefore between developing the courage to be middle-class or accepting utter failure.

SELF-DIRECTION

When I was in the fifth grade, I was shocked when I read my report card. Up to this point I had received outstanding grades in virtually every subject. But now there was a category marked satisfactory. What was more, I did not understand its meaning. Why did the teacher write that I was merely average in *Initiative*? What was "initiative"? When I found out, I was angry. How could I be marked down for doing what I had been told to do? Why, just because I didn't break the rules, was I going to be punished? This was not fair!

Many years later, when I was employed at the psychiatric hospital, a wall of photographs depicting the employees of the month initially impressed me. These, I thought, must be the most important members of the team. Nonetheless, I couldn't have been more wrong. Once I got to know these folks, I realized that most of them were nice people. But they weren't leaders. They never rocked the boat. They almost always did as they were asked. The people with influence were different. They did not require a pat on the head. Nor were they distressed if others did not like them. Prepared to be demanding, they were also prepared to deal with pushback.

Self-directed people must show initiative. They do not always wait to be told what to do. In addition, because they make independent decisions, they can tell others what to do. The result is that self-motivated experts become leaders. And as leaders, they make waves.[31] As least some of the time, they tell others what they do not want to hear. If they understand what they others don't, they must occasionally change the directions they are taking. Likewise, if they possess skills that others lack, they may need to take control. This can cause discomfort. They may be required to do it anyway. Despite resistance, the best outcome often depends on them pressing forward.

Few of us like to be disliked. Not only are we uncomfortable when we make others uncomfortable, but we fear a negative response. What if these folks fight back? What if their hostility makes us a pariah? Professional persons have to take this chance. If they are to be self-directed experts, they must sometimes make decisions that others disapprove. If they don't, if they invariably go along to get along, the consequences could be calamitous. Doing the wrong thing in order to avoid conflict is usually a prescription for folly. They must, therefore, pull up their socks and assert their priority. This sort of courage has grown ever more critical as societies have become larger and more complex.

Self-directed people must thus trust in their own judgment.[32] If they are genuine experts, they have to stand up for their expertise. If they know what they know, and also what they don't, they ought not be ashamed of asserting their convictions. Of course, everyone's competence has limits; hence errors are inevitable. Nonetheless more mistakes are made when a false modesty prevails. This means that self-directed professionals can expect disagreement. Others who know less may not realize that they know less. On the other hand, although a professional's opinions deserve respect, rubber-stamping their views is a serious miscalculation. Their subordinates too could be right. As a result, they too have a right to an opinion. The upshot is that conflict is unavoidable. If so, the courage to endure differences is essential.

Leaders must likewise take responsibility for their decisions. First of all, they must put in the effort to get things right. If they are careless, they are not being conscientious. Nonetheless, when they screw up, they must be prepared to accept the blame. They have to be willing to admit their errors. More than this, they must attempt to fix what went wrong. Should they recognize that their efforts have gone astray, they need to figure out what miscarried and how this might be rectified. Then they must implement their new plans and monitor the results to determine if they have succeeded. To do less is irresponsible.

This said, experienced leaders must realize that they have a special expertise and therefore should reject automatic accusations of incompetence. They ought not assume that they are losers merely because they have been reproached for making a mistake. For example, in baseball, a batting average of 300 is outstanding, even though this means that more than two times out of three a player goes hitless. Life too is a matter of averages. As a consequence, none of us should feel terrified by the prospect of messing up. Although our blunders demonstrate that we are not perfect, a lack of perfection does not imply that we should never take chances.

Self-directed people take risks. As a result, they can be creative. They are thus able to do the unexpected. The upshot is that they may solve problems that had not previously been solved. Nonetheless, they can go too far. In their hubris, they can overestimate their abilities. What is important is that they be honest with themselves and others. If they assess reality for what it is, including their missteps, they will probably not go too far astray. While it is crucial that they defend themselves from unfair allegations, they need to listen to what others say. After all, these folks could be right. Leaders must thus be prepared to investigate the facts. In short, they have to be willing to learn. No one, no matter how expert, is immune to error. But neither should they lose status merely because they are fallible. It is a question of percentages. If professional people know more than others, they should not be diverted from implementing their capabilities.

Self-directed individuals must also be self-disciplined. They have to be able to complete disagreeable tasks. Not everything that needs doing is fun. Some educators insist that learning should always be enjoyable. Only this, they tell us, can motivate disengaged students. Would that this were true. If it were, almost everyone would pursue a higher education. In fact, some abilities require effort to master.[33] They may also require effort to practice. Perhaps what needs doing is tedious; perhaps it is mentally fatiguing. In any event, some things must be undertaken whatever our personal mood. The tensile strength of a bridge, for instance, has to be accurately calculated. A book's bibliography must likewise be conscientiously compiled. If these tasks are not embarked upon despite their difficulty, the job will not be done. Comforting oneself that one could have completed them, if one had so desired, is not sufficient. As they say in Britain: It butters no parsnips.

Self-discipline demands self-control. There are times when we have to force ourselves to do what we prefer to pass over. How, for instance, are we to feed ourselves if we refuse to tend our garden? And can we be winners if we decline to run the race? Self-control may be difficult, but as psychologists have demonstrated, people who are unable to delay gratification are seldom successful. If they cannot prevent themselves from eating dessert before the main course, in the end they often starve to death.

Self-direction and emotional maturity are inseparable. Without the latter, there cannot be the former. People who are incapable of controlling their anger are bound to get angry at the wrong person at the wrong time.[34] They make terrible choices because they plunge into unwinnable battles. Similarly, people who are consumed by guilt punish themselves whenever they encounter opposition. At the slightest whiff of disagreement, they rebuke their alleged impertinence. Likewise, those who love with unrestrained passion are apt to attract bullies and exploiters. They do not pursue important goals because they do not want to offend others.

An inability to restrain imprudent impulses can be ruinous. Unrestrained passions preclude competent self-direction. They forfeit intelligent choice to childish impetuosity. Whatever a person's expertise, it will have flown out the window, mortgaged to caprice. As we will soon see, George Armstrong Custer was just such a person.[35] The last thing courageous people want to do is emulate his emotional liability.

Clearly, a lack of self-direction is inimical to being effectively middle-class. It interferes with establishing occupational success or familial stability. Although self-direction can be frightening, its absence is more so. Making independent choices in an uncertain environment exposes us to slipups. Not making them, however, invites other persons—who might not be friendly—to make them for us. The most reasonable course is thus to prepare ourselves to make good decisions. While not foolproof, this reduces our vulnerabilities.

THE OCCUPATIONAL FRONTIER

Once upon a time the sons of farmers became farmers. Actually, for millennia most of them were peasants who did not own the land they plowed. There were therefore few ways for these folks to improve their status. Later, many people became factory workers. They tended machines while being overseen by demanding foremen. A majority of these folks hoped that they would find remunerative life-time employment. The corporation would thus shelter them from the vicissitudes of the marketplace. Times have changed. My father was one of those caught in the maelstrom of these accelerating transformations. As technology changed, he found that he could not keep up. Betrayed by his educational and emotional limitations, he was forcibly retired before he desired.

Our techno-commercial society is awash with occupational choices and therefore with opportunities.[36] Farmers now constitute less than 2 percent of the population. Meanwhile, manufacturing jobs have also disappeared. Less than 10 percent of workers occupy them. And of these, many entail dealing with automation. Conversely, managerial jobs have exploded. There are more of these than there are factory openings. There are also millions of slots in the legal, financial, engineering, educational, and medical arenas.

These, however, come with a price. Their occupants need more than a strong back. Because these jobs entail working with people and data, they demand unprecedented levels of expertise and emotional maturity. They may also require the flexibility to change jobs or move to different parts of the country.

With so many different niches available, it is likewise difficult to select the appropriate one. Making this process even more challenging is that our young people are unaware of the possibilities. Perhaps they know what some of their relatives do for a living. Perhaps Mom and Dad brought their work home or took them to the office on school holidays. How, on the other hand, can they understand the hundreds of thousands of jobs with which they have never had contact? How do they even know what these are? Clearly what they see on television is misleading. Police work is much more tedious than it appears in crime dramas.

The consequences of this ignorance are on display at colleges across the nation.[37] Students struggle to figure out a suitable major and then, as they approach graduation, fret over how this will translate into employment. When they begin higher education, most undergraduates are influenced by their parents' ambitions. Generally advised to be practical, they gravitate toward what seems to make sense. Only gradually do some shift toward subjects that they enjoy and/or in which they excel. This swing toward personal preference becomes more pronounced once they enter the job market. Because success is contingent on motivation and competence, unless people are true to themselves, they are apt to be trapped in occupations they loathe. Struggling to endure each tedious day, they never live up to their potential.

Nonetheless it can be frightening to make personal selections. Not only might this alienate family and friends, but a lack of knowledge of what lies ahead, coupled with a dearth of experience, make it impossible to be certain of what is best. Nowadays we do not inherit social positions. Most of us are not bequeathed land or the title to a family business. We usually have to find our own way with a minimum of family assistance. The rich, needless to say, have an advantage. They are heir to money and social connections. But even they have to perform if they are to be accorded respect. In a middle-class society, our personal capacities count for more than reflected glory.

Nor does the capacity for occupational proficiency come automatically. Professionalized jobs demand meaningful skills. Doctors, lawyers, accountants, architects, scientists, and bankers are not born with these abilities. They are learned. Nor does this learning come easily. Failure is possible and is therefore frightening. Developing the social expertise to be a competent manager is a lengthy process that entails numerous lessons. Manipulating complex data so as to get the right answer is also fraught with danger. These aptitudes must nevertheless be sought if success is to follow.

Perhaps the best legacy that parents can provide their children is a capacity to be self-directed.[38] Independent decision making is a generalized skill. It is beneficial in multiple vocations. Despite that it can be unsettling. Autonomous choices sometimes go wrong. Correspondingly, because it is possible to identify the authors of these decisions, the blame can be attached to those who made them. Leaders who lack confidence are thus inclined to pass the buck. Instead of figuring out what is best and then defending their selections, they allow others to set the agenda. In this, they relinquish control and accept secondary status. A failure of nerve subsequently deprives them of the accomplishments they covet.

Meanwhile, youngsters who are taught how to make independent decisions typically grow into self-reliant adults. Having learned to cope with personal errors, they are less liable to get flustered. In most cases, a history of taking chances prepares them to survive setbacks. Parents who hope to instill self-direction proceed in several ways. First they respect their children. They treat their concerns as important and abide by their selections. This can be achieved by providing "latitude with limits." In offering areas where autonomy is encouraged, while at the same time imposing boundaries beyond which danger lurks, they provide practice in making choices in relative safety. Second, these parents offer their children guidance.[39] Rather than demand strict obedience, they talk to them. Effective learning is rarely instantaneous and therefore takes years of resolute effort. Only patience and sustained dedication make this possible.

I watched this with my brother as he taught his daughter how to drive. Our dad had been a hard taskmaster. He would accept no errors—ever. As for me, he would not let me get near the family car. I was deemed so clumsy that I was sure to have a wreck and drive up his insurance. My sister fared a little better. She was offered a lesson, but when she hit the clutch instead of the brake she was summarily ordered out of the vehicle, never to return. Joel, in stark contrast, took his daughter's mistakes in stride. He did not yell at her. He instead quietly explained what she had done wrong and allowed her to try again. His goal was to reduce her anxieties rather than exacerbate them. He also encouraged her to go on the highway, detailing ahead of time some of the difficulties she might expect to meet. No wonder she became a safe driver fairly quickly.

Yet even for those receiving the appropriate support, self-direction is intimidating. Although people learn from their mistakes, missteps are painful. Fortunately, recovering from these can increase our confidence. Such setbacks demonstrate that errors need not be fatal. They can, in fact, be instructive if they are not converted into death sentences. Nonetheless, life is unfair.[40] Children born into lower-class families are handicapped in that they are normally deprived of suitable assistance. Often left to their own devices, they never discover that they have the ability to recuperate from their blunders. As a result, they may shy away from unfamiliar ventures and when placed in positions of leadership are liable to be rigidly defensive.

Unsure of how to proceed and unable to function up to their abilities, they often look to powerful defenders to save them. The upshot is that they abdicate personal responsibility.

The government, however, can do little to inculcate self-direction.[41] Impersonal and frequently detached from everyday life, its agents generally have difficulty imparting personal strengths. Regardless of how well-intended federal policies are, they are no substitute for loving parents. Nor does the courage to deal with occupational uncertainties derive from federal transfer payments. Shoveling resources in people's direction creates dependence rather than independence. Neither can affirmative action remedy this defect. Placing people in positions for which they are unprepared actually increases the chances of failure. If they cannot win tests of strength, they will be regarded as losers. Similarly, if they cannot make appropriate choices, they will be challenged when they falter. Only adequate occupational performances rescue people from defeat.

Formal education is likewise insufficient to implant courage.[42] Merely attending school does not provide the knowledge or skills to be an effective leader. Teachers are temporary custodians. They cannot provide dependable support for students who know that they are here today but gone tomorrow. Nor can students who do not put in the appropriate effort keep up. Our society is overflowing with opportunities for those capable of grasping them. Yet government-appointed helpers cannot do the grasping. If people have the daring, they can create their own breaks. Nonetheless, they must realize that their fate depends primarily on themselves. If they are too frightened to take risks, the occupational frontier is an obstacle they will never surmount. Conversely, if they develop the courage to plunge ahead, they can accomplish objectives of which they never dreamt.

THE FAMILY FRONTIER

If occupational success in a Gesellschaft society typically eludes those bereft of bravery, so does family success. Here too we must make independent choices, which we must then self-reliantly implement. The world in which we inherited personal relationships has disappeared.[43] Once upon a time, people married because they had to. Indeed, they often wed persons their parents chose. This was the case with my grandparents. Indeed, few could create a secure lifestyle without a mate. A failure to obtain a spouse was thus perceived as catastrophic. By the same token, married couples were expected to have children. If they didn't, their neighbors would gossip. Raising a family was considered a moral duty. Childless couples were therefore pitied and/or reviled. Furthermore, out-of-wedlock parenthood was scandalous. As evidence of forbidden sexuality, it was deemed sinful. Because those in this situation became pariahs, they were frequently shipped out of town so that their condition remained secret. Or if they were adults, they might be forced to wear the scarlet letter *A*.

Today all that has changed. Neither men nor women are required to marry, and hence fewer do. Similarly, if they decide not to have children, this is regarded as their business. What's more, cohabitation[44] without marriage, as well as single parenthood, have become normal.[45] When years ago I lived with a woman with whom I was not married, this was unusual. We both felt like pioneers. Yet today almost half of all couples do so before they wed. As for divorce, it too was sinful.[46] Indeed, in England an act of Parliament was required to gain release. By my parents' day, this had changed. Given their quarrels, they thought about separating but never followed through. This solution was still only for movie stars. Nowadays, outraged strangers no longer comment upon such transgressions in hushed tones. Where once community standards were rigorously enforced, modern Americans tend to view themselves as independent operators. As a consequence, whatever consenting adults choose to do in the privacy of their own abodes is left up to them. In a free country, this too is reckoned to be an elementary freedom.

Nowadays both men and women can provide for themselves. Our market economy is so prosperous that we do not have to depend on our families of origin for financial support. No longer reliant on land inherited from despotic parents, we do not fear being disowned. Hence if Mom or Dad disapproves of our lifestyle choices, that may be uncomfortable, but it is not tragic. Nor do we require a spouse to feed and clothe us. There are more than enough jobs so that both sexes can care for themselves. Even poverty need not deter a person from setting up an independent household or raising children unaided. Government transfer payments may not be generous, but they afford sufficient resources to underwrite nonconformity. Accordingly, if we decide to eschew traditional family arrangements, we can do so without undue hardship.

Marriage and family have thus become voluntary. We now marry because we want to and stay married because we know how to. Likewise, we have children because we desire them. With birth control often readily available, accidental or unwanted pregnancies can be kept to a minimum. Nor are we forced to raise our offspring according to the old rules. Whatever our relatives and friends think, we can act as we please within the precincts of our separate homes. If we go too far, that is, if we are abusive, the authorities might interfere, yet this is the exception. We can even control what our children learn, assuming we homeschool. The upshot is that, as with occupations, we have choices to make. Do we want to marry or have children? If so, what kind of marriage and children do we want? Consequently, if we are to make good choices, we must know what we are doing and have the courage to do it well. In short, our relationships too have become professionalized.

Nonetheless, voluntary intimacy is difficult.[47] Without strict rules that are strictly enforced, we must navigate the shoals of interpersonal conflict on our own. When spouses disagree, there is usually no one else available to settle their differences. I discovered this while cohabiting. One day my girlfriend and I got into a dreadful fight. There we stood, practically toe to toe, arguing with each other. Then it dawned on me. There is no parent around to caution us to play nice. Consequently, if we did not know how to arrive at an agreement, we never would. As it happened, we did not. So immature were we that we were unintentionally cruel. Intimacy provides people the access to do each other grave harm, while closeness affords the knowledge to target a spouse's weaknesses. This makes marriage scary. Hence, individuals who do not know how to protect themselves tend to shy away. As with occupational success, information and skill are necessary to deal with these vulnerabilities.

The first step toward a viable marriage is selecting the right partner.[48] Nonetheless, because we must now achieve this on our own, mistakes are common. With so many eligible persons available and the existence of soul mates a reassuring fiction, how are we to decide? In fact, the very young are notoriously inept at this. Since teenagers are apt to fall in love with love, their romances are remarkably fragile. It takes time for people to get to know themselves well enough to ascertain what they genuinely want. It also takes time, and competence, to judge another person's character. Accordingly, discovering if a couple has enough in common, as well as if each is trustworthy, does not occur instantaneously. Courtship is a process during which welcome—and unwelcome—details come to light. Courage is therefore needed to be patient and honest. Unacceptable candidates must be identified and discarded, despite a compelling desire for affection. If not, attempts to remake an inappropriate partner are bound to fail. People do not change just because we want them to.

As for marriage, it never provides automatic salvation. Two human beings who are both striving for personal growth can assist each other in becoming more successful, but they cannot engage in the growing for one another. The best they can manage is a profitable collaboration. If they work together on shared aspirations, they can accomplish more as a team than either can alone. This, however, is not without problems. The give-and-take needed to negotiate differences depends on emotional maturity. Both parties must know their limits and be willing to relinquish some aspirations in order to fulfill others.[49] Neither will get everything he or she once dreamt of. Both must be flexible.

Nor should they expect total equality. Teamwork does not imply a 50/50 approach to every activity. Successful couples develop viable divisions of labor. In former times, the tasks assigned to men and women were traditional. My grandfather Simon had his shop where Lizzie entered at her peril. Meanwhile he had to be on his best behavior when in her domain—the kitchen. Now each couple must decide for themselves who will do what such that both accept this allocation as fair. Doing so allows them a degree of autonomy while reducing interpersonal conflicts. Nonetheless, this voluntary fairness takes courage. The temptation toward selfishness must be shunned. Unless the interests of the two are respected, lingering grievances are apt to tear them apart.

The two most significant missions upon which modern couples must collaborate are creating "a haven in a heartless world" and raising children who can eventually succeed in our techno-commercial society. The demands of the middle-class marketplace take their toll on individuals who tackle them singlehandedly.[50] It thus helps to have someone who understands and cares about us. If, at the end of the day, a spouse can unburden him- or herself to a sympathetic ear, these trials are easier to bear. Nor is supportive counsel to be spurned. A different, albeit kindly, perspective can provide unanticipated solutions. Unfortunately, these benefits aren't inevitable. The ability of dissimilar individuals to be reliably on each other's side has to be developed. Despite their differences, both partners need the determination to set their personal interests aside—at least temporarily. This too takes courage. It is not easy to relinquish cherished aspirations.

With respect to raising successful children, the starting point is a committed adult relationship. Parents cannot provide their offspring security if they are not securely bonded to each other. Nor can they offer latitude with limits if they are unable to function as a team. Youngsters learn how to be self-directed from parents who know how to be self-directed. A mother and a father who are able to be themselves, while working in tandem, can provide a model for how their children can be themselves. Such parents offer useful guidance while eschewing demands for strict obedience. They are able to respect their children's desires because their own have largely been fulfilled. It takes courage to allow one's children to surpass oneself. My father certainly could not. While most parents want the best for their offspring, a child's accomplishments can expose an adult's limitations. All of us are vulnerable; nevertheless it takes guts to accept this vulnerability.

On one extreme end of the spectrum, the free-love movement asserts that personal freedom trumps family responsibilities. Its advocates assume that if the bondage of a lifelong commitment is to be circumvented; consenting adults must be allowed to do as they please. They thus have to be permitted to engage in extramarital sex that sometimes results in unplanned births. They must also be allowed to cohabit without pledging a permanent relationship. The freedom thereby gained is supposedly genuine. It theoretically enables individuals to change their minds without negative consequences.

Except that there are negative consequences to unreliable relationships. Safe havens are not safe if a partner can walk away at a moment's notice. Nor do children acquire confidence if they grow up in an unstable household. Freewheeling cohabitation, hasty divorce, and voluntary single parenthood have long since proven detrimental to the prospects of our children.[51] Is this what decent people want? Can we, who want love for ourselves and those we care about, find the courage to restrain our impulses despite the growing opportunity to do whatever we desire? Can we achieve the personal resolution to renounce untrammeled selfishness?

Love and commitment go together. They do so between bonded adults. They do so between caring parents and their children. Being alone takes courage, but so does being with someone. Life's uncertainties throw up a multitude of challenges. Our interpersonal demands do likewise. To remain loyal therefore requires the daring to stay constant. Nevertheless, only we can find the strength to do so. Only we can develop the emotional maturity to remain faithful. Fortunately if we do, the companionship we reap is usually worth the effort. It took me years to discover this, but, much to my surprise, I am now happily married.

The middle-class frontier is thus multifaceted.[52] It necessitates that we possess the courage to save ourselves by living up to our potentials. Freud counseled that mental health entails an ability to love and to work. In a complex techno-commercial society this requires the acquisition of professionalized self-direction. If we want to be happy, we must become self-motivated experts in making sound choices. Once again, this takes courage. But if we are brave, we can liberate ourselves from the doubts that once held us back. We can become our best selves and earn the rewards available to free people. Personal liberation too is thus one of the benefits bestowed by true courage.

Chapter 10

PERSONAL LIBERATION

MAKING CHOICES

Why did they do it? Why did the folks we know as the Pilgrims make the dangerous voyage across the Atlantic Ocean?[1] The *Mayflower* was a tiny, leaky tub of a ship. Trusting it to brave the perils of a stormy sea was assuredly an act of faith. Meanwhile the New World was largely unexplored. Neither its peoples nor is resources were well understood. As for the foodstuffs necessary to survive a harsh winter, these were clearly inadequate. Starvation was not only a real possibility; it became a fact of life when scores of migrants met their deaths.

So why did they do it? They must have entertained fears. Obviously, they could not be certain that they would not drown. Nor could they be positive that they would not share the fate of the Jamestown settlers who had so recently suffered malnutrition and slaughter at the hands of unfriendly natives. In light of these risks, they must have been strongly motivated. As human beings who had never previously undertaken so hazardous a venture, they had to have had compelling reasons to take such a chance.

As most schoolchildren learn, these colonists were Puritans. They were Calvinists who were at odds with the Anglican Church.[2] Determined to be faithful to their strict Protestant creed, they had run afoul of King Charles I. Charles, whose wife was a French Catholic, sought to return England to a more traditional religion. This prompted his opponents to defy his will—to which he responded with persecutions. The Pilgrims, in short, were in search of religious freedom. They wanted to be able to choose how the pray to God in the manner dictated by their consciences.

In the New World, they found this freedom. They quickly set up their own government and houses of worship. These latter eventually became known as Congregationalist churches. This was because the members of their congregations determined how they were organized. They chose their ministers and subscribed to their own doctrines. Because they took these matters seriously, within little more than a decade of landing at Plymouth Rock, they started their own college.[3] Harvard was intended to educate pastors who could maintain the purity of their beliefs. It might have been small, a mere shadow of Cambridge University, yet it was their own.

Contemporary Americans might find it difficult to understand, but these folks cared deeply about protecting their immortal souls. They therefore insisted upon upholding the principles they held dear. If this meant jeopardizing their corporeal existence, they were prepared to do so. This is what gave them the courage to endure. It is why they were able to tame the normal fears any of us would have experienced under their circumstances.

Little more than a century and a half later, their descendants would again risk death rather than submit to arbitrary authority. New England's Sons of Liberty also took their freedoms seriously. They may have protested against a tax on tea or the requirement that they purchase stamps for legal documents, but the real issue was who was going to decide how they were governed.[4] As the legatees of the people who wrote the Magna Carta, they insisted upon defending their rights as Englishmen. The British king had long ago ceded his absolute authority to imprint his will on his subjects. He was thus not entitled to make a variety of decisions without the consent to those to whom they applied. These colonists, having become accustomed to self-government, were not about to relinquish this privilege without a fight. They would choose how they were to live, irrespective of their monarch's capricious fiats.

Yet this too entailed huge risks. Great Britain was a world power. It had a large army and the mightiest navy on the planet. Defying King George and his Parliament was not a small matter. If these rulers decided to crush opposition, they could extract a heavy price. Founding Father Benjamin Franklin learned this when, as the colonists' representative in London, he defied the king's ministers.[5] They subsequently hauled him before the Privy Council, where he was humiliated as if he had been a disobedient schoolboy. The citizens of Lexington and Concord later learned it when they faced the muskets of the regulars sent to seize their weapons. Independence would not come easily.

Why then did they continue in their rebellion? Weren't they afraid that they might be killed? If they had doubts about this, events soon proved otherwise. When Franklin warned his fellow signers of the Declaration of Independence that they had better hang together or they would surely hang separately, he was being witty, but he was not joking. His fellow patriots had signed their death warrants, and they knew it. Nor were the bloodstained footprints in the snows of Valley Forge part of a child's game. Many men died that freezing winter.[6] Many more were grievously injured. Nevertheless, for seven long years, the Continental Army held out. Despite numerous defeats, there were always enough poorly paid volunteers to maintain the struggle.

Why did they do it? Why weren't they overwhelmed by their fears? What was so important that they ignored the counsel of their more timid neighbors? Wasn't it sensible to surrender and throw themselves on the mercy of a victorious sovereign? Once again, these were men and women who sought control over their destiny. They might have been able to live securely as servants to a distant nation.

Already more prosperous than residents of the United Kingdom, they would have been comfortable in such subservience. Yet they elected not to follow this course because they prized their independence. As proud adults, they refused to live on their knees. Although they might make neophyte mistakes, these would be *their* mistakes.

The upshot, as we know, was the inauguration of the world's most vigorous democracy. The United States became the richest nation in history, as well as a bastion of liberty.[7] Countless miscalculations were made along the way; nonetheless, all in all, the government erected by the founders produced more happiness for more people than had any place ever before. Surveys repeatedly show that people who are free to be themselves are more satisfied than those who are not. Time and again this has made them willing to shed their blood in defense of their liberties.

The same impulse was revealed in opening up the continent from sea to shining sea. The westward trek was not a walk in the park.[8] Here, too, many people died in order to take control of their fate. Rather than live narrow lives in settled communities, they chose to expand their horizons. In quest of fresh opportunities, they pulled up stakes and headed into the unknown. How could they not have been afraid in doing so? When, for instance, the wagon trains trundled along the Oregon Trail, could their passengers have been oblivious of bleached bones and broken furniture that littered their path? Would they not have heard about massacres by the natives or wondered if this would be their lot? And yet they persisted and were followed by others who also persisted.

Starting a small farm or opening a new business on the frontier were hazardous enterprises. They required hard work and good luck to convert opportunity into success. Nonetheless, this gave these pioneers the latitude to make their own decisions. Whether they prospered or were forced to move on to other endeavors, they had the satisfaction of knowing that if they prevailed, they deserved the credit for doing so. Even if they failed, they could take comfort in the fact that they tried. Throughout most of history, certainly ever since the advent of agriculture, most people have been indentured to the will of others. They have either been slaves, serfs, or tenants. On the frontier, however, they were not any of these things. They were able to be their own persons.[9] They could become what they chose to be without having to genuflect to a superior. For many, this was worth the chances they took.

My grandparents, on the other hand, were not born in this country. They did not help to open up its frontier or establish its independence. Although they too came in pursuit of liberty, the oppression they fled was different.[10] The Jews had for millennia been a detested minority. As ethnic and religious outsiders, they were despised and abused by their neighbors. Unable to participate in the larger community, they were forced to live in ghettoes and take up prescribed occupations. Things had improved by the beginning of the twentieth century, but pogroms were still sweeping Eastern Europe. As dramatized in the film *Fiddler on the Roof,* merely being Jewish was an invitation to arbitrary brutality. This then was not freedom. It did not provide the right to be whatever they could become.

My Tarriff grandfather, that is, my mother's father, was doing reasonably well while in the Ukraine. He owned his own small business and had recently married. But he knew two things. One was that the czar's police might at any moment conscript him into the military. The other was that America was a land of freedom and opportunity. This made him willing to risk being turned back at the Russian border. When I was a teenager, he explained how frightening it was to be apprehended by the authorities. Once he had been thrown into jail, he did not know if this was the first step on the road to Siberia. Even so, he tried a second and a third time to find his way out. Then when he got to America, he did not speak the language. Often derided as a "kike" and a greenhorn, he nonetheless found work. Eventually he was able to begin a family, again he started his own business, and ultimately he bought his own home.

When years later he retired to Florida, I asked my grandfather Simon if he had any regrets. He told me that he didn't. His, he replied, was a good life. He had been able to make something of himself despite the obstacles he encountered. Aware that his children and grandchildren were doing better than he had, he took pride in the opportunities he made available to them. Simon did not stress his fears. Nor did he boast of overcoming them. What he emphasized was what he had accomplished. Given the freedom that he had sought, found, exploited, and bequeathed to others, he pronounced himself satisfied.

My grandmother, had she not been stricken with Alzheimer's, would also have declared nothing less. As a boy, I only thought of her as a warm, comforting presence. I never conceived of her as a young girl who had been torn from her home and deposited in a place she had not personally chosen. When today I try to visualize her alone on the Trans-Siberia Railway, my imagination boggles at the courage this took. Then, when I switch to envisioning her lying, again alone, in a hospital bed in Yokohama, ill with typhoid fever, suffering from what might have proved a fatal disease, I am stunned by what she endured. She must have been terrified. And when her hair grew back snow white, what could she have thought? Next, when she was reunited with her husband, he had to have seemed like a stranger. After this, once she got pregnant with no mother available to help deal with this stressful experience, how did she cope? Had I been in her place, would the anxiety have driven me over the edge?

Yet my grandmother did not go crazy. She was a wonderful homemaker; she was also a superb mother and grandmother. Within her limited ambit, she more than fulfilled her mission. Indeed, she often sacrificed for others and found her pleasure in ensuring that they were pleased. I will never forget her urging me to eat the sumptuous meals she prepared. "Eat, eat, mine kind!" Then, upon seeing the bright smile on her face when she realized that I was satisfied, my own contentment was amplified. These may seem like small achievements; they were not. She too had crafted independent choices that were made possible by American liberties. Although her decisions were based on a tradition derived from another continent, they were hers. And because they were, she could be happy.

THE VIRTUES OF FREEDOM

Periods of social change are pregnant with fear. When the world becomes something other than what we expect, we worry about dangers we had not anticipated and for which we may be unprepared. Such was the case for those living in the wake of the Protestant Reformation and Catholic Counter-Reformation.[11] Ordinary people could no longer be sure about what to believe regarding life or the afterlife. Hence in their anxiety they turned to war and oppression to keep their insecurities at bay. The Puritans got caught in this maelstrom. They dealt with it by running away, yet they did so in an orderly fashion. They did not merely hop on the *Mayflower*. They meticulously planned their voyage.[12] Then they built a shining city on a hill intended to provide the safety to follow their consciences. In fact, it did.

Later the authors of the American experiment got caught up in the changes wrought by the Enlightenment.[13] After the Middle Ages wound down and the Renaissance had run its course, the opening of the New World, coupled with the beginnings of industrialization, offered unprecedented opportunities. The British colonists, who at the time were clinging to the Atlantic littoral, seized upon these. They engaged in commercial ventures and political experiments that the grandees in their mother country found disquieting. Soon thereafter, in order to protect these initiatives, they found it necessary to resist English hegemony by force of arms. They literally fought for the freedom to deal with these changes in their own way. What is more, they too succeeded.

As for the intrepid souls who took on the challenges of the American frontier, they confronted a variety of unplanned difficulties.[14] As a consequence, their lives were utterly changed from what they had been in the communities from whence they migrated. Nevertheless, they adjusted. They became tougher and more daring than the homebodies. Subsequent generations would pride themselves on their forebears' independent spirit.[15] They would also follow this lead in converting their inherited autonomy into the know-how to tame a continent. These folks built railroads from coast to coast, erected skyscrapers that reached to the heavens, and sent electrical messages under the ocean to customers residing thousands of miles away. These people dreamt of starting their own enterprises and becoming their own bosses. Indeed, many of them did.[16] Thousands eventually got rich as commercial pioneers.

The American frontiersmen perceived change as providing opportunity. So did the immigrants who left everything behind in order to share in these prospects. These émigrés knew that they were cutting their ties with the traditions of their ancestors. They knew that they were entering a different world. Nonetheless, they did not yet understand the customs of their new neighbors. A strange language, legal novelties, and even unusual foods all had to be assimilated. These could be frightening, but adjustments needed to be made. Just as important, they had to prepare their children to take advantage of the unprecedented possibilities.[17] Had they simply recreated the villages of their homeland, they would have exchanged one set of limitations for another. Temporarily holding on to the old provided a safe transition, yet it needed to be relinquished so that they could move on.

In this, Americans from a variety of backgrounds wound up reinventing themselves. They became dissimilar to what their ancestors had been. Americans were a free people. They were able to take chances that others could not, partly because novel options were available and partly because the barriers that held those others back had been torn down. They could therefore fulfill their personal potentials in ways that those who preceded them could not. To do so, however, they had to overcome their fears. They had to dismantle the personal impediments that blocked their way.

Fear is the enemy of liberty. Our ingrained fears are like ramparts that separate us from what we might become. When we are afraid, we do not take chances. When we are afraid, we run away and/or engage in fights that impose additional burdens. People who are terrified of the unknown tend to hunker down. They do not explore that which is unfamiliar. Nor do they develop the skills needed to tackle untried projects. Their fears can thus be the equivalent of prison walls. They hem them in and prevent them from seeing what is on the other side. In refusing to take chances, they may be safe from dangers, but they are also separated from untold satisfactions.

Years ago the psychologist Abraham Maslow[18] speculated about what he called a "hierarchy of needs." He argued that we must first meet our basic needs for things such as food and water before we seek higher-level objectives. At the top of his pyramid he placed "self-actualization." Only when people had dealt with the former goals were they free to pursue the latter. Maslow further assumed that in a society as prosperous as our own many more millions enjoyed this opportunity than had previously. They could delve into their personal hopes and initiate the steps necessary to fulfill them. They could thus become what they had the potential to be and in the process experience gratifications denied to those who were merely trying to survive.

Nevertheless, this presupposes the courage to make independent choices and perhaps to become different than other people. Those who investigate who they are often discover that they are not what friends and relatives want them to be. The upshot is that in revealing the truth about themselves, they must sometimes defy convention. Instead of being led by others, they require the daring to be autonomous. In this, they invariably encounter moments of opposition and defeat. Mistakes are always made that must later be overcome. This is the price of personal liberation. Folks cannot fulfill their deepest dreams if they do not deal with the implied fears and failures.

As it happens, our contemporary society places a premium on becoming personally liberated. A massive techno-commercial civilization cannot maintain its integrity without battalions of professionalized organizers.[19] It requires millions of self-motivated experts to make critical decisions. These people must be trailblazers who guide the rest of us through the maze of economic, political, and social difficulties that we are forced to navigate. Essentially pioneers on the middle-class frontier, these self-directed groundbreakers must cope with changes every bit as destabilizing as those of the past.[20] Accordingly, if they are to be independent decision makers, they must possess the courage to master these vicissitudes. Were they to allow their fears to induce paralysis, they would be useless to themselves and others. Not only might they lead astray those who follow them, but they would never become self-actualized. Unwilling to recognize truths about themselves or the obstacles they encounter, they would withdraw into a self-imposed ignorance and rigidity.

Consider what successful leaders must be able to do. To begin with, they must recognize reality for what it is. Choices that are based on fantasies have a way of unraveling when they are put to the test. This means that effective leaders must identify their own and others' limitations. If they do not, they will attempt what cannot be performed in ways that do not work. The realization that things might go wrong is frightening, but this anxiety cannot be allowed to become incapacitating. If it is, essential activities will not be undertaken. Nor will a person venture into areas not previously tread. In this case, self-actualization is not possible in that the self is prevented from expanding into alien territory.

Successful leaders must also be capable of exercising initiative.[21] They need to be able to instigate novel schemes without asking permission. That which is new tends to arouse suspicions. If a program has not already demonstrated its value, some will suspect that it may not and hence they will resist implementing it. The alternative, however, is to do what has always been done. In this case, those who hold back are not leaders but followers. This is fine, as long as unexpected problems do not arise. Yet if they do, and adjustments are not made, the odds of failure escalate. Fear-induced inflexibility is usually a recipe for doing nothing—or, at least, for doing the wrong thing.

Innovative people not only take chances, they also perceive opportunities that others overlook. A century ago, many people assumed that everything that could be invented already had been. Heavier than air, flying machines were certainly not feasible, nor would anyone ever journey to the moon. The pacesetters who transcended these mental barriers did so because they were not afraid to look beyond the conventional wisdom.[22] Creativity favors the prepared mind, yet such minds are open only if they are not weighted down by fear. To "think outside the box" a person must not dread venturing into virgin terrain.

When I was in graduate school, trying to come up with a topic for my dissertation, those of us in the same boat would gather in the lunchroom to gripe about how our professors were not being helpful. Why weren't our supposed mentors suggesting promising areas of study? Why didn't they provide a rubric for deciding how to proceed? Only later did it occur to me that they were forcing us to make independent choices. They knew that the world does not provide detailed directions on how to be successful. Almost no one hands out engraved invitations to engage in groundbreaking missions. The chances are that if we do not invite ourselves, we will be left on the sidelines. This applied to those of us who hoped one day to become academics. How would we develop research agendas after we graduated and were out on our own? Leaders lead. They initiate ideas. This is why they are followed. Moreover, in exuding the confidence to take chances, they can infuse a spin-off courage in others. It is only then that teams of individuals are able to work collaboratively on complex projects.

The alternative is conventionality. To do what seems safe because it conforms to the past is to repudiate personal and/or collective growth. Had all of our ancestors followed this strategy, we would still be hunting zebras on the African savanna. Similarly, when we only depend on the good graces of others for survival, we place ourselves in jeopardy. If they do not come through, we are apt to flounder. Regrettably, our spirits are crushed and our imaginations never soar. As for liberating our inner selves, this cannot happen when we voluntarily bind ourselves to the whims of others. If we constantly fear their displeasure, we never cut loose to be ourselves. If before we act we must always make certain that others won't be offended, we are as tightly bound as any slave.

This is not idle speculation.[23] I saw the consequences of conformity when I was employed by the New York City Welfare Department. At one point, my job was to help our clients find work. We caseworkers would locate potential employers and then make interview appointments. This, however, rarely resulted in those we referred being hired. Why? The answer was simple. These folks did not want to give up their Welfare checks. Most were afraid that if they got a job, they might later lose it. Depending on government money was a safer option. The Welfare check came every month. The amount might be small, but it was reliable. Besides, under-the-table jobs could be used to supplement these benefits.

The outcome was that our clients would routinely mess up their interviews. They would say things that made them sound like poor risks. They might, for instance, talk down their abilities. Often they did not even show up for an appointment. Then, when they didn't, there was always an excuse. The alarm clock went off too late. They didn't own the proper clothing. Perhaps they had missed the bus. Somehow it was never their fault that they did not do what they promised. Maybe someone had started a fight in the neighborhood and they felt it prudent to stay at home. Or possibly they realized that the employer was a racist. Nevertheless, if they did get hired, it was amazing how frequently they were let go. For some reason the boss did not understand why they were habitually late.

In fact, dependency had become a way of life.[24] A majority of our clients had given up hope. They had long since decided that the deck was stacked against them. Afraid that they did not possess the ability to keep up with others, they withdrew from the competition. They did not plan to go to school or to work their way up from an entry-level job. To the contrary, they wanted to be saved. They hoped that a benevolent authority would swoop down and restore them to the place of honor they deserved. This, paradoxically, ensured that they would never be saved. Unwilling to contemplate rescuing themselves, they did not take advantage of the opportunities they were offered.

My clients were usually decent people. Most had good hearts and good intentions. But they were afraid. Many were deathly afraid. Convinced of their personal weaknesses and certain that injustice laid around every corner, they were unwilling to make things worse by allowing themselves to be humiliated. They thus declined to look reality in the eye.[25] It was too cruel. They would therefore not countenance taking initiatives. These invited frustration. And so they drifted. The middle-class frontier might have set a banquet before them, yet they refused to eat unless they were spoon-fed. As a result, they starved. Their anxieties were so great that they were unwilling to make the choices that would set them free. For them, the uncertainties of a society in flux represented debasement rather than opportunity. Liberty appeared to be a trap as opposed to a path toward fulfillment.

These Welfare clients were fooling themselves. They believed that they were making smart choices, but because they were unaware of the effects of dependency, they did not.[26] Their self-awareness had been compromised by a need to deceive themselves about why they weren't taking risks. The point is that another advantage of courage is personal integrity. People who have the mettle to be honest with themselves can be consistent. They can integrate the good with the bad so as to make decisions in accord with reality. Unafraid of their personal weaknesses, they are better able to surmount them.

People who have integrity can be authentic. They do not feel compelled to disguise who they are from themselves or others. This makes life easier. Freed of the need to keep track of how they have presented themselves in particular circumstances, they have more energy available to pursue other priorities. These folks can look themselves in the mirror without flinching. They are also better positioned to stand up for what they believe. Because they are aware of why they came to particular conclusions, they are able to defend them. This too is liberating. Released from the necessity of following the crowd in order to camouflage their distinctiveness, they can stand out without fear of being demolished. They know who they are; hence they know that this identity cannot be torn from them.

TWO INTREPID PIONEERS AND ME

If some people have been held back by a society that provides more choices than they can manage, others have been able to flourish. They have taken advantage of the freedom made available by American democracy and prosperity. Maslow uses the metaphor of personal growth to describe how some individuals learn to fulfill their potential.[27] He compares them to flowers that reach up toward the sun so as to share their glory with the universe. These folks typically encounter obstacles, which they overcome because they are prepared to be assertive. They become more than others because they dare more than others.

I have been fortunate enough to know a few of these people. They are not fairytale characters. Nor are they superhuman. In some ways they are so ordinary that others do not recognize them as extraordinary. Ironically the folks who are least likely to appreciate their accomplishments are those imprisoned by their own insecurities. Instead of recognizing courage in action, they suspect that good luck and unfair manipulation must have facilitated success. Were they to see the truth, they might have to admit that they were complicit in their personal failures. And so they don't. In most cases, they also stay away from the winners. They literally avoid interacting with them. Accordingly, they never discover how to deal with their own fears.

The physical frontier has long since disappeared, but the social one has not. America continues to welcome immigrants to its shores. It still permits people born into the lower classes to rise into the higher ones. Social mobility is not a myth; it is merely difficult.[28] As in former days, it requires courage to attain this success. Achievement is not a birthright. It takes work and risk-taking. Those awaiting the proverbial silver platter will have a lengthy wait. Let me provide a pair of examples. Both of these folks escaped the collectivist trap. Both became winners by dint of honorably overcoming their fears.

Robert is an immigrant to the United States. His homeland was Iran. There he went by the name of Mohammad. As a boy, he had not intended to leave, but when adulthood approached, he found himself at odds with this father. The family was prosperous and his dad wanted him to follow suit by either becoming a banker or training as a physician. The sight of blood, however, horrified Robert, as did the long hours required by a financial career. Although he did not have an alternative in mind, he knew that the medical and banking professions were not for him.

This impasse is what precipitated Robert's decision to come to America. As an educated person, he was aware of the broad opportunities available in the United States. Perhaps this might provide a way out. Not surprisingly, his father objected. After all, Robert had been admitted into an Iranian university that had a 1 percent admission rate. Nonetheless his Dad was ultimately won over.

The problem which remained was that in order to obtain an exit visa, Robert had to pass a national examination. Yet on his first attempt he failed. Happily on his second he succeeded. Then fate intervened to wipe out this victory when the results of the test were invalidated by a cheating scandal. Still, Robert was not deterred. He took the exam for a third time. Once again passing, albeit by the skin of his teeth, he was on his way to a place where he had no connections. Had he not done so, he would have been drafted into the Iranian army by 8:00 a.m. the next day.

Lacking the finances to support himself while pursuing a college education, Robert was compelled to take a job as a busboy. Unfortunately his English was so deficient that he did not understand patrons who asked for a glass of water. Had not a Persian-speaking coworker translated, he would have been adrift. Likewise unable to afford better, he was obliged to share a small apartment with a stranger. Moreover, because this flat was located miles from the nearest grocery, he had to walk there in good weather and bad. Despite these difficulties, Robert persevered. In due course, his grades earned him a degree in nuclear physics.

Eventually Robert rose to a high-level management position in the nuclear safety department for his state. In this capacity, he was responsible for making sure that its facilities met the highest standards. This was a challenging task but one he found rewarding. Then a problem arose. A new nuclear plant had been proposed. The question was, were its plans adequate? Robert examined the specifications and came to the conclusion that what was being requested was several times more expensive than was reasonable. With many hundreds of millions of dollars at stake, he could not in good conscience recommend the project. Although he was pressured by the governor to change his mind, he would not. In the end, he decided that it was better to resign than to capitulate to demands with which he morally disagreed.

It might be assumed that this was a foolhardy choice from which Robert would have difficulty recovering. This would be wrong. Robert was both talented and resilient. After obtaining an MBA, he went into the real estate business. Although this is a cutthroat field, his integrity allowed him to make decisions based on his own calculations. Robert was never one to follow the crowd; yet the upshot was that he became a millionaire. As a consequence, he was able to finance the relocation of his parents and siblings to the United States. This enabled them to escape the clutches of the mullahs with as much conclusiveness as my grandparents had earlier escaped those of the czar.

Incidentally, Robert's wife also has an inspiring story. Winnie emigrated from China to the States, also to pursue opportunities unavailable in her homeland. More fluent in English than her husband, she obtained the medical credentials he eschewed. Today a practicing physician, she too has demonstrated sustained courage under pressure. Together they are preparing their two children to take advantage of the life chances they have personally learned exist in our free country. Determined to do their best, they were not deterred by proclamations that social mobility is no longer possible. When knocked down, both demonstrated the courage to keep going.

My second example is William. He was born in the rural South.

His father was a Baptist minister who survived the Bataan Death March. William knew his father was brave, but like many sons he was excruciatingly aware of his dad's limitations. He was thus determined to surpass him. In particular, he was dedicated to being a truth teller. In time, William earned a master's degree that enabled him to obtain employment as a college administrator. His specialty was human services. In this regard, he was so competent that he rose to become the head of human resources at his university. Because he was also well liked, his future seemed assured.

Then, as often happens, something unexpected occurred. One of the professors circulated a survey instrument that asked how satisfied his colleagues were with their circumstances. This study indicated that the faculty respected their students and their fellow professors, but that they did not trust the upper administration. When the president learned about this, she was appalled. As a groundbreaking female, she was proud of having navigated the school's transition from a two- to a four-year institution. She was therefore convinced that she deserved greater appreciation. Her response was to convene a series of administrative roundtables in order to discuss what should be done.

Then, at these meetings, she went around the table to ask each of those present to affirm their loyalty to her publicly. William was summoned to one of these forums and was in his turn expected to confirm his fealty. Up to this point, there had been no dissenters. Nonetheless, William believed that this procedure was inappropriate and hence he declared that his allegiance was to the university. As he expected, the president was not pleased. Indeed, she was so displeased that he went from being favored to in the doghouse. It was now well understood that his pathway to promotion was closed.

This might have been the end of William's career. His unwillingness to sacrifice his integrity might have been an act of imprudent bravado that could have been avoided by articulating what had been desired. In fact, William's career took an entirely different turn. The same sturdy independence that impelled him to defy the president had driven him to develop a new resource-management package. He subsequently published this in a professional journal, where it attracted widespread notice. One of the people who was impressed worked in the chancellor's office of the state university system. As a result, William was offered the position of associate vice chancellor. His job was now to oversee the health programs for all of the state's public colleges.

William took the same no-nonsense attitude to this mission that he had to his previous one. He would do the right thing—even if pressured to do otherwise. As a result, he stood up to medical providers more concerned about their own bottom lines than the needs of state employees. This made him a tough negotiator, who in the end saved the state millions of dollars. So impressive was his performance that the governor appointed him to a committee commissioned with making recommendations about reorganizing other state agencies. William had not been sidetracked by his courage, but promoted to a wider stage. Courage may not always be rewarded, but it often is. The reason is that courageous people tend not to give up. They may be defeated in one venue only to find an opportunity in another.

While I cannot claim to have displayed as much bravery as either Robert or William, I would not be where I am today had I not resisted pressures to conform. As I previously recounted, many years ago I worked as a vocational counselor in upstate New York. In this capacity, I had the occasion to develop new techniques to help emotionally distressed clients overcome their shortcomings and difficulties. Unlike most of the professionals with whom I worked, my background was in sociology. This enabled me to look at problems through a different lens. Instead of understanding mental disorders as medical or psychological, I began to perceive them in a social-role context. This was an exciting breakthrough I was eager to share with others. Reinterpreting psychotherapy as a form of role change opened auspicious new avenues of approach.

The problem was that my superiors were uncomfortable with my doing something different. I was literally told not to engage in resocialization because they did not understand it. They did not ask for evidence, nor evaluate my results. They simply demanded conformity. That was when I knew I needed to move on. Although I enjoyed my work at the psychiatric facility, it would become burdensome if I could not expand my abilities. Regrettably, I was not confident I could do better elsewhere. While I did have a doctorate in sociology, there was not much call for clinical sociologists.

Nonetheless, I considered quitting my job and seeking academic employment. At this point, my uncle Milton got word of what I was contemplating. Not only was he a nice person, but I was confident that he was concerned with my welfare. So it came as a blow when I learned that he believed I should stay put. Milton had lived through the Great Depression. Having once attended a Communist Party meeting, he had also fought his way through the Red Scare. Now he occupied a secure job as a New York City bus driver. This might not have allowed him to live up to his potential, but it did enable him to buy a home and support a family. Best of all, he could sleep soundly at night, comforted in the knowledge that he was not going to be laid off.

Milton did not want me to experience the same anxieties he had when he thought that he might never land a good-paying position. He therefore drove from New Jersey to upstate New York with the express intension of convincing me to change my mind. Why, he asked, would I abandon a good-paying job, one with a wonderful pension, for something that might never happen? Why would I release a plump bird in the hand for an imaginary one in the bush? I should stay put. My work was not onerous and allowed me to live comfortably. Quitting would thus be rash. It would bespeak a childish impulsivity rather than adult responsibility.

This gave me pause. I did not have a job offer in hand. What if I resigned and went unemployed? This had happened to my dad. It could happen to me. As a consequence, I hung on for another year. But then I could take it no longer. My courage was still wobbly, yet the indignities of being forced to conform to methods with which I did not concur had piled up. And so I quit and made a crash effort to find an academic niche. Much to my surprise, I got lucky. Kennesaw State University was looking for a clinical sociologist. I had the credentials; but more than this, when interviewed I was myself. I did not pretend to be what I thought the search committee wanted. Before I made the trip to Georgia, I decided that I did not want to work at any place that did not want me for me. I had had enough of that already. In the end, I was relaxed, responsive, and apparently somewhat impressive.

Previous to this I had never been in Georgia, knew no one in Georgia, and had no full-time college teaching experience. I was taking a huge risk—one I knew my uncle and father would disapprove of. So what was the result? Well, I love college teaching and am good at it. I also love the freedom to write books; books that are out of the sociological mainstream. I also found a wife who is the love of my life. This is a winning trifecta few others can boast. Not everyone approves of me or what I do. Still I am widely respected and comfortable in my own skin. I can take pride in what I have accomplished and—on my good days—realize that if I had not demonstrated a modicum of courage, none of this would have come to pass.

CUSTER VERSUS SHERMAN

With this said, it is important to distinguish between courage and bravado. The former may be liberating, whereas the latter often is not. People who are too bold frequently do not pause to evaluate the consequences of their actions. In their brash rush to glory, they convert dangers into disasters. Good choices are usually considered choices. Rather than being impulsive, they derive from knowledge and controlled emotionality. Truly brave people have the courage to wait before they swing into action. They allow themselves to cool down before they decide on a strategy. If they do not, they generally remain trapped by their fears. Although they might seem to be brave, their boldness is a disguise for their insecurities.

George Armstrong Custer illustrates exactly what is not needed.[29] Dashing, and ostensibly fearless in battle, he epitomizes the perils of rashness. Custer was not a good student at West Point. He did not have the patience nor the personal discipline to attend to his studies or avoid breaking the cadet code of conduct. While he was a good horseman, no one expected him to become an able commanding officer.

But then the Civil War intervened. Trained commanders were required[30] and hence Custer was called to action. He made the most of it. Put in charge of a cavalry detachment, this inspired him to make bold attacks on Confederate forces. These succeeded so well that he was promoted to senior rank. Now, as the famous "boy general," he attracted national attention. Garbed in uniforms designed to accentuate his daring, he appeared to be exactly what Union victory demanded. In sum, he was regarded as a hero. The epitome of mounted glory, he was as proud of himself as others were of him.

Nonetheless Custer was not well loved by his troops. He was too careless with their lives and too sloppy in planning attacks. Concerned primarily with his personal fame, he was never a talented tactician. This trend continued once the war ended. Now assigned to frontier peacekeeping duties, he continued his pursuit of celebrity. Believed by the higher-ups to be a useful officer because he was not afraid to engage in combat, he never sought to understand his enemy or cultivate leadership qualities.

These weaknesses culminated in his defeat at the Little Big Horn.[31] Assigned to track down and confront rebellious Plains Indians, he assumed that all he had to do was to find and come to grips with them. He and his men would then charge in with guns blazing. Their courage would subsequently be so overwhelming as to sweep away any resistance. With this attitude clogging his brain, Custer did the unthinkable. He separated his forces in the face of a superior enemy. As a result, instead of having his entire command at his disposal when he met Crazy Horse, he led an inadequate remnant.

Why did he do this? Surprisingly, because, in part, he was not brave. Custer did not calculate the odds against him because he had substituted audacity for courage. Instead of contemplating dangers, he impetuously rushed into action so that he would not have to dwell on the negative possibilities. This was why he did not reconnoiter the enemy's positions. It was why he never realized that he was up against a much larger force than his own until it was too late. Truly brave people are not this reckless. They are clearheaded realists. When they take chances, they are aware of the potential hazards and make adjustments accordingly.

In the movies, the Plains Indians are wild fanatics. They circle the pioneer wagon trains, thereby allowing themselves to be shot down at leisure. In fact, this was rarely the case.[32] Because their numbers were small, they could not afford to waste lives in ill-conceived assaults. This was the case at the Little Big Horn. The Lakota, Northern Cheyenne, and Arapaho tribes surrounded Custer's men and wore them down. They used the rolling hills to provide cover. Then they shot arrows in parabolic arcs so that these showered down on their foes. They also had repeating rifles, whereas the cavalry was armed with single-shot weapons. At the end of the day, it was no contest. The Native Americans were levelheadedly brave, whereas the bluecoats were imprudently led to the slaughter.

William Tecumseh Sherman was a leader of far different character.[33] Much more in touch with his shortcomings, he did not deceive himself about impending dangers. The upshot was that he was no more imprisoned by his fears than was his friend Ulysses S. Grant.[34] He was thus able to exhibit genuine courage, thereby enabling him to achieve remarkable successes. Sherman was also a person whose temperament was revealed by the Civil War. Like Custer, he was a West Point graduate who had never previously been exposed to battle. Not unexpectedly, he wondered how well he would perform. He also pondered what it might take for the Union to achieve victory.

A man of incisive intelligence, "Uncle Billy," as his troops would later fondly call him, was petrified by what he foresaw.[35] Having been the headmaster of a Louisiana military academy, he understood that Southerners were prepared to fight. He also realized that they had the skills to do so effectively. Given these facts, a conflict between the North and South was apt to be long and bloody. This prospect precipitated anxieties that others regarded as a nervous breakdown. His superiors were therefore loath to appoint him to a major command that he might not be able to handle.

Events proved otherwise. When exposed to whizzing bullets at Shiloh, Sherman kept his head. And because he did, he was able to organize a systematic retreat on the first day of battle. Then, as Grant's point man, he oversaw the tremendous successes of the next day. After this, it was clear to all that Sherman could get the job done. His colleagues recognized it and so did he. Irrespective of his fears, he was able to control his passions so as to make sensible decisions. Sherman *was* a brave man. But he was never a rash man. A recognition of this faculty was to free him from the doubts that plagued his earlier career.

Where Uncle Billy really showed his mettle was during the Georgia campaign.[36] This began with a slow and steady advance from Chattanooga to Atlanta. Always prepared to outflank his adversary rather than waste valuable troops on a frontal assault, excepting for the debacle at Kennesaw Mountain, he arrived at his objective with his army intact. Next he settled down into a siege until his adversary, General John Bell Hood, exhibited the same sort of rashness as Custer.[37] Hood, instead of waiting for Sherman's army to exhaust itself in futile assaults on Confederate defenses, unwisely instigated frontal attacks on Union lines. Because he regarded his predecessor, General Joseph E. Johnston, as a coward for not doing likewise, he squandered his forces until they were reduced to a shadow of their former selves. This enabled Sherman to march into the deserted city with nary a casualty.

The question was what to do afterward. Sherman had a plan. He would march his army to the sea and in the process create devastation across the Georgia countryside. The problem was that he would require so many men to guard his supply lines that the remaining troops would be vulnerable to flank attacks. Sherman's answer was to cut loose from his supplies. His men would live off the land until they reached Savannah. This was a daring proposal. It was so daring that both Grant and Lincoln had their doubts.

Nonetheless Sherman persuaded them. He did so via his meticulous preparations. Because he too understood the hazards, he planned how many horses would be required, how much ammunition was needed, and what sorts of rations could be acquired. He was also thoroughly familiar with the topography. Sherman knew where his opponent's supplies were located. In addition, he feinted attacks on Macon and Augusta. These kept the enemy confused and unable to mount a counterattack. As a consequence, the march through Georgia went off without a hitch. What is more, it, and his subsequent marches through South and North Carolina, shortened the war.

Sherman was a war hero, but not because he was a superman. Rather it was because he made intelligent use of his talents.[38] He used his head and his military resources to the best advantage. In the process, he freed himself from the uncertainties that he had once experienced upon the untimely death of his father. More important, he helped free a nation from the twin curses of slavery and disunion. Indeed, without his assistance, Lincoln's "new birth of liberty" might never have come to fruition. Sherman demonstrates what people can do when they tame their fears. This was a man who took his time and did not overextend himself. He was never anything other than what he was; nevertheless, this was sufficient to render him a legend.

You and I are probably not in the same league as Sherman. Then again, we do not have to be. But neither do we have to emulate Custer. We can liberate ourselves from our demons by taking a middle course. Although we might not be as strong as we would like, neither do we have to be as weak as we may dread. Like Sherman, if we take the time to nurture our courage, we just might wind up surprising ourselves.

EPILOGUE

WHY NOT COWARDICE?

Is courage worth the price? Why should we put in the time to overcome our fears when doing so takes so much effort? Why not just live with them? Besides—dealing with our uncertainties may require us to expose ourselves to multiple dangers. Why not just hunker down and avoid the potential harm? Not everyone has to be a hero; not even an everyday hero. Nor do we all have to be leaders. Furthermore, if we are to be free, don't we also require the option of renouncing our freedoms? Doesn't it sometimes make sense to defer to those individuals who feel called upon to take risks? Let them bear the burden.

Honesty compels me to admit that most cowards survive. They generally find ways to avoid dealing with the dangers that they dread. Indeed, many people are able to escape dealing with these for a lifetime. While it is true that they must compress the boundaries of their existence in order to accomplish this, they normally can do so and get by reasonably well. Having decided to settle for less than they might become, they grow relatively comfortable within a circumscribed space. This way they know what to expect. There may be fewer moments of exultation, whereas there are also fewer disconcerting surprises. Such folks consider the trade-off acceptable. And who is to say they are wrong? If this is their choice, why should they be forced to do otherwise?

My answer is that they shouldn't. Although I personally lament their decision, it is still their decision. People have a right to be frightened. They also have a right to be unhappy. But make no mistake about it, most cowards are fairly unhappy. They are not living up to their capacities and therefore they are not obtaining the satisfactions they might otherwise obtain. Although they might not be desperately miserable, they are usually less well-off than is feasible. Precisely because they do not allow themselves to realize what is achievable or to make potentially daunting exertions, they condemn themselves to unnecessary losses.[1]

Yet if a society is permeated by cowardice, even the courageous suffer. People who are afraid to conquer their doubts are less able to contribute to the group's welfare. Hunkered down in their private storm cellars, they do not cooperate in neutralizing shared dangers.[2] No society can be great if too many of its members refuse to take risks. Such communities are unable to defend themselves from external threats. Nor are they able to take advantage of opportunities for prosperity and self-fulfillment. Collectively their economies stagnate, while personally their relationships deteriorate. Conversely, communities that work stalwartly toward common ends, while simultaneously allowing individuals to fulfill their personal promise, maximize mutual interests. They have bright futures, whereas less resilient populations cling, at best, to a respectable past.[3]

Courage is not a luxury. Neither is it an entitlement. Courage must be earned. Personally and collectively it is the key to our well-being—but only if we choose to make it so. Megyn Kelly, of Fox News, frequently laments that we have become a "cupcake nation."[4] She bemoans the fact that so many people refuse to accept risks. They apparently want to be wrapped in cotton batting so that they are never offended, or challenged, by unexpected events. She often cites the law-school students who asked to be excused from final examinations because they were so distressed by the shooting of an unarmed black man by a white police officer that they could not study. What sorts of lawyers, she asks, will these folks make? When something untoward happens in the courtroom, will they become so flustered that they cannot make a coherent argument? If so, she would not want them defending her.

Kelly sometimes muses that this might be beneficial for her children. They would not have to face stiff competition and would therefore do well. On the other hand, she knows this is not good for the nation. If we stop being the land of the brave and embrace the idea of universal safety, we will be neither safe nor prosperous. We will also be stuck in jobs we hate and families that disintegrate. Courage really is not a luxury. It can, however, be eschewed. On the personal level, cowardice can be survived despite the limitations it imposes. Even so, on the communal level, if it becomes too widespread, we are doomed. If we must always be protected from whatever makes us feel uncomfortable, it is a safe bet that one day we will be less comfortable than we currently are. Someday the wolf will be at the door. Our economy will crumble and our armies will endure the fate of the Roman legions.[5]

I know I am repeating myself, but my personal experience argues that courage is not only for a select few. Virtually all of us are capable of it if we put our minds—and hearts—to acquiring it. Nonetheless, taking the steps to become brave requires commitment. Those who do not apply themselves to what can be an intimidating and time-consuming process are bound to stumble. Many people find excuses as to why they should not proceed, whereas others pretend that they have made enormous progress when they have not. The truth is that if we remain cowards, it is because we choose to be cowards. If we are compelled to deal with the fruits of our timidity, it is not because there was no alternative. Uncertainty is part of the human condition.[6] During periods of rapid change, such as our own, doubts magnify. We can thus face up to the challenges produced by this new frontier—or we can retreat into a rationalized slumber. The choice is ours. Yet lest we forget, the repercussions of this choice are also our own. Everyday heroism is within our grasp—but so is everyday cowardice.

NOTES

CHAPTER 1: LAND OF THE FREE, HOME OF THE BRAVE

1. Paul Johnson, *A History of the American People*. New York: HarperCollins Publishers, 1997.

2. David H. Fischer and James C. Kelly, *Bound Away: Virginia and the Westward Movement*. Charlottesville: University of Virginia Press, 2000.

3. Dairmaid MacCulloch, *The Reformation: A History*. New York: Penguin Books, 2005.

4. David H. Fischer, *Albion's Seed: Four British Folk Ways in America*. New York: Oxford University Press, 1989.

5. John C. Miller, *The First Frontier: Life in Colonial America*. New York: Dell Publishing, 1974.

6. Charles C. Mann, *1491: New Revelations of the Americas before Columbus*. New York: Alfred A. Knopf, 2005.

7. S. C. Gwynne, *Empire of the Summer Sun: Quanah Parker and the Rise and Fall of the Comanches, the Most Powerful Tribe in American History*. New York: Scribner, 2010.

8. Bob Drury and Tom Clavin, *The Heart of Everything That Is: The Untold Story of Red Cloud, an American Legend*. New York: Simon & Schuster, 2013.

9. Bernard Bailyn, *To Begin the World Anew: The Genius and Ambiguities of the American Founders*. New York: Vintage Books, 2003.

10. Dan Jones, *The Plantagenets: The Warrior Kings and Queens Who Made England*. New York: Penguin Books, 2012.

11. Walter Isaacson, *Benjamin Franklin: An American Life*. New York: Simon & Schuster, 2003.

12. David McCullough, *1776*. New York: Simon & Schuster, 2005.

13. Richard Brookhiser, *Founding Father: Rediscovering George Washington*. New York: Free Press, 1996.

14. David McCullough, *John Adams*. New York: Simon & Schuster, 2001.

15. Alf J. Mapp, *Thomas Jefferson: A Strange Case of Mistaken Identity*. Lanham, MD: Madison Books, 1987.

16. Richard Brookhiser, *Alexander Hamilton: American*. New York: Simon & Schuster, 1999.

17. Ralph Ketcham, *James Madison: A Biography*. Charlottesville: University of Virginia Press, 1990.

18. James Madison, Andrew Hamilton, and John Jay, *The Federalist Papers*. London: Phoenix, 2000.

19. Fred Kaplan, *John Quincy Adams: American Visionary*. New York: Harper/Collins Publishers, 2014.

20. Benjamin P. Thomas, *Abraham Lincoln: A Biography*. New York: Modern Library, 1952.

21. T. Harry Williams, *Lincoln and His Generals*. New York: Alfred A. Knopf, 1952.

22. Doris Kearns Goodwin, *Team of Rivals: The Political Genius of Abraham Lincoln*. New York: Simon & Schuster, 2005.

23. Stephen Crane, *The Red Badge of Courage*. New York: Dover Publications, 1990.

24. Victor D. Hanson, *Ripples of Battle: How Wars of the Past Still Determine How We Fight*. New York: Doubleday, 2003.

25. Oscar Handlin, *The Uprooted*. Boston: Little, Brown, 1951.

26. James G. Leyburn, *The Scotch-Irish: A Social History*. Chapel Hill: University of North Carolina Press, 1989.

27. Noel Ignatiev, *How the Irish Became White*. New York: Routledge, 1995.

28. Irving Howe, *World of Our Fathers*. New York: Harcourt, Brace, Jovanovich Publishers, 1976.

29. Richard Gambino, *Blood of My Blood: The Dilemma of Italian Americans*. Garden City, NY: Doubleday, 1975.

30. Orlando Patterson, *Slavery and Social Death: A Comparative Study*. Cambridge, MA: Harvard University Press, 1982.

31. Adalberto Aguirre Jr. and Jonathan H. Turner, *American Ethnicity: The Dynamics and Consequences of Discrimination*, 2nd ed. New York: McGraw-Hill, 1998.

32. Melvyn L. Fein, *The Great Middle-Class Revolution: Our Long March toward a Professionalized Society*. Kennesaw, GA.: Kennesaw State University Press, 2005.

CHAPTER 2: FROM SAFETY NET TO FEATHER BED

1. Philip Freeman, *Alexander the Great*. New York: Simon & Schuster, 2011.

2. Adrian Goldsworthy, *Caesar: Life of a Colossus*. New Haven: Yale University Press, 2006.

3. Richard Brookhiser, *Founding Father: Rediscovering George Washington*. New York: Free Press, 1996.

4. Howard E. Wasdin and Stephen Templin, *Seal Team Six: Memoirs of an Elite Navy Seal Sniper*. New York: St. Martin's Griffin, 2012.

5. Carl Rogers, *On Becoming a Person*. Boston: Houghton Mifflin, 1961.

6. Edward Gibbon, *The Decline and Fall of the Roman Empire*. New York: Dell Publishing, 1963.

7. John K. Galbraith, *The Affluent Society*. Boston: Houghton Mifflin, 1958.

8. Marvin Olasky, *The Tragedy of American Compassion*. Washington, DC: Regnery Publishing, 1992.

9. Redskins Facts, www.redskinsfacts.com (accessed March 9, 2016).

10. John L. Jackson, *Racial Paranoia: The Unintended Consequences of Political Correctness*. New York: Civitas Books, 2008.

11. John Leo, *Two Steps ahead of the Thought Police*. New York: Simon & Schuster, 1994.

12. Peter Wood, *Diversity: The Invention of a Concept*. San Francisco: Encounter Books, 2003.

13. Jacques Derrida, *Deconstruction in a Nutshell*, edited by D. Caputo. New York: Fordham University Press, 1997.

14. Randall Kennedy, *Nigger: The Strange Career of a Troublesome Word*. New York: Vintage, 2005.

15. Earl Rice, *The O. J. Simpson Trial*. San Diego, CA: Lucent Books, 1997.

16. Alexis Shaw, "12 Companies That Have Cut Ties with Paula Deen," June 29, 2013, http://abcnews.go.com/Business/paula-deens-empire-continues-crumble-wake-racial-slurs/story?id=19534224 (accessed March 9, 2016).

17. Daniel P. Moynihan, *The Negro Family: The Case for National Action*. Washington, DC: US Government, 1965.

18. Robert D. Putnam, *Our Kids: The American Dream in Crisis*. New York: Simon & Schuster, 2015.

19. Alice Rossi, ed., *The Feminist Papers: From Adams to De Beauvoir*. New York: Bantam Books, 1973.

20. Catherine MacKinnon, *Feminism Unmodified*. Cambridge, MA: Harvard University Press, 1987.

21. Associated Press, "Mozilla CEO Resignation Raises Free-Speech Issues," *USA Today*, April 4, 2014, http://www.usatoday.com/story/news/nation/2014/04/04/mozilla-ceo-resignation-free-speech/7328759/ (accessed March 9, 2016).

22. Greg Lukianoff, *Unlearning Liberty: Campus Censorship and the End of American Debate*. New York: Encounter Books, 2012.

23. John P. Hewitt, *The Myth of Self-Esteem: Finding Happiness and Solving Problems in America*. New York: St. Martin's, 1998.

24. Diane Ravitch, *The Language Police: How Pressure Groups Restrict What Students Learn*. New York: Alfred A. Knopf, 2003.

25. Diane Ravitch, *The Language Police: How Pressure Groups Restrict What Students Learn*. New York: Knopf, 2003.

26. Lukianoff, *Unlearning Liberty*.

27. Richard H. Sander and Stuart Taylor, *Mismatch: How Affirmative Action Hurts Students It's Intended to Help, and Why Universities Won't Admit It*. New York: Basic Books, 2012.

28. Richard Sander, *Mismatch: How Affirmative Action Hurts Students It's Intended to Help, and Why Universities Won't Admit It*. New York: Basic Books, 2012.

29. Valerie Richardson, "Conservative Speaker at Oberlin Triggers Debate about Feminist 'Trigger Warnings,'" *Washington Times*, April 22, 2015. Christine Deneweth, "Why These Common 'Nice Guy' Behaviors Are Actually Sexist Microaggressions," *Everyday Feminism*, August 5, 2015, http://everydayfeminism.com/2015/08/for-nice-guys-who-dont-get-it/ (accessed March 10, 2016).

30. Alison Flood, "US Students Request 'Trigger Warnings' on Literature," *Guardian*, May 19, 2014, http://www.theguardian.com/books/2014/may/19/us-students-request-trigger-warnings-in-literature (accessed March 9, 2016).

31. "Valdosta State University: Freedom of Expression on Campus Limited to Unconstitutional Free Speech Zone," Foundation for Individual Rights in Education, https://www.thefire.org/cases/valdosta-state-university-freedom-of-expression-on-campus-limited-to-unconstitutional-free-speech-zone/ (accessed March 9, 2016).

32. Greg Lukianoff, *Freedom from Speech*. New York: Encounter Books, 2014.

33. Paresh Dave, "Condoleezza Rice Latest Graduation Speaker to Back Out Amid Protests," *Los Angeles Times*, May 3, 2014, http://www.latimes.com/nation/nationnow/la-na-nn-condoleezza-rice-commencement-controversy-20140503-story.html (accessed March 9, 2016).

34. Richard Pérez-Peña and Tanzina Vega, "Brandeis Cancels Plan to Give Honorary Degree to Ayaan Hirsi, a Critic of Islam," *New York Times*, April 8, 2014, http://www.nytimes.com/2014/04/09/us/brandeis-cancels-plan-to-give-honorary-degree-to-ayaan-hirsi-ali-a-critic-of-islam.html?_r=0 (accessed March 9, 2016).

35. William Eberhard, *A History of China*. London: Routledge & Kegan Paul, 1977.

36. H. Wayne Morgan, *Drugs in America: 1800–1980*. Syracuse: University of Syracuse Press, 1981.

37. Eric Burns, *Spirits in America: A Social History of Alcohol*. Philadelphia, PA: Temple University Press, 2004.

38. Morgan, *Drugs in America*.

39. Peter D. Kramer, *Listening to Prozac: A Psychiatrist Explores Antidepressant Drugs and Remaking of the Self*. New York: Viking, 1993.

40. Melvyn L. Fein, *On Loss and Losing: Beyond the Medical Model of Personal Distress*. New Brunswick, NJ: Transaction Publishers, 2012.

41. American Psychiatric Association, *Diagnostic and Statistical Manual of Mental Disorders*, 5th ed. Washington, DC: American Psychiatric Association, 2013.

42. Fein, *On Loss and Losing*.

43. American Psychiatric Association, *Diagnostic and Statistical Manual*.

44. Helen E. Fisher, *Anatomy of Love: The Natural History of Monogamy, Adultery and Divorce*. New York: W. W. Norton, 1992.

45. Andrew J. Cherlin, *The Marriage-Go-Round*. New York: Alfred A. Knopf, 2009.

46. Carol Gilligan, *In a Different Voice*. Cambridge, MA: Harvard University Press, 1982.

47. Hewitt, *Myth of Self-Esteem*.

48. Bruno Bettleheim, *A Good Enough Parent*. New York: Alfred A, Knopf, 1987.

49. James S. Coleman, E. Q. Campbell, C. J. Hobson, J. McPartland, A. M. Mood, F. D. Weinfield, and R. L. York, *Equality of Educational Opportunity*. Washington, DC: US Government Printing Office, 1966.

50. Diane Ravitch, *Left Back: A Century of Failed School Reforms*. New York: Simon & Schuster, 2000.

51. Barack H. Obama, *The Audacity of Hope*. New York: Crown, 2006.

52. Thomas Sowell, *Affirmative Action around the World: An Empirical Study*. New Haven: Yale University Press, 2004.

53. Obama, *Audacity of Hope*.

54. Fein, *Loss and Losing*.

55. Rushworth M. Kidder, *Moral Courage*. New York: William Morrow, 2006.

56. Walter B. Cannon, *Bodily Changes in Pain, Hunger, Fear, and Rage: An Account of Recent Research on the Function of Emotional Excitement*. New York: Appleton-Century-Crofts, 1929.

CHAPTER 3: INTEGRATED FEAR MANAGEMENT

1. Antonio Damasio, *Descartes' Error: Emotion, Reason and the Human Brain*. New York: Penguin, 2005.

2. Steven Pinker, *The Blank Slate: The Modern Denial of Human Nature*. New York: Viking, 2002.

3. Michael Lewis and Jeannette M. Haviland, eds., *Handbook of Emotions*. New York: Guilford, 1993.

4. David H. Barlow, *Anxiety and Its Disorders: The Nature and Treatment of Anxiety and Panic*. New York: Guilford, 1984.

5. Melvyn L. Fein, *I.A.M.: A Common Sense Guide to Coping with Anger*. Westport, CT: Praeger, 1993.

6. Melvyn L. Fein, *On Loss and Losing: Beyond the Medical Model of Personal Distress*. New Brunswick, NJ: Transaction Publishers, 2012.

7. Walter B. Cannon, *Bodily Changes in Pain, Hunger, Fear, and Rage: An Account of Recent Research on the Function of Emotional Excitement*. New York: Appleton-Century-Crofts, 1929.

8. Caroll E. Izard, *Human Emotions*. New York: Plenum, 1977.

9. Cannon, *Bodily Changes in Pain*.

10. Theodore Lidz, *The Person: His and Her Development Throughout the Life Cycle*. New York: Basic Books, 1976.

11. Helen E. Fisher, *Anatomy of Love: The Natural History of Monogamy, Adultery and Divorce*. New York: W. W. Norton, 1992.

12. Kerry W. Buckley, *Mechanical Man: John Broadus Watson and the Beginnings of Behaviorism*. New York: Guilford, 1989.

13. Doris Kearns Goodwin, *The Bully Pulpit: Theodore Roosevelt, William Howard Taft, and the Golden Age of Journalism*. New York: Simon & Schuster, 2013.

14. Rushworth M. Kidder, *Moral Courage*. New York: William Morrow, 2006.

15. John Clausen, ed., *Socialization and Society*. Boston: Little, Brown, 1968.

16. Daniel Goleman, *Social Intelligence: The New Science of Human Relationships*. New York: Bantam Books, 2006.

17. John Bowlby, *Attachment*. New York: Basic Books, 1969.

18. Michael Lewis and Carolyn Saarni, eds., *The Socialization of Emotions*. New York: Plenum, 1985.

19. Melvyn L. Fein, *Evolution versus Revolution: The Paradoxes of Social Change*. New Brunswick, NJ: Transaction Publishers, 2015.

20. Barlow, *Anxieties and Its Disorders*.

21. Melvyn L. Fein, *Human Hierarchies: A General Theory*. New Brunswick, NJ: Transaction Publishers, 2012.

22. Fein, *I.A.M.*

23. Kidder, *Moral Courage*.

24. Melvyn L. Fein, *Hardball without an Umpire: The Sociology of Morality*. Westport, CT: Praeger, 1997.

25. Sigmund Freud, *The Standard Edition of the Complete Psychological Works of Sigmund Freud*, edited by J. Strachey. London: Hogarth Press and Institute for Psychoanalysis, 1953–1974.

26. Fisher, *Anatomy of Love*.

27. Dean G. Pruitt, *Negotiation Behavior*. New York: Academic, 1981.

28. Barbara D. Whitehead, *The Divorce Culture: Rethinking Our Commitments to Marriage and the Family*. New York: Random House, 1998.

29. Arlen Thornton, William G. Axinn, and Yu Xie, *Marriage and Cohabitation*. Chicago: University of Chicago Press, 2007.

30. Melvyn L. Fein, *The Great Middle-Class Revolution: Our Long March toward a Professionalized Society*. Kennesaw, GA: Kennesaw State University Press, 2005.

31. Melvyn L. Fein, *Redefining Higher Education: How Self-Direction Can Save Colleges*. New Brunswick, NJ: Transaction Publishers, 2014.

32. Herbert A. Simon, *Administrative Behavior*. New York: MacMillan, 1947.

33. Melvin L. Kohn and Carmi Schooler, *Work and Personality: An Inquiry into the Impact of Social Stratification*. Norwood, NJ: Ablex Publishing, 1983.

34. Fein, *On Loss and Losing*.

CHAPTER 4: ENSURING SAFETY

1. Sigmund Freud, *The Standard Edition of the Complete Psychological Works of Sigmund Freud*, edited by J. Strachey. London: Hogarth Press and Institute for Psychoanalysis, 1953–1974.

2. Judith S. Wallenstein, Julia M. Lewis, and Sandra Blakesee, *The Unexpected Legacy of Divorce; a 25 Year Landmark Study*. New York: Hyperion, 2000.

3. Barbara D. Whitehead, *The Divorce Culture: Rethinking Our Commitments to Marriage and the Family*. New York: Random House, 1998.

4. Barbara Risman and Virginia Rutter, *Families as They Really Are*. New York: W. W. Norton, 2015.

5. Robert S. Weiss, *Marital Separation: Coping with the End of Marriage*. New York: Basic Books, 1975.

6. Wallenstein, *Unexpected Legacy of Divorce*.

7. Christopher Jencks, *Rethinking Social Policy: Race, Poverty and the Underclass*. Cambridge, MA: Harvard University Press, 1992.

8. David Zarefsky, *President Johnson's War on Poverty*. Tuscaloosa: University of Alabama Press, 1986.

9. Samuel A. Stouffer and Edward A. Suchman, eds., *The American Soldier: Adjustment During Army Life*. Princeton, NJ: University of Princeton Press, 1949. Paul Fussell, *Class: A Guide through the American Status System*. New York: Simon & Schuster, 1983.

10. Charles A. Valentine, *Culture and Poverty: Critique and Counter Proposals*. Chicago: University of Chicago Press, 1968.

11. Joseph T. Howell, *Hard Living on Clay Street: Portraits of Blue Collar Families*. Prospect Heights, IL: Waveland, 1973.

12. Charles Murray, *Coming Apart: The State of White America, 1960–2010*. New York: Crown Forum, 2012.

13. Kathryn Edin and Maria J. Kefalas, *Promises I Can Keep: Why Poor Women Put Motherhood before Marriage*. Berkeley, CA: University of California Press, 2011.

14. W. B. Wilcox, et al., *Why Marriage Matters: Thirty Conclusions from the Social Sciences*, 3rd ed. New York: Institute for American Values, 2011.

15. Richard Majors and Janet M. Bilson, *The Cool Pose: The Dilemma of Black Manhood in America*. New York: Simon & Schuster, 1993.

16. Melvyn L. Fein, *On Loss and Losing: Beyond the Medical Model of Personal Distress*. New Brunswick, NJ: Transaction Publishers, 2012.

17. Donald M. Gallant, *Alcoholism: A Guide to Diagnosis, Intervention, and Treatment*. New York: W. W. Norton, 1987.

18. Doris Kearns Goodwin, *No Ordinary Time: Franklin and Eleanor Roosevelt: The Home Front in World War II*. New York: Simon & Schuster.

19. Henry David Thoreau, *Walden, or Life in the Woods*. New York: Dover, 1995.

20. Doris Kearns Goodwin, *The Bully Pulpit: Theodore Roosevelt, William Howard Taft, and the Golden Age of Journalism*. New York: Simon & Schuster, 2013.

21. John Bowlby, *Attachment*. New York: Basic Books, 1969.

22. Bruno Bettleheim, *A Good Enough Parent*. New York: Alfred A, Knopf, 1987.

23. Goodwin, *Bully Pulpit*.

24. Dairmaid MacCulloch, *The Reformation: A History*. New York: Penguin Books, 2005.

25. Elizabeth Kubler-Ross, *On Death and Dying*. New York: MacMillan, 1969.

26. Sigmund Freud, *The Interpretation of Dreams*. New York: Discus Books, 1970.

27. Anna Freud, *The Ego and the Mechanisms of Defense*. New York: International Universities Press, 1966.

28. Ibid.

29. Goodwin, *Bully Pulpit*.

30. Erik Erikson, *Identity: Youth and Crisis*. New York: W. W. Norton, 1968.

31. David H. Barlow, *Anxiety and Its Disorders: The Nature and Treatment of Anxiety and Panic*. New York: Guilford, 1984.

32. Oscar Lewis, *La Vida: A Puerto Rican Family in the Culture of Poverty*. New York: Random House, 1966.

33. Steven D. Levitt and Stephen J. Dubner, *Freakonomics; a Rogue Economist Explore the Hidden Side of Everything*. New York: Harper Perennial, 2009.

34. David M. Buss, *The Evolution of Desire*. New York: Basic Books, 2003.

35. Thomas E. Bratter and Gary G. Forrest, *Alcoholism and Substance Abuse: Strategies for Clinical Intervention*. New York: Free Press, 1985.

36. Ibid.

37. Michael Lewis and Jeannette M. Haviland, eds., *Handbook of Emotions*. New York: Guilford, 1993.

CHAPTER 5: INCREMENTAL TOLERANCE

1. Malcolm Gladwell, *David and Goliath: Underdogs, Misfits, and the Art of Battling Giants*. New York: Little, Brown, 2013.

2. Ibid.

3. Ibid.

4. Richard Brookhiser, *Founding Father: Rediscovering George Washington*. New York: Free Press, 1996.

5. Gladwell, *David and Goliath*.

6. Joseph Wolpe, *The Practice of Behavior Therapy*. New York: Pergamon, 1973.

7. Irwin L. Kutash, Louis Schlesinger, et al., eds., *Handbook of Stress and Anxiety*. San Francisco: Jossey-Bass, 1980.

8. Andrew M. Matthews, Michael G. Gelder, and Derek W. Johnston, *Agoraphobia: Nature and Treatment*. New York: Guilford, 1981.

9. Michael Lewis and Jeannette M. Haviland, eds., *Handbook of Emotions*. New York: Guilford, 1993.

10. Melvyn L. Fein, *I.A.M.: A Common Sense Guide to Coping with Anger*. Westport, CT: Praeger, 1993.

11. Richard S. Lazarus, *Emotion and Adaptation*. New York: Oxford University Press, 1991.

12. David H. Barlow, *Anxiety and Its Disorders: The Nature and Treatment of Anxiety and Panic*. New York: Guilford, 1984.

13. Donald M. Gallant, *Alcoholism: A Guide to Diagnosis, Intervention, and Treatment*. New York: W. W. Norton, 1987.

14. Donald Light, *Becoming Psychiatrists: The Professional Transformation of Self*. New York: W. W. Norton, 1982.

15. Doris Kearns Goodwin, *The Bully Pulpit: Theodore Roosevelt, William Howard Taft, and the Golden Age of Journalism*. New York: Simon & Schuster, 2013.

16. Ibid.

17. Stella Chess and Alexander Thomas, *Temperament in Clinical Practice*. New York: Guilford, 1986.

18. Sigmund Freud, *The Standard Edition of the Complete Psychological*

Works of Sigmund Freud, edited by J. Strachey. London: Hogarth Press and Institute for Psychoanalysis, 1953–1974.

19. Rick A. Myer, *Assessment for Crisis Intervention: A Triage Assessment Model*. Belmont, CA: Brooks Cole, 2000.

20. E. Fuller Torrey, *Schizophrenia and Civilization*. New York: Jason Aronson, 1980.

21. Freud, *Standard Edition*.

22. Ayala M. Pines, *Falling in Love: Why We Choose the Lovers We Choose*. New York: Routledge, 2005.

23. Maggie Scarf, *Intimate Partners: Patterns in Love and Marriage*. New York: Random House, 1987.

24. Murray S. Davis, *Intimate Relations*. New York: Free Press, 1973.

25. Everitt C. Hughes, *Men and Their Work*. New York: Free Press of Glencoe, 1958.

26. Melvyn L. Fein, *Redefining Higher Education: How Self-Direction Can Save Colleges*. New Brunswick, NJ: Transaction Publishers, 2014.

27. Ibid.

28. Hughes, *Men and Their Work*.

29. Booker T. Washington, *Up from Slavery*. New York: Oxford University Press, 1985.

CHAPTER 6: EVALUATING OUR FEARS

1. Josef Breuer and Sigmund Freud, *Studies on Hysteria*. New York: Basic Books, 1957.

2. Franz Alexander, *Fundamentals of Psychoanalysis*. New York: W. W. Norton, 1948.

3. Andrew Scull, *Social Order/Mental Disorder: Anglo-American Psychiatry in Historical Perspective*. Berkeley: University of California Press, 1989.

4. Jerome Frank, *Persuasion and Healing: A Comparative Study of Psychotherapy*. Baltimore: Johns Hopkins Press, 1973.

5. Janet Malcolm, *In the Freud Archives*. New York: Alfred A. Knopf, 1984.

6. Carl Rogers, *Client-Centered Therapy*. Boston: Houghton Mifflin, 1951.

7. Carl Rogers, *On Becoming a Person*. Boston: Houghton Mifflin, 1961.

8. Sigmund Freud, *The Standard Edition of the Complete Psychological Works of Sigmund Freud*, edited by J. Strachey. London: Hogarth Press and Institute for Psychoanalysis, 1953–1974.

9. Melvyn L. Fein, *On Loss and Losing: Beyond the Medical Model of Personal Distress*. New Brunswick, NJ: Transaction Publishers, 2012.

10. Frank, *Persuasion and Healing*.

11. Donald Light, *Becoming Psychiatrists: The Professional Transformation of Self*. New York: W. W. Norton, 1982.

12. Fein, *On Loss and Losing*.

13. Maggie Scarf, *Unfinished Business: Pressure Points in the Lives of Women*. New York: Ballantine Books, 1980.

14. Elizabeth Kubler-Ross, *On Death and Dying*. New York: MacMillan, 1969.

15. John Bowlby, *Separation: Anxiety and Anger*. New York: Basic Books, 1973.

16. John Bowlby, *Loss: Sadness and Depression*. New York: Basic Books, 1980.

17. Helen E. Fisher, *Anatomy of Love: The Natural History of Monogamy, Adultery and Divorce*. New York: W. W. Norton, 1992.

18. Louis A. Zurcher, *Social Roles: Conformity, Conflict and Creativity*. Beverley Hills: Sage Publications, 1983.

19. Emile Durkheim, *The Division of Labor in Society*. New York: Free Press, 1933.

20. Romila Tharpa, *A History of India*. London: Penguin Books, 1966.

21. Gerald Handle, ed., *The Psychosocial Interior of the Family: A Sourcebook for the Study of Whole Families*. Chicago: Aldine-Atherton, 1967.

22. Melvyn L. Fein, *Role Change: A Resocialization Perspective*. New York: Praeger, 1990.

23. Melvyn L. Fein, *Human Hierarchies: A General Theory*. New Brunswick, NJ: Transaction Publishers, 2012.

24. Fein, *On Loss and Losing*.

25. Christopher Jencks, *Rethinking Social Policy: Race, Poverty and the Underclass*. Cambridge, MA: Harvard University Press, 1992.

26. Joseph T. Howell, *Hard Living on Clay Street: Portraits of Blue Collar Families*. Prospect Heights, IL: Waveland, 1973.

27. Gregory Bateson, *Steps to an Ecology of Mind*. New York: Ballantine Books, 1972.

28. John Bowlby, *Attachment*. New York: Basic Books, 1969.

29. Bateson, *Steps to an Ecology of Mind*.

30. Anna Freud, *The Ego and the Mechanisms of Defense*. New York: International Universities Press, 1966.

31. Michael Lewis and Jeannette M. Haviland, eds., *Handbook of Emotions*. New York: Guilford, 1993.

32. Melvyn L. Fein, *I.A.M.: A Common Sense Guide to Coping with Anger*. Westport, CT: Praeger, 1993.

33. Ibid.

34. Eugene B. Block, *The Fabric of Guilt*. New York: Doubleday, 1968.

35. Melvyn L. Fein, *Hardball without an Umpire: The Sociology of Morality*. Westport, CT: Praeger, 1997.

36. Ronald Potter-Efron and Patricia Potter-Efron, *Letting Go of Shame; Understanding How Shame Affects Your Life*. San Francisco: Harper & Row, 1989.

37. Scarf, *Unfinished Business*.

38. George Brown and Tirril Harris, *The Social Origins of Depression*. New York: Free Press, 1978.

39. Judith Viorst, *Necessary Losses: The Loves, Illusions, Dependencies, and Impossible Expectations That All of Us Have to Give up in Order to Grow*. New York: Ballantine Books, 1986.

40. John Clausen, ed., *Socialization and Society*. Boston: Little, Brown, 1968.

41. Fein, *I.A.M.*

42. Fein, *Human Hierarchies*.

CHAPTER 7: SORTING POTENTIAL RESPONSES

1. George H. Mead, *Mind, Self, and Society*. Chicago: University of Chicago Press, 1934.

2. Joseph T. Howell, *Hard Living on Clay Street: Portraits of Blue Collar Families*. Prospect Heights, IL: Waveland, 1973.

3. David McCullough, *Truman*. New York: Simon & Schuster, 1992.

4. C. Wright Mills, *The Power Elite*. London: Oxford University Press, 1956.

5. Simon S. Montefiore, *Stalin: The Court of the Red Tsar*. New York: Alfred A. Knopf, 2004.

6. William L. Shirer, *The Rise and Fall of the Third Reich*. New York: Simon & Schuster, 1960.

7. Montefiore, *Stalin*.

8. Ronald Potter-Efron and Patricia Potter-Efron, *Letting Go of Shame; Understanding How Shame Affects Your Life*. San Francisco: Harper & Row, 1989.

9. Eugene B. Block, *The Fabric of Guilt*. New York: Doubleday, 1968.

10. Gregory Bateson, *Steps to an Ecology of Mind*. New York: Ballantine Books, 1972.

11. Walter B. Cannon, *Bodily Changes in Pain, Hunger, Fear, and Rage: An Account of Recent Research on the Function of Emotional Excitement*. New York: Appleton-Century-Crofts, 1929.

12. Donald M. Gallant, *Alcoholism: A Guide to Diagnosis, Intervention, and Treatment*. New York: W. W. Norton, 1987.

13. Joseph Wolpe, *The Practice of Behavior Therapy*. New York: Pergamon Books, 1973.

14. Melvyn L. Fein, *On Loss and Losing: Beyond the Medical Model of Personal Distress*. New Brunswick, NJ: Transaction Publishers, 2012.

15. Melvyn L. Fein, *Evolution versus Revolution: The Paradoxes of Social Change*. New Brunswick, NJ: Transaction Publishers, 2015.

16. Fein, *On Loss and Losing*

17. Melvyn L. Fein, *Human Hierarchies: A General Theory*. New Brunswick, NJ: Transaction Publishers, 2012.

18. Helen E. Fisher, *Anatomy of Love: The Natural History of Monogamy, Adultery and Divorce*. New York: W. W. Norton, 1992.

19. Bruno Bettleheim, *A Good Enough Parent*. New York: Alfred A, Knopf, 1987.

20. Bateson, *Steps to an Ecology of Mind*.

21. Oscar Lewis, *La Vida: A Puerto Rican Family in the Culture of Poverty*. New York: Random House, 1966.

22. Annette Lareau, *Unequal Childhoods: Class, Race, and Family Life*. Berkeley: University of California Press, 2003.

23. Bernard Goldberg, *Bias: A CBS Insider Exposes How the Media Distort the News*. Washington, DC: Regnery Publishing, 2002.

24. Curt Anders, *Fighting Confederates*. New York: Dorset, 1968.

25. Fein, *Human Hierarchies*.

26. Fein, *On Loss and Losing*.

27. Melvyn L. Fein, *Role Change: A Resocialization Perspective*. New York: Praeger, 1990.

28. Ayala M. Pines, *Falling in Love: Why We Choose the Lovers We Choose*. New York: Routledge, 2005.

29. Victor D. Hanson, *Ripples of Battle: How Wars of the Past Still Determine How We Fight*. New York: Doubleday, 2003.

30. Thomas Sowell, *The Quest for Cosmic Justice*. New York: Free Press, 1999.

31. Richard N. Bolles, *What Color Is Your Parachute? A Practical Manuel for Job-Hunters and Career-Changers*. New York: Ten Speed, 2015.

32. Howell, *Hard Living on Clay Street*.

33. Melvyn L. Fein, *Evolution versus Revolution: The Paradoxes of Social Change*. New Brunswick, NJ: Transaction Publishers, 2015.

34. Melvyn L. Fein, *Redefining Higher Education: How Self-Direction Can Save Colleges*. New Brunswick, NJ: Transaction Publishers, 2014.

35. Andrew J. Cherlin, *The Marriage-Go-Round*. New York: Alfred A. Knopf, 2009.

36. Erik Erikson, *Identity; Youth and Crisis*. New York: W. W. Norton, 1968.

37. Robert S. Weiss, *Marital Separation: Coping with the End of Marriage*. New York: Basic Books, 1975.

38. Doris Kearns Goodwin, *The Bully Pulpit: Theodore Roosevelt, William Howard Taft, and the Golden Age of Journalism*. New York: Simon & Schuster, 2013.

39. Candice Millard, *The River of Doubt: Theodore Roosevelt's Darkest Journey*. New York: Broadway Books, 2006.

40. Goodwin, *Bully Pulpit*.

41. Fein, *On Loss and Losing*.

42. Elizabeth Kubler-Ross, *On Death and Dying*. New York: MacMillan, 1969.

43. Ibid.

44. Weiss, *Marital Separation*.

45. Fein, *On Loss and Losing*.

46. Melvin Gray, *Neuroses: A Comprehensive and Clinical View*. New York: Van Nostrand Reinhold, 1978.

CHAPTER 8: WINNING

1. Melvyn L. Fein, *Human Hierarchies: A General Theory*. New Brunswick, NJ: Transaction Publishers, 2012.

2. Carl von Clausewitz, *On War*. New York: Penguin Books, 1908.

3. Anselm L. Stauss, *Negotiations: Varieties, Contexts, Processes and Social Order*. San Francisco: Jossey-Bass, 1978.

4. William S. McFeely, *Grant: A Biography*. New York: W. W. Norton, 1981.

5. Curt Anders, *Fighting Confederates*. New York: Dorset, 1968.

6. McFeely, *Grant*.

7. Martyn Lyons, *Napoleon Bonaparte and the Legacy of the French Revolution*. New York: St. Martin's, 1994.

8. David Tuffley, *The Essence of Buddhism*. N.p.: Altiora Publications, 2013.

9. Dean G. Pruitt, *Negotiation Behavior*. New York: Academic, 1981.

10. Ibid.

11. Linda Waite and Maggie Gallagher, *The Case for Marriage: Why Married People Are Happier, Healthier, and Better Off Financially*. New York: Doubleday, 2000.

12. Stauss, *Negotiations*.

13. Melvyn L. Fein, *I.A.M.: A Common Sense Guide to Coping with Anger*. Westport, CT: Praeger, 1993.

14. Pruitt, *Negotiation Behavior*.

15. Daniel Goleman, *Emotional Intelligence: Why It Can Matter More Than IQ*. New York: Bantam Books, 1995.

16. Joseph T. Howell, *Hard Living on Clay Street: Portraits of Blue Collar Families*. Prospect Heights, IL: Waveland, 1973.

17. John Clausen, ed., *Socialization and Society*. Boston: Little, Brown, 1968.

18. Sigmund Freud, *The Standard Edition of the Complete Psychological Works of Sigmund Freud*, edited by J. Strachey. London: Hogarth Press and Institute for Psychoanalysis, 1953–1974.

19. Melvyn L. Fein, *The Great Middle-Class Revolution: Our Long March toward a Professionalized Society*. Kennesaw, GA: Kennesaw State University Press, 2005.

20. Orville Brim and Jerome Kagen, eds., *Constancy and Change in Human Development*. Cambridge, MA: Harvard University Press, 1980.

21. Annette Lareau, *Unequal Childhoods: Class, Race, and Family Life*. Berkeley: University of California Press, 2003.

22. Ferdinand Toennies, *Community and Society*. New York: Harper Row, 1966.

23. Lynn H. Lofland, *A World of Strangers*. New York: Basic Books, 1973.

24. Peter Wood, *Diversity: The Invention of a Concept*. San Francisco: Encounter Books, 2003.

25. Arlie Hochschild, *Facing up to the American Dream*. Princeton, NJ: Princeton University Press, 1995.

26. Simon Baron-Cohen, *The Essential Difference: The Truth about the Male and Female Brain*. New York: Basic Books, 2003.

27. Melvin L. Kohn and Carmi Schooler, *Work and Personality: An Inquiry into the Impact of Social Stratification*. Norwood, NJ: Ablex Publishing, 1983.

28. Melvyn L. Fein, *Race and Morality: How Good Intentions Undermine Social Justice and Perpetuate Inequality*. New York: Kluwar/Plenum, 2001.

29. Thomas Sowell, *Ethnic America*. New York: Basic Books, 1981.

30. Dairmaid MacCulloch, *The Reformation: A History*. New York: Penguin Books, 2005.

31. Robert Samuelson, *The Good Life and Its Discontents: The American Dream in the Age of Enlightenment 1945–1995*. New York: Times Books, 1996.

32. Doris Kearns Goodwin, *The Bully Pulpit: Theodore Roosevelt, William Howard Taft, and the Golden Age of Journalism*. New York: Simon & Schuster, 2013.

33. Bernard Goldberg, *Bias: A CBS Insider Exposes How the Media Distort the News*. Washington, DC: Regnery Publishing, 2002.

34. Melvyn L. Fein, *Redefining Higher Education: How Self-Direction Can Save Colleges*. New Brunswick, NJ: Transaction Publishers, 2014.

35. Ibid.

36. Melvin L. Kohn, *Class and Conformity: A Study in Values*. Homewood, IL: Dorsey, 1969.

37. Everitt C. Hughes, *Men and Their Work*. New York: Free Press of Glencoe, 1958.

38. Nicholas Carr, *The Shallows: What the Internet Is Doing to Our Brains*. New York: W. W. Norton, 2010.

39. Fein, *Redefining Higher Education*.

40. Fein, *Human Hierarchies*.

41. Ibid.

42. Dan Jones, *The Plantagenets: The Warrior Kings and Queens Who Made England*. New York: Penguin Books, 2012.

CHAPTER 9: SAVING OURSELVES

1. Lynn H. Lofland, *A World of Strangers*. New York: Basic Books, 1973.

2. Melvyn L. Fein, *The Great Middle-Class Revolution: Our Long March toward a Professionalized Society*. Kennesaw, GA: Kennesaw State University Press, 2005.

3. Emile Durkheim, *The Elementary Forms of Religious Life*. New York: Free Press, 1915.

4. Karen Armstrong, *A History of God: The 4000 Year Quest of Judaism, Christianity and Islam*. New York: Ballantine Books, 1993.

5. Alan Wolfe, *The Transformation of American Religion: How We Actually Live Our Faith*. New York: Free Press, 1993.

6. T. S. Ahston, *The Industrial Revolution 1760–1830*. New York: Oxford University Press, 1965.

7. Daniel Chirot, *Social Change in the Modern Era*. New York: Harcourt, Brace, Jovanovich, 1986.

8. Adam Smith, *An Inquiry into the Nature and Causes of the Wealth of Nations*. London: W. Strahan & T. Cadell, 1776.

9. Doris Kearns Goodwin, *The Bully Pulpit: Theodore Roosevelt, William Howard Taft, and the Golden Age of Journalism*. New York: Simon & Schuster, 2013.

10. Ron Chernow, *Titan: The Life of John D. Rockefeller*. New York: Random House, 1998.

11. Maury Klein, *The Change Makers: From Carnegie to Gates*. New York: Times Books, 2003.

12. Ron Chernow, *The House of Morgan: An American Banking Dynasty and the Rise of Modern Finance*. New York: Grove, 1990.

13. Goodwin, *Bully Pulpit*.

14. Robert S. McElvaine, *The Great Depression: America 1929–1941*. New York: Times Books, 1984.

15. David Zarefsky, *President Johnson's War on Poverty*. Tuscaloosa: University of Alabama Press, 1986.

16. Peter H. Schuck, *Why the Government Fails So Often: And How It Can Do Better*. Princeton, NJ: Princeton University Press, 2014.

17. Drew Griffin, Nelli Black, Scott Bronstein, and Curt Devine, "Veterans Still Facing Major Medical Delays at VA Hospitals," updated October 20, 2015, http://www.cnn.com/2015/10/20/politics/veterans-delays-va-hospitals/ (accessed March 9, 2016).

18. Thomas B. Edsall, "Why the IRS Scandal Won't Go Away," *New York Times*, February 25, 2014, http://www.nytimes.com/2014/02/26/opinion/edsall-why-the-irs-scandal-wont-go-away.html (accessed March 9, 2016).

19. Ilya Shapiro, "Stopping the EPA from Regulating Puddles," CATO Institute, May 10, 2013, http://www.cato.org/blog/stopping-epa-regulating-puddles (accessed March 9, 2016).

20. Anjali Shastry, "House Passes Bill to Streamline Firing, Demotion at VA: Democrats Balk, Accuse Union-Busing," *Washington Times*, July 29, 2015. Peter H. Schuck, *Why the Government Fails So Often: And How It Can Do Better*. Princeton, NJ: Princeton University Press, 2014.

21. Friedrich A. Hayek, *The Fatal Conceit: The Errors of Socialism*. Chicago: University of Chicago Press, 1988.

22. Cyril Northcote Parkinson, *Parkinson's Law*. Cutchogue, NY: Buccaneer Books, 1996.

23. Cass Sunstein, *Simpler: The Future of Government*. New York: Simon & Schuster, 2013.

24. Christopher Lasch, *The Culture of Narcissism: American Life in an Age of Diminishing Expectations*. New York: Warner Books, 1979.

25. Paul Johnson, *A History of the American People*. New York: HarperCollins Publishers, 1997.

26. Fein, *Great Middle-Class Revolution*.

27. Ibid.

28. Melvin L. Kohn, *Class and Conformity: A Study in Values*. Homewood, IL: Dorsey, 1969.

29. Everitt C. Hughes, *Men and Their Work*. New York: Free Press of Glencoe, 1958.

30. Melvin L. Kohn and Carmi Schooler, *Work and Personality: An Inquiry into the Impact of Social Stratification*. Norwood, NJ: Ablex Publishing, 1983.

31. Arnold M. Ludwig, *King of the Mountain: The Nature of Political Leadership*. Lexington: University of Kentucky Press, 2002.

32. Magali S. Larson, *The Rise of Professionalism: a Sociological Analysis*. Berkeley: University of California Press, 1977.

33. Melvyn L. Fein, *Redefining Higher Education: How Self-Direction Can Save Colleges*. New Brunswick, NJ: Transaction Publishers, 2014.

34. Melvyn L. Fein, *I.A.M.: A Common Sense Guide to Coping with Anger*. Westport, CT: Praeger, 1993.

35. Bob Drury and Tom Clavin, *The Heart of Everything That Is: The Untold Story of Red Cloud, an American Legend*. New York: Simon & Schuster, 2013.

36. Fein, *Great Middle-Class Revolution*.

37. Fein, *Redefining Higher Education*.

38. Annette Lareau, *Unequal Childhoods: Class, Race, and Family Life*. Berkeley: University of California Press, 2003.

39. Ibid.

40. Joseph T. Howell, *Hard Living on Clay Street: Portraits of Blue Collar Families*. Prospect Heights, IL: Waveland, 1973.

41. Edward Zigler and Jeanette Valentines, eds., *Head Start: A Legacy of the War on Poverty*. New York: Free Press, 1979.

42. Fein, *Redefining Higher Education*.

43. Ayala M. Pines, *Falling in Love: Why We Choose the Lovers We Choose*. New York: Routledge, 2005.

44. Arlen Thornton, William G. Axinn, and Yu Xie, *Marriage and Cohabitation*. Chicago: University of Chicago Press, 2007.

45. Robert D. Putnam, *Our Kids: The American Dream in Crisis*. New York: Simon & Schuster, 2015.

46. Barbara D. Whitehead, *The Divorce Culture: Rethinking Our Commitments to Marriage and the Family*. New York: Random House, 1998.

47. Andrew J. Cherlin, *The Marriage-Go-Round*. New York: Alfred A. Knopf, 2009.

48. Pines, *Falling in Love*.

49. Dean G. Pruitt, *Negotiation Behavior*. New York: Academic, 1981.

50. Putnam, *Our Kids*.

51. W. Bradford Wilcox et al., *Why Marriage Matters: Thirty Conclusions from the Social Sciences*, 3rd ed. New York: Institute for American Values, 2011.

52. Fein, *Great Middle-Class Revolution*.

CHAPTER 10: PERSONAL LIBERATION

1. Paul Johnson, *A History of the American People*. New York: HarperCollins Publishers, 1997.

2. Dairmaid MacCulloch, *The Reformation: A History*. New York: Penguin Books, 2005.

3. Fredrick Rudolph, *The American College and University: A History*. Athens: University of Georgia Press, 1990.

4. Bernard Bailyn, *To Begin the World Anew: The Genius and Ambiguities of the American Founders*. New York: Vintage Books, 2003.

5. Walter Isaacson, *Benjamin Franklin: An American Life*. New York: Simon & Schuster, 2003.

6. Richard Brookhiser, *Founding Father: Rediscovering George Washington*. New York: Free Press, 1996.

7. Johnson, *History of the American People*.

8. Bob Drury and Tom Clavin, *The Heart of Everything That Is: The Untold Story of Red Cloud, an American Legend*. New York: Simon & Schuster, 2013.

9. Seymour M. Lipset, *American Exceptionalism: A Double-Edged Sword*. New York: W. W. Norton, 1996.

10. Irving Howe, *World of Our Fathers*. New York: Harcourt, Brace, Jovanovich Publishers, 1976.

11. MacCulloch, *Reformation*.

12. Johnson, *History of the American People*.

13. Bailyn, *To Begin the World Anew*.

14. S. C. Gwynne, *Empire of the Summer Sun: Quanah Parker and the Rise and Fall of the Comanches, the Most Powerful Tribe in American History*. New York: Scribner, 2010.

15. Lipset, *American Exceptionalism*.

16. Maury Klein, *The Change Makers: From Carnegie to Gates*. New York: Times Books, 2003.

17. Howe, *World of Our Fathers*.

18. Abraham Maslow, *Motivation and Personality*. New York: Harper & Row, 1954.

19. Magali S. Larson, *The Rise of Professionalism: A Sociological Analysis*. Berkeley: University of California Press, 1977.

20. Melvyn L. Fein, *The Great Middle-Class Revolution: Our Long March toward a Professionalized Society*. Kennesaw, GA.: Kennesaw State University Press, 2005.

21. Everitt C. Hughes, *Men and Their Work*. New York: Free Press of Glencoe, 1958.

22. Walter Isaacson, *Innovators: How a Group of Hackers, Geniuses, and Geeks Created the Digital Revolution*. New York: Simon & Schuster, 2014.

23. Charles Murray, *Losing Ground: American Social Policy*. New York: Basic Books, 1986.

24. Ibid.

25. Joseph T. Howell, *Hard Living on Clay Street: Portraits of Blue Collar Families*. Prospect Heights, IL: Waveland, 1973.

26. Charles Murray, *Coming Apart: The State of White America, 1960–2010*. New York: Crown Forum, 2012.

27. Maslow, *Motivation and Personality*.

28. Robert D. Putnam, *Our Kids: The American Dream in Crisis*. New York: Simon & Schuster, 2015.

29. Drury and Clavin, *Heart of Everything That Is*.

30. T. Harry Williams, *Lincoln and His Generals*. New York: Alfred A. Knopf, 1952.

31. Drury and Clavin, *Heart of Everything That Is*.

32. Ibid.

33. Robert L. O'Connell, *Fierce Patriot: The Tangled Lives of William Tecumseh Sherman*. New York: Random House, 2014.

34. William S. McFeely, *Grant: A Biography*. New York: W. W. Norton, 1981.

35. O'Connell, *Fierce Patriot*.

36. Ibid.

37. Curt Anders, *Fighting Confederates*. New York: Dorset, 1968.

38. O'Connell, *Fierce Patriot*.

EPILOGUE

1. Judith Viorst, *Necessary Losses: The Loves, Illusions, Dependencies, and Impossible Expectations That All of Us Have to Give up in Order to Grow*. New York: Ballantine Books, 1986.

2. Charles Murray, *Coming Apart: The State of White America, 1960–2010*. New York: Crown Forum, 2012.

3. Melvyn L. Fein, *Evolution versus Revolution: The Paradoxes of Social Change*. New Brunswick, NJ: Transaction Publishers, 2015.

4. "'In America, WE Have Grit': Megyn Takes on Students Seeking Exam Delays," *Fox News Insider*, December 11, 2014, http://insider.foxnews.com/2014/12/11/america-we-have-grit-megyn-takes-students-seeking-exam-delays (accessed March 9, 2016).

5. Edward Gibbon, *The Decline and Fall of the Roman Empire*. New York: Dell Publishing, 1963.

6. Melvyn L. Fein, *On Loss and Losing: Beyond the Medical Model of Personal Distress*. New Brunswick, NJ: Transaction Publishers, 2012.

INDEX